IN THE
SHADOW
OF THE
DEVIL

IN THE SHADOW OF THE DEVIL

WILLIAM K.M. BRECKENRIDGE
in
FIELDING HURST'S
First West Tennessee U.S. *Cavalry*

JOHN D. TALBOTT, J.D.

BRAYBREE
Publishing

Copyright © 2021 John E. Talbott
All rights reserved

Published by BrayBree Publishing Company LLC
FIRST EDITION

No part of this book may be reproduced, stored in or introduced into a retrieval system or transmitted in any form or by any means (electronic, mechanical, photocopying, recording, or otherwise) without the prior written permission of the publisher and copyright owner.

The scanning, uploading, and distribution of this book on the Internet or through any other means is not permitted without permission from the publisher and copyright owner.

ISBN-13: 978-1-940127-17-0

Printed in the United States of America

BRAY BREE
BrayBree Publishing Company LLC
P.O. Box 1204
Dickson, Tennessee 37056-1204

Visit our website at www.braybreepublishing.com

Dedicated to the memory of two people who were my steadfast supporters and who encouraged my love of Civil War history because of their own dedication to the subject:

Quentin Hayes Hayre (1921–2000)
Myrvin Gray Harris (1929–2016)

Their support for my studies and desire to write is never forgotten. This work is affectionately dedicated to their memories.

CONTENTS

Introduction ix

CHAPTER 1
Two Men, A National Conflict, and Storm Clouds 3

CHAPTER 2
Building a Regiment Amid Controversy 24

CHAPTER 3
Out of Control 54

CHAPTER 4
Taking Charge 80

CHAPTER 5
On The Move 94

CHAPTER 6
Three Pivotal Days and The Mile Marker Murders 133

Chapter 7
Riding Toward a Legacy.. 166

Chapter 8
The Last Duty... 179

Chapter 9
Drifting into History's Shadow... 198

Epilogue...206

Bibliography..233

Index...245

INTRODUCTION

When it comes to history and its telling, I dislike strongly the term "revisionist." To me, it implies to the reader that someone is changing history or retelling it to suit some purpose or to achieve some agenda. Indeed, people often do everything they can to provide the "proper" spin on the subject of their interest. This leads us to one overriding question: is it so hard to accept that history is, by and large, simply an incomplete story that, from time to time, will be supplemented by new discoveries and long-hidden records and manuscripts? The answer seems far simpler than the question itself often implies. It seems to me that the puzzle that is history is seldom ever completed. If a subject is fortunate enough, it may be revisited enough so that further research and what I term "academic archeology" may supplement and accurately enhance the story until it becomes as complete as possible. In short, often newly discovered sources shed new light on events and force us to rethink our positions on a subject.

The story of Fielding Hurst, the U.S. First West Tennessee Cavalry (later renamed the Sixth Tennessee Cavalry), and the story of the Union-Confederate struggle in West Tennessee is one of those subjects. So many stories abound about the man, the regiment, and the times that it has become difficult to sort truth from fiction. Certainly, valiant efforts have been made over the years and many less so. Local "historians" and purveyors of legend and lore have distorted and exploited the image of Hurst the devil and painted both him and his soldiers as no less than sadistic. Others have taken a more sympathetic view while still admitting that both Hurst and some of his officers and soldiers were guilty of some level of transgression against local Confederates and their supporters.

Fortunately, there has been academic research and writing by writers and historians who have striven to give the historically minded public the truth as best they could discern it. Both Gary R. Blankenship and Kevin D. McCann worked hard in different decades to document the truth as it could be determined in those times. Still, one must wonder if the essence of the story has been fully and accurately told. As stated earlier, the story of any historical character, event, or group is constantly evolving as new discoveries are made. As each individual writer or historian strives to capture the essence of a subject, they do so with the tools and resources available. Fortunately, sometimes we are just fortunate enough to see the release of heretofore unknown documentation, relics, and other items that help continue the development of the person's or the event's story.

Indeed, this work does not purport to correct or disprove any portion of either Blankenship's treatise on Hurst or McCann's history of the U.S. Sixth Tennessee Cavalry. That may, however, indeed occur of its own volition as this account unfolds. Simply stated, this account does offer another viewpoint. It presents the observations and opinions of an actual participant of the war and a contemporary comrade of Hurst and the soldiers of the regiment: Lieutenant Colonel William K.M. Breckenridge. More importantly, it reveals the vital role he played in the formation, preparation, and provision of the regiment, a role heretofore not known. Further, it sheds a new light on a controversial personality and the Southern Unionist regiment by a man who personally knew Fielding Hurst and the men of the First West Tennessee Cavalry collectively and individually.

One of the more recently released records reviewed in this work will be Breckenridge's letters and journal. This journal is one of several historical records that was not previously available when others sought to record the history of the First West Tennessee Cavalry/Sixth Tennessee Cavalry and the life of Fielding Hurst. Other documents include various service records of men whose roles were previously unknown or overshadowed and selected Southern Claims Commission records. These were directly consulted to give a more complete history of the regiment, Hurst, and Breckenridge himself.

It is fortunate that Breckenridge kept a journal. To better understand the man, his antagonist Fielding Hurst, and the regiment they tried to lead together, that journal will serve an invaluable resource to be counted with others. It was a journal that he didn't chose to begin until March 31, 1863. He simply went about his work until events in his life and his career warranted the need to keep a record and chronicle these events. Its existance had not been known for almost 150 years. Breckenridge's unpretentious yet remarkable journal finally saw the light of day with the donation of a scanned copy to the Tennessee State Library and Archives in 2012.

As to the major primary source for Breckenridge, beginning in 2013, I spent some seven years slowly but surely transcribing and researching the letters and journal entries contained in Breckenridge's Daybook. This daybook contained often no discernible order at times, but it was fortunate that the dates of documents and entries were noted. I chose to transcribe this valuable document and history is richer for the correspondence, orders, and journal entries contained within. The transcription and research process assisted me in making better sense of the activities of Breckenridge, Hurst, and the regiment itself. In the journal portion of the Daybook, Breckenridge chronicled his labors, his frustrations, his successes, his failures, the crimes of his colleagues, and the events of the day. Still more importantly, he shed light and a new perspective on one of the most controversial cavalry regiments of the Union Army.

In examining Breckenridge's journal as one of my sources, there were questions to ask and examine: Are Breckenridge's assessments correct? Is he biased? Does he have a proverbial "ax to grind" or a personal grudge? Indeed, that is for the student of history to determine. However, regardless of any other consideration, Breckenridge has one advantage over all students and academics who have written about Fielding Hurst thus far: he personally knew and worked with Hurst. Further, he knew and led the men of the First West Tennessee Cavalry. I say he led the men for a reason. It seems that Breckenridge often took the reins of the regiment when Hurst was nowhere to be found. Those facts make him far better qualified to criticize, assess, and report on the daily actions of both the regiment and its commanding colonel.

Perhaps Breckenridge finally gives us just what we have desperately needed and sought for better than 150 years: a clear voice of a contemporary of Hurst. Indeed, Breckenridge experienced frustration, anger, perhaps envy, and certainly exasperation with Hurst. But otherwise, he was fiercely dedicated to the cause of the Union, a cause that would ultimately claim his life. Throughout his journal, we learn that Breckenridge was making every effort to make a difficult situation work. We are fortunate in that he carefully and regularly kept his journal from the organization of the regiment until his death on October 15, 1863.

One of my primary goals in this book is to finally shine a historical light on a man long hidden in the shadows of history and the shadow of Fielding Hurst. Breckenridge has long been robbed of recognition for his contributions to both the Union cause and the establishment and leadership of the First West Tennessee Cavalry. Through this book it is my goal to remedy that deficiency, that failure of history. The story of the soldiers of the First West Tennessee Cavalry is also integral to the story of Breckenridge himself. The men who served honorably under him and Hurst and those who committed what was tantamount to war crimes with the blessings and under what appears to be direct orders of Fielding Hurst have to be examined as well. Service records and other governmental records have proven extremely valuable in clearing away the fog and mystery that have long enshrouded the history of the regiment and Breckenridge himself.

Those interested in the subject of Hurst and the First West Tennessee Cavalry/Sixth Tennessee Cavalry are divided into two polarized and distinct camps. There are those who willingly and recklessly demonize the man, soldier, and leader Fielding Hurst. There are also those who are slowly rising to the cause of defending Hurst who could be in danger of acting as apologists for him, an equally dangerous position. In fact, Hurst deserves neither demonization nor canonization. It must be clearly stated that neither position is helpful or constructive to the task of understanding either the times or the personalities.

History and the individuals who make it do not exist in a heaven and hell world. Its characters are seldom, if ever, black and white or that simple. One of the refreshing qualities of Breckenridge is his apparent honesty and the sincerity in his "voice" as evidenced on the written pages of his journal. Although it soon becomes clear that he doesn't respect Hurst, Lt. Colonel Breckenridge nevertheless respects the cause which they mutually espouse. One feels they are looking into the soul of the man as he pours out his innermost thoughts and opinions onto paper.

The terrible acts of Hurst have been raised to levels that even the worst criminal might not aspire and could not perhaps obtain. Still, it is folly to treat him as a misunderstood leader who didn't know how to adequately express himself. Hurst was, in fact, a very determined personality during a very controversial era. The level of his fidelity to his position of leadership appears somewhat questionable now in light of Breckenridge's emergence. There appear many unsavory characteristics shining through in Hurst's character as a result of the close analysis of both Breckenridge's journal and the available service records. Other records such as depositions in the Southern Claims Commission give interesting and otherwise little known facts. In Breckenridge's journal, there are hints of cowardice on Hurst's part, direct accusations of theft and pillage, and suggestions of desertion, as well as irresponsible attitudes and behaviors. Many sources appear to verify Breckenridge's observations.

On the other hand, Hurst's acts were hardly more noteworthy, violent, or ungentlemanly than his Confederate counterparts. The period from late 1862 to the spring of 1865, the period in which the U.S. First West Tennessee Cavalry largely operated, was one of almost true anarchy in West Tennessee. There was little if any certainty in the day-to-day lives of rural West Tennesseans or even town and city dwellers. Many individuals regularly committed acts of destruction that might have otherwise seemed extraordinary under other more normal circumstances.

For the critics of the regiment and its leadership, it might be surprising to learn that Hurst's men often disagreed with his orders and tactics. Breckenridge himself frequently cited the displeasure of the enlisted men toward the actions of Hurst and his closest subordinates.

Indeed, Breckenridge himself paints the picture of a group of conscientious soldiers who are suffering under the leadership of a far less savory man than himself. For the potential apologists, it becomes evident from Breckenridge's telling that a very radicalized and reckless man is leading this Southern Unionist regiment in a very torn region, one that needs no more turmoil than humanly necessary.

Still, despite the great temptation to concentrate solely on Hurst and his actions, it would be rendering a terrible disservice to Breckenridge himself. This work is designed not to be used simply to better determine the personality and habits of Fielding Hurst, but to give a glimpse and sound of a new voice on the American Civil War itself. Breckenridge's voice and his record as a leader should not be lost in the search for Fielding Hurst. Instead, it should be magnified in an effort to give the historically minded reader a new source of information regarding a horrible event about which we thought we knew so much. In fact, the story of war-torn West Tennessee has really yet to be told, especially that area that Hurst himself called home.

In the final analysis, it is my desire, my hope, and my goal to see that Lieutenant Colonel William K.M. Breckenridge emerges from the dustbin of history to trumpet a "new" voice, one which we have not heard before. The emergence of his perspective and an accurate record of his leadership is long overdue. More importantly, it is my goal to present my research in a manner that allows all of us to better glimpse the activities of an irregular and controversial Union cavalry regiment in an uncertain and dangerous time in American history

In the pages that follow, we will return to the battlefields, wagon roads, forests, and small towns and villages of the past. Here we shall join the fighting men of U.S. First West Tennessee Cavalry as they head out on picket duty, lie up in their tents during summer downpours, tidy up their camps, and get drunk on peach brandy. Here on the pages of this work, you will learn of Breckenridge's exhaustive efforts to equip and arm the First West Tennessee Cavalry and his willingness to share his men's privations while Fielding Hurst sleeps a mile away from camp in his featherbed. You will learn that Breckenridge, the regiment's second-in-command, disdains the stealing of citizens' valuables by certain members of the regiment. We also learn that many of the men—if not most—find

Hurst's behaviors and those of his immediate cronies reprehensible. That new disclosure is heartening.

I should let you, the reader, in on a little secret of my own. In the process of my research into this book, I often came across mention in Breckenridge's journal of a villainous young solider by the name of Tom Walker, whom I later discovered to be a young lieutenant named Benjamin Thomas Walker. This soldier was often detailed by Hurst and another officer, William Jay Smith, to loot and burn the homes and farms of individuals in West Tennessee, normally Confederates or Confederate sympathizers. According to Breckenridge's journal, Walker was usually accompanied by one or more others as he wreaked havoc upon citizens in West Tennessee. Soon, history and my own genealogy would collide.

As my research continued, I occasionally "chased a rabbit" in the form of looking into the service records of my own ancestors who served in the First West Tennessee Cavalry. One afternoon in a lull in my work, I decided it was long past time that I researched the elder brother of my own great-great grandfather. I knew little about Isaac T. McIntyre and wanted to fill in the great gaps that existed in my information about this uncle who died in 1864 and was buried in the National Cemetery in Memphis, Tennessee. I pulled Isaac's compiled military record and got a swift and harsh kick in the gut. I learned that Isaac was an accomplice to Walker's war crimes and was personally selected by Hurst to transfer to the same company as Walker and thereafter detached to accompany Walker on his missions. It was one of those moments when my own history was revised and—for the sake of historical accuracy and honesty—I had to swallow whatever familial pride previously existed toward Isaac, and put him on record for history and expose his own part in a dark and terrible chapter in history. I would not have it any other way. Such are the dangers of shaking the limbs of the family tree.

As you prepare to allow yourself to stroll back into history, I ask only that you keep an open mind as to the information with which you find yourself confronted. Many who read this book will begin with firm prejudices on either side of the conflicts. Some may have a very negative view of the regiment and Fielding Hurst. To you, I would ask for a careful evaluation of what you read and allow yourself to determine if your opinion is based on fact or fable. Some may feel Hurst has been grossly mistreated by history. To you, I would say largely the same thing. Ultimately, I want all who read this work and consider its merits to concentrate on the contributions, actions, accomplishments, and attitudes of Lieutenant Colonel William K.M. Breckenridge. An evaluation of this officer is long overdue and history owes him that obligation, if nothing else.

JOHN E. TALBOTT, J.D.

IN THE SHADOW OF THE DEVIL

1

TWO MEN, a NATIONAL CONFLICT, and STORM CLOUDS

On October 11, 1863, a sick and war weary Union officer watched his men march by under the command of a man he neither liked nor respected. The last year of his life had been frustrating and filled with both successes and setbacks. But as Lieutenant Colonel William Kibben Matthews Breckenridge watched from his hotel window, one can only imagine what went through his mind. He may have thought about home and family or worried about the men he had led for more than a year. Perhaps his mind drifted back to the last war his country had called upon him to fight. That was in Mexico more than fifteen years before. Maybe he thought back to his days on the frontier at Fort Larned, Kansas. The fact remains that we will never know other than what he penned in his journal.

To better understand Breckenridge's role in the U.S First West Tennessee Cavalry, one must understand and better appreciate his background. In fact, that very background is key to understanding the man and the events that molded his career during the American Civil War. One must understand how his experiences came to be used in the formation of a controversial Southern Unionist regiment later known as the Sixth Tennessee Cavalry. Breckenridge was an experienced Army officer. His career may be the best detailed aspect of his life. His personal life and his background, however, are as murky as the history of the regiment he helped to form and lead.

Breckenridge was born in 1825 in Maury County, Tennessee.[1] According to the late John Sickles, a descendant of Breckenridge, the future soldier was the son of David and Hannah Breckenridge. Interestingly, he was named for Hannah's first husband, the late William Kibben Matthews.[2] According to Sickles, Breckenridge was a Lowland Scot.[3] At one time, he worked in an apothecary, though he was by career a military man.[4] His experience would serve him well beginning in 1862 and be severely tested. Aside from his parentage, little else is known about his early life prior to joining the army. He may have apprenticed at the age of fifteen and was living away from his parents.[5]

In 1846, President James Knox Polk, also from Maury County, led the United States into war with Mexico. Though seldom studied by today's youth in school, the Mexican War was a watershed moment for the still fledgling nation. The causes of this war—which a young officer name Ulysses S. Grant thought wicked—were central to the annexation of Texas.[6] Polk himself believed fundamentally in the country's westward expansion, whether by peaceful negotiation or military means.[7]

---

1. John Sickles, *A Chronological Sketch of the Life of William Kibben Matthews Breckenridge* (Merrillville, Indiana: Self-published, 2011).

2. Ibid.

3. Ibid.

4. Register of Enlistments in the U.S. Army, 1798–1914. National Archives Microfilm Publication M233, Roll 81. Records of the Adjutant General's Office, 1780s–1917, Record Group 94. National Archives and Records Administration, Washington, D.C.

5. Sickles, *Breckenridge*, 1.

6. C. Vann Woodward, ed. *White House Under Fire, Responses of the Presidents to Charges of Misconduct* (New York: Dell Publishing Company, 1974), 30–38. John S.D. Eisenhower, *So Far from God: The U.S. War with Mexico, 1846–1848* (Norman, OK: University of Oklahoma Press, 1989), 17–26.

7. Dale L. Walker, *Pacific Destiny: The Three-Century Journey to the Oregon Country* (New York: Forge Press, 2000), 375. Eisenhower, *White House Under Fire*, 17–25.

Ultimately, with Mexico viewing Texas as its territory wrongfully seized by its northern neighbor, war became inevitable.[8]

As 1846 faded into 1847, more and more Tennesseans were drawn into the conflict. Breckenridge was among them. He enlisted in the United States Army on September 30, 1847, in Lewis County, Tennessee.[9] He served as a private in Company A (Capt. Leftwich's Co.) of the Third Tennessee Infantry. He worked as a hospital attendant (or steward) in a military hospital at Molino Del Ray, Mexico, in March and April of 1848.[10] He missed the Battle of Molino Del Ray, which occurred on September 8, 1847. Present at that battle, primarily observing, was General Winfield Scott, "Old Fuss and Feathers" himself.[11] Breckenridge's service was somewhat brief; he was mustered out and discharged from the service at Memphis, Tennessee, on July 22, 1848.[12] Whether he entered private life for a significant period of time or just for a while, it is not known.

Breckenridge's private life is somewhat of a mystery. The records evidencing that private life show just how complicated it was. He never mentioned his wife or children in his wartime journal and he never recorded any letter to his spouse or from her in it either. It seems, on its face, an odd situation. Research has yielded some answers. The situation between Breckenridge and his wife was a strained one for the times. He married Dicey Wilson in Lawrence County, Tennessee on July 3, 1851, with minister J.C. Sparkman officiating.[13] Perhaps the couple married

---

8. Ibid.

9. Compiled Service Record of William K.M. Breckenridge. Compiled Service Records of Volunteer Soldiers Who Served During the Mexican War in Organizations from the State of Tennessee. Records of the Adjutant General's Office, 1762-1984. Record Group Number RG 94. Series Number M638. NARA Roll 7. National Archives and Records Administration; Washington, D.C.

10. Breckenridge Compiled Service Record.

11. Walker, *Pacific Destiny*, 17–25.

12. Breckenridge Compiled Service Record.

13. Byron Sistler and Barbara Sistler, *Early Middle Tennessee Marriages, Volume 1, Grooms*. (Self-published, 1988), 60. Claude A. Carter, Lawrence County, Tennessee Marriage Records, 1818–1923. Self-published, 1979. Reprinted with permission. Lawrenceburg TN: The Family Tree Press, 1992. Tennessee State Marriages, 1780–2002. Tennessee State Library and Archives, Nashville TN, microfilm.

because she was pregnant out of wedlock. Their child, William Daniel Breckenridge, was born on March 15, 1852.[14]

However, the marriage didn't last long. In 1869, an individual familiar with the situation stated that they were personally acquainted with the Breckenridges during the time they lived together. He declared that he knew that Dicey Breckenridge had two children in adultery since the birth of William Daniel Breckenridge and that the Breckenridges did not live together any longer than fifteen days after their marriage.[15] The same individual further stated the couple did not claim the other children, only William Daniel Breckenridge.[16]

Dicey Breckenridge abandoned her son when he was only about nineteen months old.[17] In 1871, Breckenridge's sisters, Milly Patterson and Nancy Patterson, testified as follows:

> That during the continuance of their marriage there were born unto them one child only, to wit: William D. Breckenridge. That the said W.K.M. Breckenridge and his said wife separated about the time of the birth of said child, and the said Dicy not being a suitable person to have care and custody of a child abandoned the said William D. at the age of seventeen to nineteen months said child was raised by Mrs. Angelina McNeill until he was in his eighth year. We further state that the said Dicy has been gone from this country for many years and contributed nothing to the support of her said child after the first abandonment and after he was taken to the house of Mrs. McNeill.[18]

---

14. W.K.M. Breckenridge Pension Papers. Army Pension, Declaration of Guardian of Orphan Child. National Archives and Records Administration, Washington, D.C.

15. Sickles, *Breckenridge*. Army Pension, Declaration of Guardian of Orphan Child,

16. Breckenridge Pension Papers

17. Sickles, *Breckenridge*, 1.

18. Breckenridge Pension Papers

Following the war, it appears that Dicey Breckenridge made an effort to draw a pension on W.K.M. Breckenridge, a pension which should have gone to William Daniel Breckenridge, but she was unsuccessful.[19]

In any event, Dicey abandoned the couple's son around late 1853 or early 1854. However, it appears that Breckenridge was still at home at the time. It was shortly after the abandonment that Breckenridge appears to have joined the United States Army once again, leaving his son in the care of family. In 1860, Dicey was maintaining her own residence in Wayne County, Tennessee, and was working as a seamstress.[20] The 1860 Census gives a hint as to perhaps why Dicey abandoned William Daniel Breckenridge in or around late 1853 or early 1854. Living with her in 1860 were her illegitimate son, James N. Breckenridge, only five years old, and an Elizabeth Y. Wilson, who was twelve when the census was taken.[21] According to contemporaneous family sources in 1871, this child did not belong to William K.M. Breckenridge.

In 1860, Breckenridge's son, William Daniel, was living with his paternal grandfather, David Breckenridge, and William K.M. Breckenridge was winding up his service on the frontier. All of this personal instability would account for why Breckenridge never mentions home, his wife or his children in his journal. By 1862 and 1863, they were a part of a dark past. In fact, the only mention which Breckenridge makes of his family in his journal is a mention of his father, David, and then only once and not by name. More interestingly, there exists no record that he traveled home or attempted to travel home to check on his family.

On September 25, 1855, Breckenridge enlisted in Company C of the Second Dragoons. His enlisting officer was a Captain Taylor and he signed up in St. Louis, Missouri.[22] He was still a young man, tall with a ruddy complexion, and long removed from the man who eight years later was tired and frail of health watching his men march by his window

19. Email from Frank Breckenridge (great-great-grandson of William K.M. Breckenridge) to the author, August 14, 2020.

20. Eighth Census of the United States, 1860. Series Number M653, Records of the Bureau of the Census, District 8, Lawrence County, Tennessee. National Archives and Records Administration, Washington, D.C.

21. Ibid.

22. Register of Enlistments in the U.S. Army, 1798–1914. National Archives Microfilm Publication M233, Roll 81. Records of the Adjutant General's Office, 1780s–1917. Record Group 94, National Archives and Records Administration, Washington, D.C.

without him.²³ The Second Dragoons were a colorful unit with a colorful history and already had such a history by the time of Breckenridge's enlistment in the regiment. Breckenridge was becoming a part of a regiment that saw its first combat in June 1836 during the Second Seminole War. Their next combat role was during the Mexican War. The Second Dragoons' history during that conflict was central to the invasion of Mexico by United States forces.

By the time Breckenridge had enlisted in the regiment, the Second Dragoons were actively engaged in protecting American settlers on the nation's new frontier. The lands had been acquired in the Treaty of Guadalupe Hidalgo. Prior to his involvement with the First West Tennessee/Sixth Tennessee Cavalry, Breckenridge was stationed at Fort Larned, Kansas, a remote outpost far from the hills of Middle Tennessee. There he became a seasoned soldier, acquiring the kind of impromptu military education that would serve him well in his future dealings with Fielding Hurst.

The Fort Larned that Breckenridge found in 1859 was a vastly different outpost than it would become after 1861. The post as it remains today is the preserved fort of the post-1861 era. Fort Larned was an outpost on the Pawnee River along the Santa Fe Trail. Today, it is a National Historic Site and wonderfully preserved with nine original buildings constructed of native stone, including two barracks buildings and post hospital, two company officers' quarters, the commanding officer's quarters, a shops building, two commissary buildings, and the quartermaster's storehouse.²⁴

This post is a far cry from the Fort Larned experienced by Breckenridge. When he left there in September of 1860, it consisted of an officer's quarters, combined barracks and storehouse, a guardhouse, two laundresses' quarters, and a hospital. These structures were inadequate for their purpose—sod houses and adobe dwellings which surely made for an uncomfortable existence. He had to make do with a tent in rains and winds and summertime humidity like that back home. Still, to get a better idea of what Breckenridge endured while at Fort Larned, a look at the sketches and drawings of Private Robert F. Roche would help. A soldier in Company G of the Second Infantry, Roche was stationed at Fort Larned during the same period as Breckenridge. He drew a number of sketches and il-

23. Ibid.

24. Leo E. Olivia, *Fort Larned: Guardian of the Santa Fe Trail* (Topeka: Kansas State Historical Society, 1982), 27–40.

Fort Larned, Kansas
Author's Collection

lustrations of the post between the period of May–November 1860.[25] At that time, there was significant standing timber around the post. Today, Fort Larned is in the midst of a windswept plain, the only substantial vegetation being that growing along the Pawnee River.[26]

Breckenridge most likely had an interesting experience at Fort Larned. According to James M. Fugate in his *Scouting Adventures in 1853*, Kansas at that time was "one vast wild plain, over which roving bands of hostile Indians were constantly cutting off emigrant and freight trains on their way to New Mexico and the Californias."[27] Major John C. McFerran in his *Report and Journal, 1865*, commented on the building of Fort Larned, giving one a better idea of what Breckenridge saw and experienced.

> Fort Larned is a post of four companies, some sixty-five miles by the ridge road and one hundred miles by the river road, below Fort Dodge. It was built in 1858, '59, and '60, of logs set endwise in the ground and roofed with earth. It is on the Pawnee fork, but too far from the road, is surrounded by an abundance of fuel, water, and good grazing. Hay can be cut within a few miles of the post, at a cost, I should think, of about twenty dollars per ton, delivered. It is a proper place for

---

25. Ibid, 12–15. Copies of Roche's sketches can be found on these pages.

26. The author traveled to Fort Larned, Kansas, in the summer of 2017 to gain a better understanding of Breckenridge's posting prior to the Civil War as well as the history of Fort Larned.

27. Marc Simmons, ed., *On the Santa Fe Trail* (Lawrence: University of Kansas Press, 1986), 29.

a military post, and should be the depot of supplies for any troops acting against Indians on that line...²⁸

Breckenridge mustered out of the service on September 25, 1860, at Fort Larned, as an orderly sergeant. Then he came back East. Yet he wasn't finished serving his country. He would have learned something about Army bureaucracy and the military structure during his years as a professional soldier. Those skills would be useful in the new war that was brewing.

As the war clouds loomed and the country was being torn apart from within, no one could escape the turmoil. The divisions within the nation spared few Americans. Breckenridge was no different. As a Southerner, he naturally fell under suspicion by the military. No sooner had he been discharged from the Army than he was accused of being a secessionist. This charge was a severe accusation in the months after Fort Sumter and the onset of the Civil War. Breckenridge was arrested on November 9, 1861, and confined to a prison in Washington, D.C. According to the *Official Records of the War of the Rebellion:*

> This person [W.K.N. Breckinridge] was arrested November 9, 1861, and confined in the Thirteenth Street Prison by order of Major General McClellan. He was seen on the 8th of November with General McClellan's staff by Dr. C.A. Henry, formerly deputy marshal of Nebraska Territory, who remembered him as an orderly sergeant of Company C, Second U.S. Dragoons. Breckenridge was at that time a bitter secessionist; claimed to be a cousin of Vice-President Breckinridge and stated that he had a commission from the State of Tennessee in the rebel army. He was released by order of General Porter November 13, 1861.²⁹

---

28. Ibid, 101.

29. *The War of the Rebellion: A Compilation of the Official Records of the Union and Confederate Armies, Series II, Volume 2* (Washington, D.C., Government Printing Office, 1891), 316. (Hereafter referred to as *OR*.) Incidentally, Breckenridge is often referred to as "W.K.N. Breckinridge" or "W.K.N. Breckinridge." He is also identified by his regiment and company in this reference to an arrest. The regiment, company, and officer's rank are Breckenridge's. There is little doubt that the two are one and the same. The generals mentioned in this report were closely aligned. Major General George B. McClellan and Brigadier General Fitz John Porter were both in Washington,

Breckenridge was also found on a list of persons received at the Old Capitol Prison. Perhaps this charge of disloyalty to the Union laid the groundwork for at least part of his later difficulties with Fielding Hurst. It is ironic that he would face such accusations in the same period of time that Hurst was being persecuted by secessionists in McNairy County for his outspoken support for the preservation of the Union.

Many individuals in 1861 found themselves scrutinized on both sides of the conflict. In this respect, Breckenridge and Hurst had something in common: both were jailed for suspicion of their beliefs. Hurst was imprisoned and accused by local Confederates of being a Unionist and anti-secessionist, which he was indeed.[30] Breckenridge was jailed and accused of being a "bitter secessionist" and disloyal citizen, which he was not. No man could have been so bitterly secessionist and then work so assiduously to raise a Union Army regiment of cavalry, as Breckenridge shortly would. In fact, time would eventually prove just how loyal Breckenridge was to his Army and his nation.

It is important for the reader to understand the personalities and backgrounds of these two men whose activities will ultimately comprise the majority of this work. They were very different in many aspects. Breckenridge's background, as much of it as is known, was not affluent. He did not come from money or privilege and his station in life was humble. He was a career soldier and accustomed to adhering to the rules of an established military structure.

Fielding Hurst was another story entirely. As a farmer, surveyor, and attorney, he had attained more than modest wealth. His personality seemed tailor made for the role he would soon play and the legacy he would eventually establish, whether fair or not. Hurst was a fierce supporter of the American Union, but he was enigmatic in so many ways. Despite his Unionist beliefs, he was a slave owner, possessing no fewer than 23

D.C., in November 1861, transferring raw recruits into the force that would become the Army of the Potomac. Porter became fiercely loyal to McClellan as their association grew. Ezra J. Warner, *Generals in Blue: Lives of the Union Commanders*. Baton Rogue: Louisiana State University Press, 1964, 378–379.

30. Kevin D. McCann explained the seed of Fielding Hurst's extremely partisan views and his resulting treatment by local Confederate officials in his work, *Hurst's Wurst: Colonel Fielding Hurst and the Sixth Tennessee Cavalry, U.S.A* (Dickson TN: McCann Publishing Company, 2007), 10–13.

slaves in 1860.³¹ Perhaps his personality combined with his strong beliefs led to the explosive circumstances in which he found himself. Hurst was no affable person. He was, according to the eminent Tennessee attorney and jurist John A. Pitts, "a very sensible man, though full of prejudice, fractious and litigious, utterly devoid of any sense of humor, serious on all subjects."³² That very personality description seems apt in light of events pertaining to Hurst both before and after the war.

Hurst's apparent boldness as well as his personality were likely provocative to his neighbors and the secessionist leaders of McNairy County, Tennessee, where Hurst lived and thrived financially. To better understand Hurst's hardening and quickly radicalizing views, one must understand the atmosphere of its county seat, Purdy, in 1861. Though today a relative wide spot in the road, at that time it was a seat of power in rural West Tennessee. The area's antebellum congressman, John Vines Wright, a favorite son and resident of the village, had left office in March 1861. He, his brother Marcus Joseph Wright, and their boyhood friend, Dew Moore Wisdom, were among the spirited young secessionists who were putting together units for the new Confederate Army. Purdy was in many ways emblematic of small Southern towns who put their collective hearts into the new Confederate States of America.

As this secessionist fervor swept the town of Purdy, Fielding Hurst endured far more serious encounters with his oppressors than did Breckenridge. While Breckenridge spent only a few short days in jail, Hurst was arrested three times between the summer of 1861 and February of 1862.³³ He certainly wasn't alone. Hurst attested to the means by which Confederates forced locals in his area to contribute to their cause: "Union men was [sic] compelled to lay out, leave the Country, go to prison, or enlist in the Rebel Army."³⁴

---

31. Eighth Census of the United States, 1860. Series Number M653, Record Group Number 29, United States of America, Bureau of the Census. National Archives and Records, Washington, D.C.

32. John A. Pitts, *Personal and Professional Reminiscences of an Old Lawyer* (Kingsport TN: Southern Publishers, Inc., 1930), 184.

33. McCann, *Hurst's Wurst*, 10.

34. Deposition of Fielding Hurst. Southern Claims Commission. Claim No. 17782. Claim of Pitser M. Cheshier, Claim Date: December 5, 1872, NARA Publication Number M1407, Roll No. 014, National Archives and Records Administration, Washington, D.C.

Col. Fielding Hurst
Author's Collection

One example of how local Confederates often threatened residents to contribute to or join their cause is the story of Mary Swain, who also lived in McNairy County.[35] Her husband, William W. Swain, left home when the war started and traveled north to Illinois to join the Union Army.[36] He participated in the battles for Forts Henry and Donelson but took ill and was discharged in Cincinnati, Ohio.[37] He returned home in October 1862 and went to work scouting for the Union Army. He was later killed at Eastport, Mississippi, on February 14, 1864.[38] Swain's activities made him a target of local Confederates. When the news first came back in 1861 that Swain had gone north to join the Union Army, they threatened his wife with the confiscation and sale of the family farm for the benefit of the Confederate Army and government.[39]

In June 1862, Confederate Major Houghton went to Mrs. Swain's home and informed her that if her husband didn't return and give himself up to Confederate Army, Houghton and his men would burn everything the Swains owned.[40] In 1864, another group of Confederate soldiers under the command of an officer named Skinner visited Mrs. Swain and gave her ten days to leave her premises or they would drive her out of her house and "burn up the place."[41] Worse still, Skinner threatened to take her daughter to prison until her husband gave himself up.[42] Mrs. Swain further recounted that she was harassed many times and "was disabled from raising (or having) a crop raised when they taken my horses and

---

35. Mary Martha Caroline Alexander Swain (May 25, 1825–March 9, 1893) was married to William W. Swain. Born about 1826, there is some dispute as to the death date of William Swain. According to some family sources, he died on February 17, 1862. According to Mary Swain herself, her husband died on February 14, 1864.

36. Deposition of Mary Swain. Barred and Disallowed Case Files of the Southern Claims Commission, 1871–1880. Records of the U.S. House of Representatives, 1789–2015. Record Group Number 233. Series Number M1407. National Archives and Records Administration, Washington, D.C.

37. Ibid.
38. Ibid.
39. Ibid.
40. Ibid.
41. Ibid.
42. Ibid.

when our cows were taken. My children suffered from want of milk and butter."⁴³ Mrs. Swain's story was not an isolated one.

Fielding Hurst had no intention of having any of the options of flight, forced conscription, acquiescence, or prison, forced upon him. Still, according to Hurst himself, "I was forced to leave my house, and otherwise abused, had my family abused, and property destroyed."⁴⁴ He claimed specifically that he was imprisoned three times: in September 1861, in late November 1861, and again from December 16, 1861 through January 27, 1862, the latter imprisonment stemming from a trial held by a Confederate court.⁴⁵ A thorough account of the trials of Hurst, both literally and figuratively, may be found in McCann's *Hurst's Wurst: Colonel Fielding Hurst and the Sixth Tennessee Cavalry, U.S.A.* Following the last period of incarceration, he was released to return home to Purdy.⁴⁶

Following Hurst's return, he discovered that his local secessionist neighbors had pillaged his farm.⁴⁷ No sooner had he come back than he was arrested once again by Confederate authorities and sent to Columbus, Kentucky.⁴⁸ Within a short time, Hurst managed to escape his captors.⁴⁹ The ransacking of his property, his arrest, and the clear intentions of local and regional secessionists to permanently eliminate him could only have succeeded in further embittering him. They certainly helped set the course for his future actions.

As Hurst was returning home for good from custody, events detrimental to Confederate hopes were hurdling down the tracks. In February 1862, Forts Henry and Donelson fell to Union naval and armed forces, opening up the Tennessee and Cumberland Rivers for navigation and invasion. As Union forces made their way south toward Pittsburg Landing and beyond, Hurst and other ardent Unionists became more encouraged. Confederate control in Hurst's own home county, McNairy County, and

43. Ibid.

44. Deposition of Fielding Hurst. Southern Claims Commission. Claim No. 17782. Claim of Pitser M. Cheshier, Claim Date: December 5, 1872. NARA Publication Number M1407, Roll No. 014, National Archives and Records Administration, Washington, D.C.

45. McCann, *Hurst's Wurst*, 10–12.

46. Ibid.

47. Ibid, 12–13.

48. Ibid, 13.

49. Ibid.

surrounding areas was about to become extremely tenuous. The very men who had persecuted him were about to realize their Southern Confederacy was far more vulnerable than they may have been willing to acknowledge or even realize.

In March of 1862, as events were gathering steam for a decisive and explosive clash at a church called Shiloh in nearby Hardin County, Hurst assembled a group of scouts, all Southerners and loyal to the Union cause.[50] This task wasn't as daunting as it might seem. Certain sections of West Tennessee were just as divided as families everywhere in the war-torn nation. McNairy County in particular had distinct divisions within it. When Abraham Lincoln was elected president in 1860, Tennessee was confronted with the burning question of secession from the Union. Determining the answer to that question required one of two events or both to occur: (1) a convention to determine the secession question, or (2) a referendum putting the question to a direct vote by the people (a white male population).

Unlike other Southern states, the issue of secession was not an open and shut case in Tennessee. There was no overwhelming drive to leave the Union simply because of Lincoln's election. The course of action was rather cautious with an eye toward reconciliation and remaining in the Union. Despite his own prejudices and hot rhetoric, Tennessee Governor Isham G. Harris proposed to the legislature that the question be submitted to the voters whether a convention should be held to consider secession.[51] It was rejected by some 9,000 votes.[52] Hurst's own McNairy County also voted against the convention.[53] Some Unionists in Tennessee felt they had achieved a great victory, but the issue was far from settled.[54]

Events continued to occur elsewhere that would help decide the state's course. On April 12, 1861, Confederate forces opened fire on Fort Sumter in Charleston Harbor and took the fort from the Federals the

50. Ibid, 14.

51. Sam Davis Elliott, *Confederate Governor and United States Senator Isham G. Harris of Tennessee* (Baton Rogue: Louisiana State University Press, 2010), 60–66. Thomas Perkins Abernathy, *From Frontier to Plantation in Tennessee: A Study in Frontier Democracy* (Memphis TN: Memphis State College Press, 1955), 329–345. Robert E. Corlew, *Tennessee: A Short History*. 2nd Edition. (Knoxville: University of Tennessee Press, 1990), 284–297.

52. Corlew, *Tennessee*, 291.

53. Abernethy, *From Frontier to Plantation*, 343.

54. Corlew, *Tennessee*, 291.

next day.⁵⁵ This event catapulted matters even faster. Lincoln's reaction was to call for volunteers to suppress the rebellion.⁵⁶ This call spurred Governor Harris to inform the president that "Tennessee will not furnish a single man for the purpose of coercion but fifty thousand if necessary for the defense of our rights and those of our Southern brothers."⁵⁷ Lincoln's call for troops not only incensed Harris but pushed Tennessee over the edge toward secession. In June of 1861, the issue went directly to the people once again with a different result. The choice was overwhelming now, 104,913 for secession and 47,238 against.⁵⁸ The question now was a matter of Tennesseans' support of their state government.⁵⁹ Both West Tennessee and Middle Tennessee voted almost overwhelmingly for secession, but there was dissent in a number of counties along the Tennessee River and its vicinity.⁶⁰ Though McNairy County voted for secession, there were many like Hurst, especially in parts of its north and central sections, who fervently opposed secession. Eventually, their fervor would show in their support of and enlistment in Union regiments.⁶¹

In fact, McNairy County was as much a hotbed for loyalist Unionists as it was for rebellious Confederates. Its loyalists were every bit as ardent as its most renowned Unionist, Hurst himself, although their tactics were usually different. Many of them traveled north to Southern Illinois to escape the regional turmoil, any of innumerable dangers, or especially forced conscription into the Confederate Army. A number of north McNairy Countians weathered the war years there including John A. McIntyre, George Bulliner, and Isabel Jane Coleman and her children. Interestingly, all of these individuals are buried within feet of one another

---

55. E. Milby Burton, *The Siege of Charleston, 1861–1865* (Columbia: University of South Carolina Press, 1970), 43–51.

56. Shelby Foote, *The Civil War, A Narrative: Fort Sumter to Perryville* (New York: Random House, 1958), 51.

57. Ibid, 52.

58. Corlew, *Tennessee*, 294.

59. Abernethy, *From Frontier to Plantation*, 340–341.

60. Ibid, 342.

61. A review of the service records on file in the National Archives gives ready evidence of Union support in McNairy County, Tennessee, as well as the large number of U.S. Army headstones in cemeteries across the county.

in north McNairy County's Mount Carmel Cemetery.[62] There is no way to know how many sought refuge within the confines of northern states but in the case of McIntyre, he was just a young teenager sent there by his father, the influential Unionist Robert Thompson McIntyre. Coleman, who would one day become young McIntyre's mother-in-law, apparently emigrated while her husband, John, was serving as a nurse in the Washington Hospital in Memphis.[63]

There are examples of loyal Unionists who went to greater lengths to serve their nation in its greatest period of turmoil. A prime example of strength under adversity was Nancy Webster, another north McNairy Countian. She was a resolute supporter of the Union. Her sons Daniel and William served in the Seventh Tennessee Cavalry, a Southern Unionist regiment under the leadership of Colonel Isaac R. Hawkins, also known as "Hawkins' Tories."[64] According to Mrs. Webster, her sons "had to leave home to keep from being forced in the Rebel Army."[65] She didn't know what became of them until she heard they had already joined the Union Army.[66] Mrs. Webster herself was active on behalf of the cause. She testified after the war that she carried victuals to the troops and the sick and wounded at Pittsburg Landing after the Battle of Shiloh.[67] She stated further: "I carried the food to the tents which they called the Hospital but do not know what command the men belonged to or where they were from. It was enough for me to know they belonged to the Union Army."[68]

Mrs. Webster's visit to the battlefield to minister to the wounded afforded her a look at history being made. The tent hospital she saw was the first of its kind in American history, the first consolidated tent hospital

---

62. John E. Talbott, J.D. *A Sacred High Place: A History of Mount Carmel Cemetery & Meetinghouse, McNairy County, Tennessee* (Dickson TN: BrayBree Publishing Company, LLC, 2012), 37–38; 68–86.

63. Ibid.

64. Deposition of Nancy Webster. Southern Claims Commission Approved Claims, 1871–1880, Claim No. 17793, Claim Date: December 5, 1872. National Archives and Records Administration, Washington, D.C.

65. Ibid.

66. Ibid.

67. Ibid.

68. Ibid.

on an American battlefield.[69] She traveled from her home near White Oak Creek in the community known as Rocky Knob in the far northern reaches of McNairy County.[70] Upon her arrival and trek through the battlefield area to the tent hospital, she saw carnage of proportions not previously seen on American soil. Undoubtedly, her desire to serve the Union cause was resolute and firm to have been willing to witness such human suffering and lend her hand to assist.

Mrs. Webster's patriotism existed in both word and deed. "I advised my husband and sons to stand by the old flag," she wrote.[71] She was "for the Union all the time, State or no State."[72]

> I can't describe my feelings over the defeat of the Union Army at Bull Run. And it is about as hard to tell how glad I was over our success at the other times and places, it is enough to say I was hurt at the one, and elated at the other.[73]

Like many of her neighbors, Mrs. Webster was threatened with arrest and imprisonment by area Confederates, not to mention having her property plundered.[74] But the threats were never enough for her to give up her sentiments.[75]

Mrs. Webster's son William became a Rebel soldier for a while. The story she told of his predicament is a compelling one and similar to those witnessed and heard by Breckenridge. She was resourceful, traveling to Henderson Station to convince her son to desert the Confederate Army. She hoped to get her son to the Union gunboats on the Tennessee River,

---

69. Captain John H. Fahey, MC USN (Ret.), "Bernard John Dowling Irwin and the Development of the Field Hospital at Shiloh." *Military Medicine*, 171, no. 5 (May 2006), 345.

70. Deposition of Nancy Webster.

71. Ibid.

72. Ibid.

73. Ibid.

74. Ibid. Mrs. Webster stated that the Rebels took a mule from one of her sons, William Webster, in May 1863.

75. Ibid.

thus assuring his safety from Confederate conscription.[76] She later recalled the situation in 1872:

> My son William enlisted in the Rebel Army and was considered a Rebel soldier for a while, and I used my influence with him to desert and he did so at my request, and he and Daniel went away together and joined the Union Army. William never left the county nor never done any service. This was all before the Union Army came into this part of the country. William was only 17 years of age and was persuaded by his rebel companions of the neighborhood to join the Rebels and he done it without my knowledge or consent. He lives now at Trunnels Cross Roads [today known as Trundle Crossroad] in Seveere [Sevier] County in the Eastern part of this State. I had no chance to use my influence with him. He was hired out away from home, and when I heard he had joined the Rebels I went to Henderson Station and persuaded him to come home and then I got him to come home and then I got him and Daniel and leave the country. And that their intentions was to go North and about 3 months after they left I heard they were both in Col. Hawkins's Regiment.[77]

Mrs. Webster's sacrifice included the loss of her husband, also named William Webster. He had enlisted in the First West Tennessee Cavalry, but took ill and never served.[78] She was a strong woman. A story about a horse taken by the First West Tennessee Cavalry demonstrates her view on her own position in the world and her willingness to face down even Fielding Hurst. Her story provides a number of interesting details that paint a picture of life in war-torn West Tennessee during the period following the collapse of the Confederate regime in McNairy County and surrounding areas.

---

76. Deposition of Jessie J. Clemmons. Southern Claims Commission Approved Claims, 1871–1880. Claim No. 17793. Claimant: Nancy Webster, Claim Date: December 5, 1872. National Archives and Records Administration, Washington, D.C.

77. Ibid.

78. Deposition of Nancy Webster.

Mrs. Webster sent her sons John and Marion on an errand. They were about one mile from Johnson's Mill near the Rocky Knob community, when they encountered a group of Union soldiers on the road who were in a great hurry.[79] Two of them, brothers Elijah and Jessie Clemmons, were sent by Colonel Hurst himself to arrest three Rebels in the far northern reaches of McNairy County.[80] The Union scouts were hastily trying to get back to their camp at Purdy, as they feared an attack from the rear.[81] The Websters met the Union scouts and their prisoners about a half mile from White Oak Creek just a short distance from the Tennessee Valley Divide,[82] known by generations of locals as Dividing Ridge.[83] One of the Rebel prisoners was making trouble and refused to walk.[84] Fearing a possible attack, the Union soldiers ordered Marion Webster to dismount and turn his horse over to the prisoner to ride.[85] Marion did so and ultimately the horse was shot accidentally when a Union soldier in camp dropped his revolver. The hammer struck a small stump and discharged, lodging in the horse and eventually killing it.[86] Mrs. Webster went directly to Fielding Hurst, addressed the issue with him, and he gave her an "old broken down horse" that was no longer of any use to the Army. She rode it home but it died shortly thereafter.[87]

Mrs. Webster's sacrifice to the Union was larger still. One son, Daniel, was later captured and imprisoned at Andersonville Prison in Georgia.[88] He was one of the fortunate ones who survived. One of the Union soldiers

79. Deposition of John Webster, Southern Claims Commission Approved Claims, 1871–1880. Claim No. 17793. Claimant: Nancy Webster. Claim Date: December 5, 1872. National Archives and Records Administration, Washington, D.C.

80. Ibid.

81. Deposition of Jessie J. Clemmons.

82. Ibid.

83. The author grew up within a few miles of Dividing Ridge. He was taught its significance as a geological formation that divides the drainage of waters between the two great rivers that form the east and west borders of West Tennessee. All waters flowing or falling on the west side of Dividing Ridge eventually make their way to the Mississippi River and all waters flowing or falling on the east side of the ridge eventually make their way to the Tennessee River.

84. Deposition of Jessie J. Clemmons.

85. Ibid.

86. Ibid.

87. Deposition of Nancy Webster.

88. Deposition of Jessie J. Clemmons.

who requisitioned Mrs. Webster's horse, Jessie J. Clemmons, testified generally that he had known Mrs. Webster "to visit the army and do whatever she could for the sick and wounded." He surmised her reasons were to learn the prospects of Union success.[89] Clemmons also recounted that he had heard of Mrs. Webster being treated "very badly" by one of the Ethridges, another local family nearby, simply because "she was a Union woman."[90] Her lengthy story is recounted here to demonstrate the atmosphere and conditions of relations between people in West Tennessee generally and specifically McNairy County, Hurst's place of residence and the scene of his own alleged persecution.

In March 1862, Fielding Hurst and his gathering of Unionists offered their services as scouts and spies to the Union Army.[91] Between March and June, they served in an unofficial capacity, providing intelligence and assistance to the invading Northerners. They happily harassed Confederate troops, destroying communication lines and rail lines and disrupting their supply lines. Their knowledge of their native soil was advantageous to their Union allies.[92] Despite their usefulness to the cause, Hurst and his men also established their proclivity for straying from the main army and pursuing their own objectives.[93] This habit would later cause Breckenridge major concerns.

With the Confederate tide having receded into Mississippi following their defeat at Shiloh and Andrew Johnson installed as military governor of Tennessee, Hurst was ready to formally raise a regiment. On July 23, 1862, he and Henderson County native James Tarkington, having raised enough recruits to form five companies, sought commissions from Governor Johnson to form a regiment.[94] The plan was for Tarkington to serve as colonel and Hurst as lieutenant colonel. This arrangement changed when Tarkington withdrew for unknown reasons as the plans

89. Ibid.
90. Ibid.
91. McCann, *Hurst's Wurst*, 14.
92. Ibid, 15.
93. Ibid.
94. Ibid, 16.

for the regiment formalized.[95] On August 12, 1862, it was Hurst who received the commission as colonel.[96]

It may be asked why so much attention is given to Fielding Hurst, the issue of secession, and the situation in West Tennessee. After all, the subject of this work is William K.M. Breckenridge. But to understand Breckenridge, the predicament he would face, and his level of frustration, it helps to understand the political climate in Tennessee in 1861 and 1862, the situation facing those Tennesseans who remained loyal to the Union, and the background of Hurst. Ultimately, Breckenridge and Hurst would be partners in the endeavor of building the First West Tennessee Cavalry. These matters would factor heavily into the controversies and incidents that so frustrated and taxed the energies of Breckenridge.

Breckenridge's background as a professional soldier was helpful to Hurst and the Union Army as the U.S. First West Tennessee Cavalry was being raised and equipped. Hurst was essentially a politician and an aggrieved citizen. Breckenridge possessed something far more valuable than a grudge. He had knowledge, experience, and an understanding of the Army bureaucracy and rules. Taxed as his talents would be, Breckenridge used his training to equip and help lead the First West Tennessee Cavalry. In fact, it appears that his expertise was desperately needed in 1862 and beyond. His involvement proved helpful to Hurst and the new regiment as it struggled to attain legitimacy and a role in the conflict in the months after the evacuation of West Tennessee by the regular organized Confederate forces following the Union victory at Shiloh.

Before they could fight or attempt to rid the region of Rebel guerillas, the regiment had to attain its official status and be properly equipped and accoutered, which it was not following the enlistment of the first six companies of men. As October 1862 dawned, Breckenridge was fully engaged in preparing the First West Tennessee Cavalry for its purpose of aiding the Union Army in West Tennessee and north Mississippi.

95. Ibid.
96. Ibid.

2

BUILDING a REGIMENT amid CONTROVERSY

August 1862–February 1863

No previous work has extended credit to Lieutenant Colonel William K.M. Breckenridge for his role in organizing and equipping the new First West Tennessee Cavalry in the fall of 1862. Little credit has ever been ascribed to Breckenridge generally; his death during the war robbed him of either fame or infamy. Indeed, his involvement in the organization and actual leadership of the unit largely appears nowhere other than in a few entries of the *Official Records of the War of the Rebellion*, compiled and published by the War Department in the decades after the war. Fielding Hurst gave little credit to Breckenridge in life and certainly none in death, obliterating his labors on behalf of the regiment. His death from disease in October 1863 effectively silenced him.

Had it not been for the journal Breckenridge began keeping in March 1863, such would have remained the case. It was a moment of incarceration that prompted him to begin recording his activities on behalf of the regiment as well as his observations of what others were doing to its detriment. The journal chronicles the growing pains of a new, irregular, volunteer Union regiment in what may be considered the worst of times in Civil War-era West Tennessee. His words offer a perspective long unknown to previous histories of operations in Middle and West Tennessee.

The exact moment at which Hurst and Breckenridge agreed to work together to organize the regiment is unknown. There appears to be no information that explains how the two men came to know one another. With the emergence of Breckenridge's journal, using language employed by him, it appears they "consolidated" on September 20, 1862, and began working together from that moment.[1] However, it is certain that Breckenridge's efforts on behalf of the regiment predated his actual enlistment. According to his compiled service record, he was appointed to serve by Fielding Hurst on November 13, 1862, but was "absent on detached business."[2] Yet, according to the same records, he was mustered in on November 15, 1862, at Bolivar, Tennessee.[3] This contradicts Breckenridge's own accounting of events. Too much should not be made of this disparity. After all, Hurst would withhold Breckenridge's commission until September 13, 1863, shortly before his death and almost a full year after his agreement with Hurst.[4]

According to Breckenridge, Hurst felt that Breckenridge was "best acquainted with military affairs" and in the best position to assist in equipping the regiment.[5] His activities on behalf of the new regiment carried him to Washington, D.C., St. Louis, and back to West Tennessee, as well as points in between.[6] It can only be assumed at this point that his duties included procurement of supplies, arms, and munitions. Breckenridge indicates in his journal and his letters that he and Hurst had an agreement about a month after the initial formation of the regiment. Hurst would recruit men and Breckenridge would maneuver the Army bureaucracy to procure the necessary arms and supplies needed to operate.

    1. Lt. Col. William K.M. Breckenridge Civil War Daybook, 1862–1863. Tennessee State Library and Archives. Hereafter cited as Breckenridge Day Book.

    2. Service Record of William K.M. Breckenridge. Compiled Service Records of Volunteer Union Soldiers Who Served in Organizations from the State of Tennessee. Publication Number M395, NARA Catalogue No. 300398, Record Group 94, Roll 0051. National Archives and Records Administration, Washington, D.C.

    3. Ibid.

    4. Breckenridge Day Book, 197.

    5. Ibid, 190.

    6. Ibid.

Hurst had already been recruiting men for the new regiment. Between August 11 and September 21, he had raised six companies, A through F.[7] These new recruits came largely from McNairy County and nearby areas.[8] The raising of that many companies indicated the type of resistance to Confederate authority that existed in that one county in West Tennessee. The recruits were from a variety of backgrounds. While most were farmers and farm laborers, there were other professions represented as well. Many of the initial officers of the regiment were well known and respected men. Hurst was successful in recruitment, but such efforts were of little use if men had no horses, arms, or munitions with which to fight.

Therefore, Breckenridge set to work on his end of the bargain. By October 1862, he had traveled to the nation's capital on behalf of the new regiment. While he was in Washington, it appeared that a breakdown in communication and cooperation was occurring for the first time between the two men. It would not be the last time that Hurst failed to communicate with his second-in-command. Breckenridge wrote to Hurst from Washington on October 12:

> Washington City, D.C.
> Oct. 12th, 62
>
> I take my pen in hand this morning to inform you that I have been here since last Tuesday a week ago and have written and telegraphed to you all most [sic] every day and have not heard from you yet. I want the Mustering Officer certificate showing that the regiment is mustered into the U.S. Service and then I can begin to get along here and try and get back as I come by St. Louis. I there had the promise of all that we wanted but the arms, and the horses I will bring as I come back. Please let me hear as soon as possible by telegraph about the certificate so that I can get away for I am out of money and would like to get away as soon as possible and if don't hear by the 15th, I shall start for St. Louis and leave this until I get the horses home and then come back. I wish I had have done that at first but as I am here I had better get it

---

7. *Tennesseans in the Civil War: A Military History of Confederate and Union Units, Part I* (Nashville TN: Civil War Centennial Commission), 1964, 333.

8. Ibid.

Lt. Col. William K.M. Breckenridge
Author's Collection

all fixed before I leave and then I will have nothing to do but get our men drilled. So no more at present but remain yours,

Respectfully,
Wm. K.M. Breckenridge
Lieut. Col. 1st West Tenn. Cav.[9]

Hurst appeared to make no effort to remain in contact with Breckenridge. Perhaps he was taking matters into his own hands. Apparently, he and certain soldiers were stealing horses from the citizens in the countryside. From the existing correspondence and records, it is clear that Hurst was procuring horses for his new regiment by stealing them from civilians.[10] This issue came to the attention of Major General Ulysses S. Grant, who addressed it with Brigadier General John Alexander "Black Jack" Logan.[11]

> Complaints are constantly coming to me of depredations committed by Hurst's men on Citizens [sic] through the country. They go about the country taking horses wherever they find them. They must desist from this practice or I will disband the whole concern. When horses are claimed by citizens, and there is no satisfactory reason why they should be taken, have them returned.[12]

This behavior or acquiescence to such behavior as looting and confiscation by Hurst would prove to be a point of contention between Hurst and Breckenridge. The letter makes it clear that Breckenridge was going

---

9. Breckenridge Day Book, 183. This letter—like many others recorded in Breckenridge's journal—are not recorded or otherwise documented in the *OR*. This is not unusual as many documents were never recovered or otherwise submitted in this record for various reasons.

10. McCann, *Hurst's Wurst*, 20.

11. John Alexander "Black Jack" Logan (1826–1886), a native of southern Illinois, had previously fought in the Mexican War. He was an elector for Democrat James Buchanan and served as a member of Congress on the Free-Soil Democrat ticket. A vociferous supporter of the Union, Logan was a supporter of Democrat Stephen A. Douglas. By this time, he was a veteran of the battles of Bull Run, Belmont, and Fort Donelson. In October 1862, Logan commanded a brigade and division of Grant's Army of the Tennessee. See Warner, *Generals in Blue*, 281–282.

12. John Y. Simon, ed. *The Papers of Ulysses S. Grant, Volume 5* (Carbondale: Southern Illinois Press, 1973), 195–196.

to extreme efforts to procure supplies. He needed Hurst's assistance, but received little or none.

It wasn't until October 25 that Hurst finally responded. He wrote about the regiment's mustering officer's certificate, but did not address his lack of communication.

> Head Quarters Bethel Tenn.
> Oct. 25th 1862
>
> Col. Breckenridge
> Dear Sir
> Our Captains has [sic] never been able to make accurate Muster in Rolls for the reason there [sic] men are on detached duty everlastingly. Must you have complete mustering rolls or will the certificate of the officer who sworn them in stating the number and date of oath be sufficient State to me by tomorrows [sic] mail precisely what is required and what will answer. If I can effect anything by coming to you I will come a [sic] Monday.
>
> Yours truly
> Fielding Hurst
> Col Comg.
> 1st Regt. West Tenn. Cav.[13]

There were many moving parts to building a regiment. Some required the assistance of others besides Breckenridge and Hurst. Breckenridge's surviving correspondence shows that he was busy. He received a report from Captain William E. Houston, who would serve as quartermaster on the Field and Headquarters Staff. Apparently, Houston was assisting him in locating certain blacksmithing tools needed to repair wagons, caissons, gun carriages, as well as helping the farriers in caring for the regiment's horses. At this point, Houston had no success in procuring the tools in question or any information about them.

---

13. Breckenridge Day Book, 184. This letter is not recorded or otherwise documented in the *OR*.

Registered Letter
Office of the Adams Express Company[14]
    Jackson Tenn. 1862
Col. Breckenridge
I cannot find the Blacksmith tools nor the man that had them in charge. I think they have been shipped to bolivar or some other point the Station agent have known nothing about them. The railroad agent, who was here the evening we was here together, is away. He knows the man you spoke to about the tools.[15]

                                Yours very Respectfully,
                                Capt. Wm. E. Houston[16]

By October of 1862, despite setbacks and issues seemingly beyond Breckenridge's control, the First West Tennessee Cavalry was operating and becoming a regiment of Union cavalry. On the 28th, he received word from St. Louis, the headquarters for General Henry W. Halleck's army, that his efforts were beginning to come to fruition. The regiment would be receiving in short order at least part of its request for horses and mules with more to follow in the coming days. This must have been most welcomed news for Breckenridge.

    Oct. 28th 1862
By Telegraph from St. Louis
                                To Col. Breckenridge
                                1st West Tenn. Cavalry
Four Hundred 400 horses shipped up to Saturday the other 400 will send this week, the mules today.
                                        G.W. Ford [17]

14. Ibid, 183. The Adams Express Company was a freight and cargo transport business established in 1854. Though founded in the Northeast, it had penetrated deeply into the South by the time of the Civil War. The company still exists today and is one of the oldest companies traded on the New York Stock Exchange.

15. The exact date of this letter is unknown, but it is recorded in Breckenridge's journal among other correspondence dated October 1862.

16. This letter is not recorded or otherwise documented in the OR.

17. This telegraph letter is not recorded or otherwise documented in the OR. The name G.W. Ford appears in records that are contained there. Ford was appointed by General William S.

BUILDING A REGIMENT AMID CONTROVERSY

Breckenridge struggled from the beginning of his service with the First West Tennessee Cavalry. In the "registered letter" below recorded in his journal, he sets forth the problems he has tried to correct. Already the regiment did not enjoy the best reputation even with its superiors. As an officer and a professional soldier, Breckenridge seemed duty bound to both report his observations of regimental problems and to report the individuals responsible. Hurst was not immune. This letter is not found in the *Official Records of the War of the Rebellion*. It cannot be certain that it was sent, yet Breckenridge recorded it in his journal nonetheless. The letter begins with the rumors and "talk" surrounding the regiment. Such rumors and talk would intensify following Breckenridge's death a year later. He sets forth a history of regimental issues. The letter was likely not written until March 1863, but it provides an account of his frustrations and the conditions prevalent in the First West Tennessee in 1862 and 1863, the years of Breckenridge's involvement. Certain events recorded in the letter that occurred after October 1862 will be discussed in other portions of this work.

Registered Letter[18]

General Sir

I learn this evening that there is some considerable talk around H.D.C. about our regiment the 1st West Tennessee Cavalry. I am well aware that they have not done as well as they might, but then I cannot think the officers and men are to be blamed for it all in the first place. When Colonel Hurst and myself consolidated on the 20th of September last he told me that there was nothing to do but draw the equipment and he said as I was best acquainted with military affairs I had best go and get the supplies and so me and him went to Jackson on the 22nd and there the requisitions was made out and I drew what I could there, then I went to Columbus and got what I

Rosecrans as the Military Harbor Master for St. Louis in 1864. He was involved in the transport of military goods and supplies as early as 1861. *New York Times*, July 24, 1864.

18. Breckenridge Day Book, 190–192. Like so much of his correspondence as recorded in this journal, this letter is not contained in the *OR*. The identity of the Union general to whom it is addressed is not disclosed. It is very possible that he is writing the officer most immediately superior to him in the winter of 1862, Brigadier General Benjamin H. Grierson.

could there.[19] Then to St. Louis and then to Cincinnati, then to Washington City, D.C. and thought I had everything for the Regiment. I then come by St. Louis and brought down some horses.[20] While at Washington and St. Louis, I wrote and telegraphed several times but got no answer from him or the regiment and when I got to Columbus I learned that the Colonel had been under arrest nearly all the time I was gone for burning a house near Bethel. And as soon as General Grant found that I was at Columbus hurried me here to take command as there had been no one take command that had any experience and there had been no drill and the men had become dissatisfied and commenced deserting and some two companies had left Captain Hayes[21] & Smiths[22] and had gone to the 2nd Tennessee Cavalry and when I went to them at Trenton to try and get them back they said if I was a going to command the Regiment they would come but to serve under Colonel Hurst they never would and I told them I felt honor bound to help him make up the Regiment. There was another trouble in camp. Captain Roberts wanted to go to the 2nd Tennessee and it was all I could do to get him and his men to stay but I got them to organize and agree then.[23]

19. At this time, Columbus, Kentucky, was a thriving river town and the headquarters and northern terminus of the Mobile & Ohio Railroad. Surrounded by the high bluffs of the Mississippi River, it was known as the "Gibraltar of the Mississippi." The town and its location was highly prized by both sides. It fell early in the war into Union hands. See Nathaniel Cheairs Hughes Jr., *The Battle of Belmont: Grant Strikes South* (Chapel Hill: The University of North Carolina Press, 1991), 36–44.

20. Breckenridge struggled to procure horses legitimately through the Army bureaucracy while Hurst and others were engaged in stealing and requisitioning them from local civilians.

21. The identity of this Captain Hayes and his unit is unknown.

22. Later in the war, while still enlisted, Captain Francis A. Smith was a member of the Tennessee Legislature.

23. *Tennesseans in the Civil War*, 333. Captain Elijah Roberts was one of the commanders of Company E, First West Tennessee/Sixth Tennessee Cavalry. It was organized at Bethel Station, Tennessee, on September 18, 1862. Roberts was a 33-year old farmer from Wayne County, Tennessee, who enlisted in September 1862. He served until November 1864 when he was discharged by reason of disability. Compiled Service Record of Elijah Roberts. Compiled Service Records of Volunteer Union Soldiers Who Served in Organizations from the State of Tennessee. Publication Number M395, Catalogue Identification Number 300398, Roll 0059. National Archives and Records Administration, Washington, D.C.

Then there was another difficulty, there was these men the most of whom were enlisted by the Colonel said they was not sworn in for only 12 months and that he had promised them when he went home they should go and so the men would go off and stay a few days and come back again. So when I went to take command there was not more than half the men in camp and after the six companies was organized the Colonel was away the most of the time and I tried to get up the muster rolls and the books in some shape and have drill and I hadn't a man that knew anything about drill or papers but I done the best I could while I had command but about the 12th of December I was sent out on a scout and then I was sent over on Tennessee River and was ordered by General Grant to report to General Dodge on the Forrest expedition and I scouted up and down the Tennessee River and as Forrest returned East, me and him had a brush near Bath Springs and when Colonel Lawler come on with his forces I give him all the assistance I could and when I left I was ordered to Corinth then to Pittsburg Landing to guard the transports when they come up and there I was in a storm with my men and not a tent nor hadn't even had one since I left camp in December but not a murmur out of my men for they were in the country where their families and friends were and they could give them some protection as the guerillas have taken nearly all the families have where their husbands and friends are in our regiment and left them to shift for themselves and all they want is to be armed and equipped so as they can get Revenge and when I was ordered back here it caused the men to complain at having to leave their families with no protection. General, it is hard to soldier when your wife and children are safe at home and have their friends around and plenty to eat but when you go to your tent of a night or out on your post and get to thinking of dear ones at home and not know but what they are turned out of doors or without something to eat as an old lady I have heard of this evening. She had but one son and two daughters and the Rebels would not let him stay at home and so he come and joined our Regiment and they then went and burned her house and told her that if she went in another they would burn it and warned her if the neighbors that if they helped her they would burn their houses and so she is now living in a shed and praying that Union troops will come give her some assistance. And another man that him and two of his sons had to come and join us they have taken all they had the Post report from that side of River was that they had cotton seed for a bed and one blanket for his wife and three children and there is lots more cases but I mention these two to let you know what my men have to bare and now they have been out almost 5 months and no equipment yet or not only 100 old saddles that the 4th Ill. [Illinois] had threw away and they were give us. there has not been a day but what but there has been all the saddles that could be gathered on duty and sometimes the pickets have to go barebacked all the time I was on Tennessee River the Colonel was at his residence in Purdy and no one here see to getting anything done or having the men drilling so as to make them of use and ever since I have been back I have been on a scout every day and night until last Wednesday night I was out trying to catch Richardson and my horse fell and hurt me so bad I have been laid up ever since not able to ride and at Head Quarters the other evening there was a talk got up about our pickets and the talk I did not like for I thought the officers of the Regiment were more to blame than the men and so I sent in my resignation thinking I would rather be a private in a Regiment where there is order than to be Lieut. Colonel where there is none. My first years in the Regular Cavalry larnt [taught] me there was but one way to have a good regiment and was strict discipline and then when you want a man to do duty he is ready and you can depend on him.

This unreported letter by Breckenridge contains significant information regarding the problems he is encountering at the outset of the regiment's formation. He begins by imploring his superior, whom he does not identify, not to blame the soldiers and officers for its shortcomings while recognizing that some issues need to be addressed. However, he immediately shifts the blame to the shoulders of Colonel Hurst. Whether this is fair or appropriate is subject to examination and question. There is an apparent difference in the early activities of both men according to Breckenridge's account. His activities to this point included procuring regimental equipment and supplies, which necessitated travel to Columbus, Kentucky, the headquarters of the Mobile and Ohio Railroad, then to St. Louis, and Washington, D.C. This was no small task in 1862. The railroad was more convenient, but travel was still somewhat slow and laborious. Breckenridge noted to his superiors that Hurst would not stay in contact with him despite all of his own efforts to remain in touch. Upon Breckenridge's return to Columbus, he learned that Hurst's silence wasn't the result of being preoccupied with regimental affairs and the normal business of war. Instead, he had been under arrest for arson. This is an early example of Hurst's wartime behavior that went beyond matters of war. Throughout his journal, Breckenridge chronicles Hurst's behaviors, shortcomings, unethical behaviors, and actions that would be considered tantamount to war crimes.

The issue of Hurst's arrest is an interesting one and dates are important here. From the wording of the letter, it appears that it occurred sometime after September 20, 1862, following Breckenridge's departure for Washington. No correspondence or record of this arrest is documented in the *Official Records*, but there is a record of correspondence regarding a potential court-marital in a September 27, 1862, letter from Colonel Isham Nicholas Haynie, Forty-Eighth Illinois Infantry, to Brigadier General John A. Logan in Jackson, Tennessee.[24]

> Jackson, Tenn. Sept. 27, 1862
> By Telegraph From Bethel
> To Brig.-Gen'l John A. Logan,
> Com'ding at Jackson, Tenn.
> Col. Hurst requests to be sent up to Jackson under arrest. Can I do so? I think it best.
> I. Haynie
> Col. Comdg.

24. Compiled Service Record of Fielding Hurst. Compiled Service Records of Volunteer Union Soldiers Who Served in Organizations from the State of Tennessee. Publication Number M395, Catalogue Identification Number 300398, Roll 0055. National Archives and Records Administration, Washington, D.C.

One can only imagine the frustration felt by Hurst's superiors at this point. Breckenridge's reference to the burning of a house by Hurst is the first such reference chronologically; it wouldn't be the last. However, it is important because it shows that his pattern of behavior and his record of actions against civilians is already established as early as September 1862. Not only was his second-in-command concerned about such behavior and the reputation it lent to the regiment, but his superiors as well.

HURST'S ENFORCERS:
ISSAC T. MCINTYRE AND BENJAMIN T. WALKER

In this case, Hurst had been arrested for setting fire to a home near Bethel Station, Tennessee, in McNairy County. Breckenridge never divulged whose home was burned. However, it must have been a serious matter to the Federal authorities. Exactly who was involved in this incident or other simultaneous burnings is not divulged by Breckenridge, but research has yielded at least two other participants: Private Isaac T. McIntyre and Private Benjamin T. Walker. Both were young men, though Walker was considerably older than McIntyre. Isaac McIntyre had been recruited by his neighbor, Captain Horry Hodges, and was a fair, red-headed eighteen-year old in 1862.[25] Walker was twenty-six years old when the arson occurred.[26] According to the service records of both men, they were arrested for burning two houses in or near Bethel Station on September 25, 1862. The charges and specifications against McIntyre and Walker read as follows:

> Charge and Specification against Isaac T. McIntyre, Private in Capt. Thompson's Company A, 1st Regt. West Tennessee Cav. Vols.

---

25. Compiled Service Record of Isaac T. McIntyre. Compiled Service Records of Volunteer Union Soldiers Who Served in Organizations from the State of Tennessee. Record Group Title: Records of the AGO, 1780s–1917. Record Group 94, Series Number M395, Roll: 0057. National Archives and Records Administration; Washington, D.C.

26. Compiled Service Record of Benjamin T. Walker. Compiled Service Records of Volunteer Union Soldiers Who Served in Organizations from the State of Tennessee. Record Group Title: Records of the AGO, 1780s–1917. Record Group 94, Series Number M395, Roll 0061. National Archives and Records Administration; Washington, D.C.

Charge

Specification—In this that the said Isaac T. McIntyre, Private in Capt. Thompson's Company A, 1st West Tennessee Cav. Vols. did in an unlawful riotous and unsoldierly manner at the County of McNairy near Bethel, Tenn. on the 25th of Sept. 1862 at night commit the crime of arson by burning the house of one Gardner Gill at said County then occupied as the residence and dwelling house of one A.A. Sanders and thereby destroying said house and the monies, property, household and kitchen furniture, clothing, beds, bedding and effects there situated and did then and there turn the family of said Sanders in the most rude and ruthless manner out of doors. All this at Bethel, Tenn.

I.N. Haynie
Col. 48th Illinois Infy.
Comdg. Post[27]

Charge and Specification against B.T. Walker, a private of Capt. Hodges Company "B" 1st Regt. West Tenn. Vol. Cav.

Charge

Specification – In this that the said B.T. Walker, Private in Capt. Hodges Company "B" 1st Regt. West Tennessee Cav. did in an unlawful riotous and unsoldierly manner at the county of McNairy near Bethel, Tenn. on the 25th of Sept. 1862 at night commit the crime of arson by burning the house of one Gardner Gill at said county then occupied as the residence and dwelling house of one A.A. Sanders and thereby destroying said house and the monies, property, household and kitchen furniture, clothing, beds, bedding and effects there situated and did then and there turn the family of said Sanders in the most rude and ruthless manner out of doors. All this at Bethel, Tenn.

I.N. Haynie
Col. 48th Ill. Infy.
Comdg. Post[28]

27. Isaac T. McIntyre Compiled Service Records.
28. Benjamin T. Walker Compiled Service Records.

According to Breckenridge, Hurst's arson supposedly occurred in the days following September 20, 1862. There is a distinct possibility that this is the same incident or a related incident, given the dates involved. A better understanding of the victims helps reveal the motives for it.

A.A. Sanders is Aaron A. Saunders (or A.A. Saunders). He was a Baptist minister and merchant who was profiled in General Marcus J. Wright's 1882 work *Reminiscences of the Early Settlement and Early Settlers of McNairy County, Tennessee*. According to Wright, Sanders was of "a delicate frame, but had excellent business capacity."[29] From 1844 until 1856, he served as the County Court Clerk of McNairy County. The motivation for this attack may have been his political and social views at the time of the war. According to Wright, Sanders was a staunch supporter of the Southern cause and an advocate of slavery.[30] In 1860, he owned four female slaves ages 24, 13, 12, and two years of age.[31] McIntyre's and Walker's crime against the Sanders family seems especially brutal when considering the members of the Sanders family at the time of the incident. According to the 1860 Federal Census, his household consisted of the following: Sanders and his wife Elizabeth, their sons, Edward L. (age 22), Sargent D. (age 20), Andrew (age 9), and Aaron (age 6); their daughters Rebecca E. (age 17), Mary S. (age 14), and Isabella M. (age 3).[32] Thus, McIntyre and Walker would have been brutally making children homeless as young as five years of age.

Gardner Gill was another victim of McIntyre and Walker. A veteran of the War of 1812, he was an eldery man approximately 73 years of age, having been born about 1788.[33] Historian A.W. Stovall in his *Notes on McNairy County* states his birth date as June 15, 1779.[34] Gill and

---

29. General Marcus J. Wright, John E. Talbott, J.D., and Kevin D. McCann, eds. *Reminiscences of the Early Settlement and Early Settlers of McNairy County, Tennessee* (Dickson TN: Bray-Bree Publishing Company, LLC, 2012), 21.

30. Ibid.

31. Eighth Census of the United States, 1860. McNairy County, Tennessee. Series Number M653, Records of the Bureau of the Census, National Archives and Records Administration, Washington, D.C.

32. Ibid.

33. Gill's age was taken from the various U.S. Censuses, which are consistent as to his age and birth year.

34. Nancy Wardlow Kennedy, *Antiquities of McNairy County, Tennessee: McNairy County History 1823–1876, Notes of Ancil Walker Stovall* (Selmer TN: Self-published, 2001), 8.

Sanders had at least one thing in common. Both were slave owners. Gill owned two slaves in 1860, a 21-year old female and a two-year old male child.[35] His holdings had decreased significantly since 1850 when the previous slave census had been taken. That year, he owned eleven slaves: nine females (ages 35, 26, 12, 10, 9, 8, 6, 4, and 1) and two males (ages 17 and 6).[36] It appears that Gill was quite wealthy, owning 731 acres in McNairy County in 1862.[37]

The attacks on Sanders and Gill were by no means isolated incidents in West Tennessee. They are representative of the types of warfare Hurst and his subordinates waged upon Confederate citizens. Interestingly, there is no indication in McIntyre's military record that he was ever disciplined for his alleged actions but only that he was charged.

Issac McIntyre was the son of a prominent resident of north McNairy County, Robert Thompson McIntyre.[38] Issac's grandfather and namesake had witnessed a Revolutionary War battle on his own grandfather's farm back in North Carolina. Thus the lessons of America's struggle for independence were engrained into his family lore.[39] To Isaac's father, the Union was a sacred thing. Robert Thompson McIntyre was an ardent Unionist and abolitionist. One of his friends and business associates was a man named Ichabod (Achabod) Brown, a free black man.[40] McIntyre was a Republican in politics, a member of the McNairy County Quarterly Court, and an acquaintance of Sanders.[41] During the war, Issac's brother John Absalom McIntyre was sent north to work in a munitions

35. Ibid.

36. Seventh Census of the United States, 1850. McNairy County, Tennessee. NARA Microfilm Publication M432, Record Group: Records of the Bureau of the Census, Record Group Number 29. National Archives and Records Administration, Washington, D.C.

37. Records of the Internal Revenue Service. Record Group 58. National Archives and Records Administration, Washington, D.C.

38. Talbott, *A Sacred High Place*, 71–74.

39. Ibid.

40. Robert Thompson McIntyre and Ichabod Brown (also known as Achabod Brown) were closely associated for approximately thirty years. Brown has also been identified as a "mulatto" and as a "Mongrel" by General Marcus J. Wright in his *Reminiscences of the Early Settlement and Early Settlers of McNairy County, Tennessee*. The two men both owned the same grist mill and gin at various times. McIntyre acted as Brown's attorney-in-fact in Brown's later years when he was being persecuted by local Confederates and secessionists.

41. Ibid.

and powder factory in Illinois.[42] Most assuredly, Gill and Sanders represented everything McIntyre had been taught to oppose.

Little is known about Benjamin T. "Tom" Walker, outside of Breckenridge's journal and Walker's own military service record. Unlike McIntyre, Walker was court-martialed for his crimes.[43] The proceedings were convened at the West Tennessee District Headquarters in Jackson, Tennessee, by Special Order No. 6 on October 26, 1862. There is no indication in Walker's record that he was found guilty or punished by the court-marital tribunal. In fact, per Special Order No. 6, it was ordered that Walker be released from confinement and returned to duty by command of Major General Stephen Hurlbut.[44] While Breckenridge gives an account of atrocities that Walker committed, Walker's service record reveals how he was able to operate with a shield of immunity. It was Hurst and William Jay Smith who detailed him to rob from local citizens. The record couches their permission in a more official manner without, of course, any reference to Walker's actual activities.

Walker entered the service at Bethel, Tennessee, on August 25, 1862, for a period of three years. There was a delay in mustering men in as reflected in Breckenridge's journal and Walker was not mustered into service until October 13, 1862, at the age of twenty-five. On December 9, 1862, he was promoted to the rank of sergeant. He rose to First Lieutenant of Regimental Commissary on February 17, 1863, a promotion made by Colonel Hurst himself that made him a part of the Field and Staff officers.[45] This promotion is intriguing. The commissary was responsible for the regiment's foodstuffs and related supplies. Appointing Walker to the Commissary cloaked him in a position that made procurement of food and supplies a priority. In wartime, a regimental commander could use a resourceful man to scour the countryside for supplies by any means. His activities could be concealed in the guise of official capacity, thus officially justifying what would otherwise be criminal activity.

Activities such as those of Walker, McIntyre, Hurst, and Smith did not go unnoticed during the course of the war. According to Breckenridge, General Grant himself was concerned about the lack of adequate

42. Ibid, 68–69.
43. Benjamin T. Walker Compiled Service Records.
44. Ibid.
45. Ibid.

Pvt. Issac T. McIntyre
Author's Collection

command over the regiment in both Breckenridge's and Hurst's absences. Grant expressed his concern to Major General William S. Rosecrans about Hurst's failure to follow orders given him by Major General Stephen A. Hurlbut.[46] This would not be the last time that Hurst would cause great consternation to his superiors in the Union Army.

In his journal, Breckenridge documents the dissatisfaction among the soldiers of the First West Tennessee Cavalry. They were quite unhappy with Hurst's behaviors and were now deserting. Breckenridge specifically identifies two companies unders Captains Hayes and Smith that had deserted and joined the U.S. Second West Tennessee Cavalry. Breckenridge recounted that he traveled to Trenton, Tennessee, to convince these men to return to the regiment but they were hesitant to do so. They were emphatic in their opposition to serving under Fielding Hurst, a reoccuring sentiment over the next several months.

Perhaps some of Breckenridge's comments and observations are tainted by self-serving motives or outright resentment toward Hurst. Then again, he was writing for his own purposes. He could not have any expectation that others would one day read his thoughts and observations recorded in his private journal. Even if there is the appearance that Breckenridge has a proverbial ax to grind with Hurst, he dispels the notion by explaining that he felt honor bound to assist him.

Breckenridge set forth a number of difficulties besetting the First West Tennessee during his and Hurst's respective absences. At the time, the regiment consisted of six companies: A, B, C, D, E, and F. Captain Elijah Roberts of Company E asked to transfer to the Second West Tennessee Cavalry. Breckenridge left the impression that it was hard for him to convince Roberts and his men to stay and serve under Hurst. Many soldiers who had been personally recruited by Hurst were promised they only had to serve a period of twelve months and could leave and go home at any time. Breckenridge's job was made even more challenging because these men were volunteers who were untrained and knew nothing about military life.

Breckenridge did not begin his journal until March 1863. Thus the handwritten duplicates of his incoming and outgoing correspondence are needed to determine his activities between December 1862 and that time. He provided a number of important details, including reports of

---

46. Simon, ed., *Papers of Grant* 5, 196.

SGT. BENJAMIN T. "TOM" WALKER TOMBSTONE
Author's Collection

a scouting expedition toward the Tennessee River in search of General Nathan Bedford Forrest and his army. According to Breckenridge, he and his party made their way up and down the river seeking him out and at one point almost engaged the Wizard of the Saddle.

Afterwards, Breckenridge was ordered to Corinth, Mississippi, and then to Pittsburg Landing to lead a guard for the Union transport ships traveling along the Tennessee River. He often mentioned these gunboats in his journal. He also acknowledges briefly the privations of his men and their good fortune to be in the vicinity of their homes. This was important to Breckenridge because these men's families were suffering at the hands of Confederate guerillas who terrorized the local Unionist families. The husbands and sons of these families, now members of the First West Tennessee, wanted them armed to protect themselves from these rogue guerilla forces, especially since they couldn't be home to protect them. Breckenridge appealed to his superiors of the need to assist these soldiers' families. He uses an anonymous example of a soldier of the regiment whose mother's home was burned, making her homeless.

Breckenridge offered another example of the crimes committed by Confederate guerillas in the area around the Tennessee River. He felt it was important for his superiors to understand the privations and abuse to which his men were exposed during the course of the war. Here Breckenridge took the opportunity to complain about the failure of the Army to provide saddles and other basic equipment to his men. Such privations by the regiment seem more in keeping with the type of existence experienced by the Confederate Army. Once again, he lodged a complaint against Colonel Hurst. While he was working hard to carry out orders, Hurst was comfortable at home in his Purdy mansion as the men went without his leadership or direction. Breckenridge had no desire to command a regiment with no order and one in which none could be expected due to lack of leadership. It is evident that he was disturbed by these circumstances and that his relationship with Hurst, such as it was, was deteriorating.

One of the functions of the First West Tennessee Cavalry was to combat and ferret out Rebel guerillas. The presence of the regiment, as well as other Union Army units, also provided a measure of comfort for Union loyalists who lived in fear of either conscription by the Confederate Army or destruction and theft of their property. Over time, they

THE HOME OF COL. FIELDING HURST IN PURDY, TENNESSEE
(Liz Bourner)

captured and turned over a number of guerillas and other prisoners. On or about December 16, 1862, the First West Tennessee took a prisoner by the name of Richard Rogers. Apparently, Rogers was a rather indolent man who was actively hiding Confederate guerillas. It was not unusual for citizens on both sides to harbor individuals. Various parts of West Tennessee switched hands back and forth. There were times when Confederate sympathizing citizens harbored Confederate soldiers and Union-leaning citizens harbored their young sons to protect them from being forced into Confederate service.

On December 16, Breckenridge wrote to the Provost Marshal regarding Rogers. He leaves no doubt that Rogers was a very perturbed man and had no patience for Breckenridge's questions. The following correspondence does not exist in the *Official Records*, but only in his journal.

> Head Quarters 1st West Tenn. Cavalry
> Bolivar, Tennessee Dec. 16th 1862
>
> Captain Stephens
> Provost Marshal
> Sir
>
> I send you a prisoner Richard Rogers. He has taken the oath. He has a son with the guerrillas and is accused of concealing stolen property & harboring guerillas and after I had searched his house I said to him he had been accused of harboring Guerillas and if I heard any more of it I would arrest him & he said I could arrest him & be damned. I then told him I had addressed him as a Gentleman and wanted a civil answer. When he told me he did not care a damn. I then told him if he gave me another such a reply I would take him along he said I could take & be damned. I arrested him and since I learn that Mr. Harris says he saw him with the Guerillas.
>
> Very Respectfully
> W.K.M. Breckenridge
> Lieut. Col. 1st West Tenn. Cavalry[47]

---

47. Breckenridge Day Book, 185.

This letter provides a glimpse of the acidic and acrimonious attitudes often typical of local Confederate sympathizers. Given the reputation afforded to the First West Tennessee Cavalry early in the war, such attitudes were not unexpected. Events such as the burning of the Gill and Sanders homes had already occurred by the time of the events described in Breckenridge's correspondence to the Provost Marshal. It is also his first reference in his journal to guerillas in southwest Tennessee. With the Federal occupation of the region following the Battle of Shiloh in April 1862, Confederate guerilla activity would prove harassing and lead to more desperate behavior by both sides.

Beginning in December, Breckenridge's activities shifted from organizing to leading men in action. He led them along the Tennessee River to determine enemy troop movements. On the 20th, he was operating on White Oak Ridge in Hardin County. His activities were the subject of a letter to Brigadier General Jeremiah Cutler Sullivan.

> Bolivar, Tenn., December 20, 1862 – 1 A.M.
> Brigadier-General Sullivan:
> Lieutenant-Colonel Breckenridge, First West Tennessee Cavalry, from White Oak Ridge, Hardin County, sends courier that rebels under General Morgan are to join cavalry force at Trenton; are fortifying at Kelly's old road track, 8 miles from Clifton. Have considerable artillery and reserve at Clifton.
> W.L. BARNUM,
> Acting Assistant Adjutant-General[48]

In late December, the Union command expected action. On the 28th, orders were sent to both Hurst and Breckenridge from Brigadier General Mason Brayman. Special Order No. 82 revoked all furloughs and leaves and ordered all absent officers back to camp.[49] The First West Tennessee Cavalry was about to encounter action in Hardin County.

---

48. *OR*, Series I, Volume 17, Part 2, 444.
49. Breckenridge Day Book, 180.

ACTION AT CLIFTON, TENNESSEE

On December 31, after a successful raid into West Tennessee, General Nathan Bedford Forrest began his withdrawal back into middle Tennessee. Federal troops attempted to stop Forrest at a little place called Parker's Crossroads in Henderson County. They weren't successful, but it was a spirited and strongly fought battle. There are many accounts of Forrest's West Tennessee raid and the Battle of Parker's Crossroads. For an account from the Confederate perspective, one can consult Jordan and Pryor's *The Campaigns of Lieut. Gen. N.B. Forrest and of Forrest's Cavalry*. For an academic perspective, one may review Dr. Lonnie E. Maness' *Lightning Warfare: Forrest's First West Tennessee Campaign—December 1862*.

On January 1, 1863, Forrest's command was on the move toward Clifton, Tennessee. Following a halt in the march to parole prisoners, Forrest was informed by scouts that a heavy force was on its way from Purdy to intercept his command. Some 1,200 cavalry crossed his line of march. Colonel George B. Dibbrell charged directly through the Union center while Colonel Jacob B. Biffle and Colonel James W. Starnes charged the Union right and left. Soon thereafter, the road was cleared. According to Forrest biographer Captain J. Harvey Mathes:

> The Federals lost some twenty killed and wounded and about fifty prisoners, while the Confederates did not lose a man. However, Lieutenant-Colonel W.K.M. Breckenridge, commanding the Sixth Tennessee Union Cavalry, reported only six prisoners lost on this occasion.[50]

Historian Robert Selph Henry reported substantially the same account with slight variations for Forrest's stopping on the road before reaching Clifton. According to Henry:

> After a halt for feeding men and animals, and attention to the wounded who had been brought off, the column marched out toward Clifton. On the morning of New Year's Day 1863, they met head-on Colonel William K.M. Breckenridge's Union

---

50. Capt. J. Harvey Mathes, *General Forrest* (New York: D. Appleton and Company, 1902), 92–93.

cavalry regiment, sent up from below by Dodge, and brushed it aside in sharp little fight.[51]

Historians Eddy W. Davison and Daniel Foxx, in their work *Nathan Bedford Forrest: In Search of the Enigma*, write of the engagement at Clifton. As was often the case with Forrest, Union commanders reported that his army was "broken up."[52] Following Breckenridge's defeat by an army that was supposedly broken up and otherwise depleted, historians Davison and Foxx speculated that perhaps Breckenridge subconsciously rehearsed "what he would say to [Jeremiah Cutler] Sullivan if the two ever again met."[53] In any event, Forrest wasn't stopped and he crossed back into Middle Tennessee.

Breckenridge's official account of the engagement is below. It differs from other accounts and gives a far more personal account of the skirmish.

> Report of Lieut. Col. William K.M. Breckenridge, Sixth Tennessee Cavalry (Union), of skirmish near Clifton, January 1, 1863.
>
> Saltillo, January 2, 1863.
>
> Sir: I have just received your dispatch of the 1st instant. I sent you a dispatch on the night of the 31st December, giving you the incidents of that day. On the morning of the 1st, a very short time after sunrise, our pickets were driven in by Forrest's advance. We first made an effort to form on a hill, which is shown in diagram, but the timber was so thick that we could not get a line to do any execution. I then fell back to the foot of the hill, leaving some men to skirmish with them until others were formed. About this time I received information that it was Forrest's whole force. I then changed position, forming company in the rear of company to get them all off without exposing our rear. It would have been all right had it not been that one of the companies that was in the rear did

---

51. Robert Selph Henry, *First with the Most Forrest* (Indianapolis IN: The Bobbs-Merrill Company, 1944), 120.

52. Eddy W. Davison and Daniel Foxx, *Nathan Bedford Forrest: In Search of the Enigma* (Gretna LA: Pelican Publishing Company, 2007), 120.

53. Ibid.

not receive the order to fall back until they were exposed very much to the enemy's fire. The first orderly failing to reach them, from some cause that I do not know of, I sent another order to fall back, which reached the commander of the company while the enemy were demanding a surrender of the whole command; in the meantime the enemy were making an attempt to surround the company, which being perceived they galloped off, losing about 6 men as prisoners. We killed 6 and wounded some others of the enemy. We made our retreat on the Decaturville road, to the right of the enemy, getting in their rear to annoy him all we could. We found that his rear was moving at a very rapid rate and followed them within a short distance of the river, and found that they had been advised that their rear was followed. I did not deem it prudent to follow farther. I propose to reconnoiter the country in the vicinity of Clifton again, and will remain till I hear from you. If you send the artillery we can use it to good advantage.

The above hasty report is respectfully submitted.

W.K.M. BRECKENRIDGE,
Lieutenant-Colonel, Commanding.
Brigadier-General Dodge.[54]

Despite the "hasty" nature of his report, Breckenridge still provides significant details of the Clifton skirmish.

In the early days of the First West Tennessee Cavalry, the regiment experienced a degree of privation in that it lacked necessary supplies, a constant frustration for Breckenridge. Worse still was the lack of pay for long periods to the officers and enlisted men. In the communication with General Grenville M. Dodge below, Breckenridge discloses that he has backtracked from the Tennessee River to Adamsville, Tennessee, for lodging there until he can feasibly return to Pittsburgh Landing. At this time in January 1863, he was contending with reports of Rebel guerillas operating along the river.

---

54. *OR*, Series 1, Volume 17, Part 1, *590*.

Adamsville, January 15, 1863

General Dodge, Corinth, Miss.:

Sir: The river raised 4 feet last night; that leaves it now about 12 feet above low water mark. No boats as yet, on account of the bad weather, and having no tents or no houses to put up in I was compelled to fall back to Adamsville, where I could get house-room and forage. I will move back to Pittsburgh Landing as soon as the tents come or the weather gets favorable. I am informed that there are about 200 guerillas back of Savannah and about 800 at the Red Sulphur Springs; the latter I don't credit. Have you ever heard from General Grant in regard to the balance of those four companies that are with me? I am informed that the greater part of the troops across the river are ordered to meet Bragg at Chattanooga.

Yours, truly,

W.K.M. BRECKENRIDGE,
Lieutenant-Colonel, First West Tennessee Cavalry[55]

One of the more frustrating aspects of the *Official Records* is the frequent gaps in the documented correspondence. In the above letter between Breckenridge and Dodge, there is a reference to additional correspondence with General Grant, but the trail ends there.

Approximately one week later, Breckenridge reported that Captain Nathan M.D. Kemp was operating on White Oak Creek, north of Savannah and west of Hookers Bend on the Tennessee River. His journal discloses that the First West Tennessee Cavalry operated significantly in the regions north of Savannah and further north towards Clifton and Saltillo. He had taken eight prisoners and learned significant information as to the possible current position of Forrest.

Adamsville [Tenn.], January 21, 1863.

General Dodge:

Sir: I have been on White Oak to see what Captain Kemp was doing, and to order him up to Pittsburg Landing. As you

---

55. *OR*, Series I, Volume 17, Part II, 564. See also notation in Compiled Service Record of Nathan M.D. Kemp. National Archives and Records Administration, Catalogue No. 300398, Record Group 94, Roll 0055.

ordered me to Bolivar, I have taken 8 of General Bragg's men on the trip, and I am informed by two reliable citizens that General Forrest, Colonel [J.B.] Biffle, and another colonel (I can't recollect his name) are camped 4 miles from Clifton, on what is called the Elliot Farm. I am also informed that their intentions are to guard the river against our crossing to re-enforce General Rosecrans. One man reports that they were going to take this country as quick as General Grant got all his forces in Mississippi.

Yours, truly,

W.K.M. BRECKENRIDGE,

Lieutenant-Colonel Sixth Tennessee Cavalry

N.B. – On hearing the reports from Clifton, I thought it best not to remove Captain Kemp from White Oak until I heard from you.[56]

In late January, Colonel Elliot Warren Rice wrote to General Dodge from aboard the Steamer *Raymond*. Nothing could be ascertained regarding this particular ship. However, it is apparent that it was operating on the Tennessee River at this time. Rice informs Dodge that he is sending Breckenridge up the river to Perryville, Tennessee, to scout for information and enemy troops.

Steamer Raymond,
Hamburg, January 27, 1863

Brig. Gen. Grenville M. Dodge,

Commanding District of Corinth:

Sir: As I informed you by dispatch last evening, I had my force on board, ready to start, but the fog was so thick the boat could not be got underway until early this morning. When about 5 miles from here, the starboard wheel broke down, in consequence of some damage it received in starting; it was not possible to repair it, or to go on up the river with only one wheel, and barge in tow, so, much to my regret, I was obliged to turn back to Hamburg. I had everything arranged, I believe, for a successful thing; but this accident, to

---

56. *OR*, Series I, Volume 24, Part 3, 4.

my great disappointment, has prevented the accomplishment of our designs. The gunboat Robb has, however, continued on as far as she can go over the shoals, and will destroy any flats that may be found. She will return this p.m., and will then probably go on down the river with convoy. I do not think, from what information I can get, there is any force now at Savannah. Colonel Breckenridge will go with them as far as Perryville, and return across the country, and report to you anything of interest he may find. The train left this morning, and I shall send the Seventh Iowa and Eighty-first Ohio and section of artillery after them. The Fifty-second Illinois is retained here until you can send 30 wagons more for the balance of the stores. Either the quartermaster is much to blame in loading or else there was much more than was supposed. A section of artillery remains here, and some cavalry. Scouts have been sent along Chambers' Creek this morning, and others over the river.

I am, very respectfully, your obedient servant,

E.W. RICE,
Colonel, Commanding.[57]

Seeing Breckenridge referenced to as the officer leading the First West Tennessee rather than Hurst is a steady trend during the first year of its existence. It gives the appearance that two polarizing figures are at work in the regiment. Breckenridge is leading the sanctioned movements and activities of the regiment; Hurst's activities are less visible. However, it will be those elusive activities by Hurst and his trusted subordinates that will most severely test Breckenridge's leadership skills.

---

57. *OR*, Series I, Volume 23, Part II, 19.

3

OUT *of* CONTROL

March 1–April 1, 1863

By March 1863, the First West Tennessee Cavalry was stationed at Bolivar in Hardeman County, Tennessee. They were unwelcome to some in West Tennessee. A writer for the pro-Confederate Memphis *Daily Appeal* opined from Okalona, Mississippi, on March 6, 1863:

> Bolivar is now cursed with the presence of about two thousand Abolitionists, mostly Tories from the State of Tennessee. Freeling [*sic*] Hurst, the notorious Tennessee traitor, is there with his regiment of renegade Tennesseans. Of all the villains that ever existed from the birth of Adam to the present time, Freeling [*sic*] Hurst is cunning, mean and contemptible. His principal warfare is made on defenseless women and children. He does not countenance an honest man nor associate with one who recognizes one principle of right and justice.[1]

---

1. Memphis *Daily Appeal*, March 17, 1863.

The month of March also found the situation within the regiment seemingly beyond the reach and control of Breckenridge. Because Hurst outranked him, there was little he could do to stop illicit activities sanctioned by Hurst himself and carried out by his trusted subordinates. As events progressed and conditions deteriorated, Breckenridge became more tormented internally. The letters he recorded in his journal detailed the growing frustration with his plight. He had volunteered to fight for the preservation of the Union and the flagrant abuses he was seeing and hearing did not befit the cause for which he was serving. March 1863 also found Breckenridge contending with disheartened and angry enlisted men who were just as outraged as he at the activities of a few. His concerns were valid and shared by Hurst's superiors within the Union Army ranks.

Fortunately, Breckenridge kept a close accounting of events and recorded his letters and responses from his superiors, including General Mason Brayman. What follows is a timeline of events in March 1863 as established by the available correspondence and found in both the *Official Records* and Breckenridge's journal. On March 3, he reported to General Brayman the frustration felt by his men, as well as himself, at the actions of Hurst in the midst of anticipated action.

> Registered Letter
> Bolivar, Tennessee
> March 3rd 1863
> General Bra[y]man
> Sir
> I left here on the 24th in person and offered to reinforce Col. Hurst at Pocahontas and got there about 8 or 9 o'clock P.M. When I got there the Col. was gone. Captain Hodge[s] and balance of the officers informed me that he was gone to Purdy to get reinforcements and the men was very much disheartened about the Col. leaving them when they were expecting an attack every minute they appeared ready for a fight and said they intended to die there before they would give up to Street. The next morning about 8 A.M. Major Love with 175 cavalry come in from the Junction[2] and none of us knew what

2. Grand Junction, Tennessee.

to do. Captain Hodge said the Col. would be back there by 9 A.M. and we waited until ½ past 10 when I ordered the men to mount and was a coming to Bolivar and just as we were about to start the Col. come and took command and in a short time captain — with his Company come and then they all left for Ripley and out 8 miles Major Love left us.

Yours very Respectfully,
W.K.M. Breckenridge[3]

Breckenridge divulges valuable information about the situation within the regiment at this time, but some commentary is required. The Captain Hodge to whom Breckenridge refers is Captain Horry Hodges, a native of north McNairy County and a neighbor to Isaac T. McIntyre. Captain Hodges was an organizer of the First West Tennessee Cavalry and, in fact, recruited many of its soldiers, including McIntyre. Hodges joined on August 25, 1862, at Bethel, Tennessee.[4] At the age of 29, he was mustered in as captain of Company B for a period of three years.[5] His brother, Elijah James Hodges, would eventually be elevated to the same rank. Both Hodges brothers were imposing figures, Horry standing at six feet and Elijah even taller at six feet, six inches tall.[6] They came from a family with Revolutionary roots that was militarily active for at least two generations.

In his letter to General Brayman, Breckenridge also hints at the possibility of cowardice on the part of Hurst. During the period of August 1862 until October 1863, Breckenridge is the officer actually leading the regiment in legitimate maneuvers and in times of danger. He implies that Hurst always seems preoccupied with personal matters. These include

---

3. Breckenridge Daybook, 186. This letter does not appear in the *OR*, but only in Breckenridge's journal.

4. Compiled Service Record of Horry Hodges. Compiled Service Records of Volunteer Union Soldiers Who Served in Organizations from the State of Tennessee. Publication Number M395, National Archives Catalogue ID 300398, Record Group 94, Roll 0055. National Archives and Records Administration, Washington, D.C.

5. Ibid.

6. Ibid. Compiled Service Record of Elijah J. Hodges. Compiled Service Records of Volunteer Union Soldiers Who Served in Organizations from the State of Tennessee. Publication Number M395, National Archives Catalogue ID 300398, Record Group 94, Roll 0055. National Archives and Records Administration, Washington, D.C.

Capt. Horry Hodges Tombstone
Author's Collection

his activities with William Jay Smith and Tom Walker among others. Here for the first time, Breckenridge refers to the notorious Confederate guerilla fighter, Solomon Street.

SOLOMON G. STREET

Solomon G. "Sol" Street was known as a notorious Rebel guerilla. A native of Hardeman County, Tennessee, he was raised in Tippah County, Mississippi.[7] He doesn't appear to have entered the Confederate service very early. He originally enlisted in Company A of the Second Mississippi State Cavalry at Ripley, Mississippi, on December 16, 1862, for a period of twelve months.[8] Street and Hurst employed a sort of tit-for-tat engagement with one another. Street was known to venture up into Tennessee to conduct raids. By mid to late March, Hurst himself was down in Mississippi and had been since March 22, 1863.[9] A writer for the Memphis *Daily Appeal* wrote from Panola, Mississippi, on March 30:

> Hurst's cavalry continue their depredations in the neighborhood of Ripley, Miss. The burning of a portion of the town has been confirmed.
>
> At latest dates there were but a few troops at Memphis, but reinforcements were expected.
>
> Two boats have passed up the Tallahatchie, and several have gone down, loaded with stores, ambulances, etc.
>
> Two Yankee yawls came seven miles above the mouth of Coldwater. They appeared to be scouting along the bank of the river.
>
> Two gunboats from the pass have arrived at Memphis for repairs.[10]

---

7. McCann, *Hurst's Wurst*, 28.

8. Compiled Service Record of Solomon G. Street. Compiled Service Records of Confederate Soldiers Who Served in Organizations from the State of Mississippi. Series Number M269, Roll 15. National Archives and Records Administration, Washington, D.C.

9. McCann, *Hurst's Wurst*, 30.

10. Memphis *Daily Appeal*, March 31, 1863.

Hurst was exacting significant damage in the area of Ripley, Mississippi, stealing horses and cotton and then making his way back toward Pocahontas, Tennessee.[11] The foray into north Mississippi was an eventful one. As he arrived at Pocahontas, action was imminent. Sol Street was prepared to meet Hurst in battle. He and his men were north of Hurst and preparing to take back some of the horses and cotton that Hurst had captured.[12] A detachment of Street's guerillas pushed past the First West Tennessee Cavalry on March 24 and slogged through the Muddy Creek bottoms, capturing eight of Hurst's rear guard.[13]

Street and his guerillas then attempted to overpower the First West Tennessee but found themselves outnumbered and unable to achieve their goal of defeating Hurst.[14] Both leaders, Hurst and Street, feared they were outnumbered by the other but, in fact, Hurst held the superior numbers. Still, he sought reinforcements from General Brayman thinking his enemy had a force some four hundred strong, a gross overestimation.[15]

There are instances in Breckenridge's journal when events pertaining to him and the First West Tennessee Cavalry are recorded in separate pieces of correspondence that confirm the version contained in the *Official Records*. Hurst's situation on March 24—seeking reinforcements in his fight against Street—is one of those. Breckenridge is commanded by General Brayman to reinforce Hurst at Pocahontas. The unpublished order as found in Breckenridge's journal is as follows:

> Head Quarters Post of Bolivar
> Bolivar, Tenn. March 24th 1863
> Lieut. Col. Breckinridge [*sic*] will accompany the expedition ordered this morning in aid of Col. Hurst.
> M. Bra[y]man
> Brig. Genrl. Comg.[16]

---

11. McCann, *Hurst's Wurst*, 30.
12. Ibid.
13. Ibid.
14. Ibid.
15. Ibid.
16. Breckenridge Daybook, 180.

This order provides additional information for a corresponding communication that does exist in the *Official Records* that is dated the same day. Between the two documents, a better understanding of the circumstances for which Colonel Hurst required the assistance of Lt. Colonel Breckenridge is gained. The published communication is as follows:

> Bolivar, March 24, 1863
> Brigadier General Sullivan:
> Colonel [Fielding] Hurst, with 100 West Tennessee Cavalry, is fighting about 400 at Pocahontas, and has sent for help. I send all I have, and have telegraphed to La Grange and Grand Junction to send a re-enforcement.
> M. Brayman,
> Brigadier-General.[17]

Hurst was then engaged at Pocahontas, located near the McNairy County line. Pocahontas was a small village in the most southeastern corner of Hardeman County. Established in 1828, it was located at the intersection of Muddy Creek and the Big Hatchie River.[18] By 1874, less than ten years after the end of the war, the village had about 350 citizens, which is believed to be somewhat comparable to its population at the time of the war.[19] The important Memphis and Charleston Railroad (which later became the Southern Railway) ran through Pocahontas.[20] On March 25, Major General Stephen Hurlbut received the following briefing:

> La Grange, March 25, 1863
> Major-General Hurlbut:
> Information just received from General Brayman, at Bolivar, says:

---

17. *OR, Series I, Volume 24, Part 3*, 137.

18. Eastin Morris, *The Tennessee Gazetteer or Topographical Dictionary, 1834* (Nashville TN: W. Hassel Hunt & Co., 1834), 235.

19. J.B. Killebrew, A.M. and J.M. Safford, PH.D., M.D. *Introduction to the Resources of Tennessee* (Nashville TN: Tavel, Eastman & Howell, 1874), 1084.

20. Elmer G. Sulzer, *Ghost Railroads of Tennessee* (Bloomington: Indiana University Press, 1975), 178.

> Thirteen guerillas just arrived. Sent in by Colonel Hurst at Pocahontas. They left last night. No re-enforcements had then arrived. Fifteen more prisoners sent to Bethel. Our loss, 1 private killed. Colonel Miller, of the rebel forces, killed. Sol. [G.] Street said to be desperately wounded. No danger.
> M. Brayman
> Wm. Sooy Smith[21]

This communication between Union commanders is more significant than meets the eye. Popular legends over the last century and a half since the war alleged that Hurst and men from the First West Tennessee Cavalry brutally murdered prisoners captured in battle. However, this official communication details the safe arrival of thirteen guerillas captured at Pocahontas. Fifteen more prisoners were sent to Bethel, Tennessee, making a total of 28 prisoners taken to appropriate Federal posts. These documents cast doubt on those popular legends. What is more convincing is the fact that they were taken during a fight with the notorious guerilla Solomon G. Street. That Hurst and his men sent these particular prisoners to safety at Federal posts is telling. These were men who were especially despised by Hurst and his cohort, William Jay Smith.

Further, there are plenty of examples documented by Breckenridge of officers in his regiment being disciplined for infractions and misdeeds. This proves that some efforts were made to correct infractions in the regiment. The following letter pertains to Captain David J. Dickerson of Company F:

> Head Quarters Post of Bolivar
> Bolivar, Tenn. March 24th 1863
>
> Special Order
> No. 66
> Capt. D.J. Dickerson, Co. F, 1st West Tenn. Cavalry having been charged with disobedience of orders and insubordination, you will place him under arrest. He will deliver his sword at these Head Quarters and remain in close confinement at his quarters until further orders.[22]

21. Ibid, 147.
22. This man is also identified as Captain David J. Dickerson.

> By order of
> Brig. Genl. M. Bra[y]man
> John Pitts [?]
> AAA General

Lieut. Col. Breckinridge
1st West Tenn. Cavalry[23]

This unpublished Special Order found in Breckenridge's journal orders him to arrest Captain Dickerson. Exactly what orders Dickerson disobeyed or the insubordination allegedly committed are not revealed. However, Dickerson's own service record shows his arrest with a notation of him being present for duty but "in arrest" in March 1863.[24] There is no record of a court marital; his service record shows that his career not only continued but that he was sent by Hurst personally to recruit men in Nashville in August 1863. Dickerson himself was recruited by Breckenridge when the regiment was formed.[25]

UNDER ARREST

Amidst the disorganization and misbehavior by both enlisted men and officers, Breckenridge also had to deal with matters pertaining to his own commission as lieutenant colonel and his struggle to keep order while having his own authority regularly undermined by Hurst and his closest subordinates. Breckenridge wrote to General Brayman discussing his frustration with the failure of his commission to be formally approved and delivered. This letter, which is not included in the *Official Records*, is very frank and makes no pretense to be discreet. Breckenridge is direct in his allegations against Hurst.

> Head Quarters 1st West Tenn. Cavalry
> Bolivar Tennessee March 24th '63

---

23. Breckenridge Daybook, 181.

24. Compiled Service Record of David J. Dickerson. Compiled Service Records of Volunteer Union Soldiers Who Served in Organizations from the State of Tennessee. Records of the AGO, 1780s–1917. Record Group 94, Series Number M395, Roll 0052. National Archives and Records Administration, Washington, D.C.

25. Ibid.

General Bra[y]man
> Sir

There appears to be some difficulty about my commission and I understand that Col. Hurst said I never would get one. He said that you were the cause of my not getting one and, General, I would like to know whether I am to have one or not as I think it very hard after the service that I have done and the hardships I have went through to be treated in this way and if the muster of Col. Dickey is not legal and is said to have a commission. I think I had better try something else for a living for I cannot get a ration or anything from the Government without paying the cash and then work all the time and board myself and get neither thanks nor pay. I can't stand it but I think General Grant's order for muster and Col. Dickey mustering me, I think quite sufficient Though there is so many turns and so much were working that I cannot tell it is strange to me that Col. Hurst promised to send for mine on the 21st of September last and then Col. Dickey on the 13th of Nov. and it has not come and others sent for in December has got here already and if I am to work and spend my money and time for the benefit of others I cannot think it fair and don't feel disposed to be made a tool of for others not while I live in a free country and no [know] myself

> Yours very Respectfully
> Wm. K.M. Breckenridge[26]

Breckenridge's concerns regarding his commission are not reflected in his military service record. This is not unusual. Military records from the Civil War are sparse in their content. Breckenridge's record in particular is sparse. He had to pay his own way and use his own resources in the course of his duty. One can only imagine the indignation that Breckenridge felt at having to pay for his own rations while seeing Fielding Hurst, William Jay Smith, and their underlings plunder the homes and farms of citizens throughout the countryside.

Breckenridge appears to have been an individual who took himself, his duty, and his obligations extremely serious. He seemed tormented by

26. Breckenridge Daybook, 186.

the events around him. What follows is a stream of consciousness narrative written in his journal. There is no evidence that he ever delivered this communiqué to anyone in particular. No doubt it was written to express his most private thoughts on the struggles he was facing in late March 1863. Extreme exasperation can be sensed in the seasoned officer's written voice. Breckenridge was a veteran of the Mexican War and the Indian Territories. He was one of the few trained and experienced officers of the First West Tennessee Cavalry. Therefore, his frustration is even more disturbing. Given the efforts he made to organize and supply the regiment, his frustration is likely warranted.

The communiqué is entitled "The Soldier's Dream." The emotion vented within it is raw and bluntly honest in its expression.

Head Quarters 1st W.T. Cavalry
Bolivar, Tenn. March 24th 1863

The Soldier's Dream

To the men of the Regiment, gentlemen and fellow Soldiers I have been a working day and night to try and get you armed & equipped on the 20th day of September last when Col. Hurst and I joined together. The understanding was that I was to go and get what Stores we needed and he was to stop with the Regiment and have it mustered into the service by the time I came back and what did he do. Nothing, he got under arrest and when I was at Washington I telegraphed and wrote and got no answer and there I waited twenty five days and then written for him to either meet me at St. Louis or write and he never done either and at St. Louis I telegraphed for me to meet me at Columbus and when I got there I learned for the first time that there had not been nothing done in this Regiment and that two Companies had left the Regiment on account of the way they had been treated and others wanting to leave. I came here and went to work and things sorter started and got six companies mustered in the service and commenced to drill and the men commenced running away and I done all I could to stop them but the Colonel would not stay in camp and the men kept a going all the time and whenever one would get tired he would fall out as fast as he could and stepped away until he got ready to come back and when I went out on the Tennessee River in the first of the Winter he went to Purdy and stopped there until I come back and in place of his trying to get us to stay on the River where we could give some aid to our Friends and Families he was trying all the time to get us all back to bolivar and why didn't he come here and stop and have the men a drilling and try to make them as comfortable as possible but no he stopped in Purdy and slept on his feather bed and kept men enough there to guard him while me and the rest of us were trying to get our country clear of the Guerrillas riding night and day and him a writing to every day to come to bolivar and me under orders from General Dodge and him a saying that if did not obey him that he would get some one that would that he would be damned if any officer could belong to his Regiment without obeying him I never thought of disobeying a superior but then I cannot obey two at once when their orders are different and it had not have been for him we would have been on the Tennessee River now and would have cleared all this time and would have not have left Bethel if it had not have been for him then General Dodge would have kept us if he had not have made such a fuss about trying to get the Regiment organized and what he has done since he come back from the River nothing only come home and back and keep up a fuss with someone and the camp he has kept us in is enough to make every man sick and the appointing Smith Major who ever heard of the like and then to appoint Morris when there is plenty of men here as good as him and far better to my notion and if they are not, I think Tennessee had better quit the job.[27]

Breckenridge argues the case against Fielding Hurst, portraying him as an individual engaged in personal agendas who is pursuing his own personal business and greed rather than the business of building up the regiment. He makes it clear that Hurst is not willing to share in the privations of his men. His actions and misdeeds are causing the men to lose faith in their purpose. He details the desertion of two companies,

27. Ibid, 187–188.

which would constitute mass desertion, a telling event. Breckenridge further divulges that the unit did not actually begin to function as a cohesive regiment until he arrived from his work in Washington, D.C., and St. Louis. His reporting that Hurst would not stay in camp and would instead return to his home is in keeping with the habits of a man not interested in the administrative and practical tasks of leading a cavalry regiment. It would seem more in keeping with someone using the opportunity to enrich himself and his friends.

In December of 1862, while Hurst is enjoying the comforts of home, his men are operating on the Tennessee River, enduring privation and shortages in camp, and constantly worrying about guerilla attacks. All the while, Breckenridge is trying to balance the management of the regiment from his very shaky position as lieutenant colonel while leading his men in action and receiving competing and contradictory orders from two superior officers, Hurst and General Grenville Dodge.

Ultimately, Breckenridge is clearly arguing the position that Hurst is not fit for command and appoints faithful retainers over more qualified and responsible men. He closes by stating that if better men are not available to command and serve, the Union cause is in trouble.

This communiqué was penned on March 24, 1863. In its form, it appears to be an address to the men. Did he give it? Or did it remain private, confined only to the pages of his journal? It is not known with certainty. However, he did give some indication of his displeasure and disappointment by reporting it to the authorities above him. Five days later, on March 29, Breckenridge was ordered under arrest by Colonel Hurst. The order, which is not contained in the *Official Records*, reads as follows:

> Regimental & Battalion Orders
> Head Quarters 1st West Tenn. Cavalry
> Bolivar, Tenn. March 29th 1863
> Regimental Order
> No. 19   Lieut. Col. W.K.M.
> Breckinridge 1st Regt. West Tenn. Cavalry is ordered under arrest. He will be confined to the limits of his camp.

> By order of
> Fielding Hurst, Col.
> Comg. Regiment
> S.L. Warren Adjt.[28]

The order does not divulge the reason for the arrest, but Breckenridge himself recorded that it was for reporting Hurst to their superior officers. In retrospect, this action by Hurst is by no means surprising. Hurst's personality was the type that sought retribution against those who offended or injured him.

Beginning March 29, Breckenridge was confined to his tent. With nothing else to do but brood over the regiment's predicament and his own, he spends a good deal of time writing in his journal. His entry for March 30 is his first actual diary entry. Perhaps he felt the necessity to document the events occurring around him for his own protection. His first entry is mostly illegible, but the closest transcription verifies that the regiment—or part of it—was at Pocahontas and on the Hatchie River. According to Breckenridge, his men were expecting an attack "every minute."[29]

While under arrest, he copied a poem into his journal, one penned by a clergyman, The Reverend Enos Guinn, pertaining to the great sectional and national conflict. Why he included it in the journal is not known unless it was simply of interest to him and one he found worthy of study and recollection.

> March 31st 1863
> Union War Hymn of Measures[30]
>
> No. 1   Columbia fled from Britain's yoke
>   By Wisdom tyrant's chains were broke
>   Old North Carolina shouted with zeal
>   Remember the Battle of Bunker Hill.

---

28. Ibid, 182.
29. Ibid, 139.
30. Ibid, 140–141.

2nd   Old South Carolina nullified
And for her subjects did provide
Mississippi forsook the Lord
And broke the Tennessee Union cord.

3rd   Old Isham Harris found he was beat
Took the bank and left the seat
To tell you the trust he's acted the pup
The Union boys will never give it up.

4th   Louisiana, she's forgat
The battle fought by Jackson's hat
And by his hero's mighty wail
Preserve the girls and cotton bales.

5th   They have Jeff Davis for their king
On us destruction did he bring
He's numbered thousands with the dead
While Southern children cry for their bread.

6th   Poor widows cry, no husbands by
To see them and hear their cry
A little morsel they have bought
But they must eat it without salt.

7th   A heavenly breeze blew over the plain
Which roused Columbia's sons again
From northern lands and plains we came
The land of liberty to gain.

8th   In Tennessee we pitched our tents
And met the rebels' stout defense
Through heat and cold we've all went
Much time and blood already spent.

9th   But God will crown the Union men
The Constitution he'll defend

                This holy law will give a right
                To those who volunteer and fight.

10th   The state guard tho good looks anew
                The holy cause still to pursue
                The officers that guide the lamp
                That rouse thy soldier's barren camp.

11th   Will shine upon the same old tree
                That gave our fathers' liberty
                The holy cause we must obtain
                By it our fathers' freedom gain.

12th   Columbia's son will make their beds
                With lasting honors on their heads
                And when the last loud cannons roar
                I hope we'll meet on Canaan's shore.

13th   And dwell with Christ around the throne
                Where none but Union men are known
                And when the dreams of life are past
                I hope we will meet in Heaven at last.

Beginning on March 31, Breckenridge began keeping more steady and routine journal entries. Sitting in his tent under confinement, he ruminates on his predicament and the causes of it. He seems quite content on resolving the problem and getting himself exonerated. During this time, he pens numerous entries and writings in which he catalogues the crimes, issues, and controversies tearing the First West Tennessee Cavalry and its leadership apart.

>   March the 31st 1863
>   31st Still under arrest and in my tent and there is a general court martial on hand and Q.M. [Quartermaster] Smith or Petty Coat Smith is before it today for trial for stealing petticoats and other things and I have called on the Col. for a copy of the charges against me but haven't got them yet and

have wrote to Gen. Brayman and am awaiting for the Col. to forward it but I haven't heard from him yet and don't expect him to send it up but if he doesn't I shall write to the General tomorrow again and see if that can get through and if it don't I shall try General Grant. Hainz come and stayed with me and give me all the news from the Tennessee River.[31] The Rebels are a running all the Union men in that country and if there is isn't something done to help them there will be no crops raised there this year.

As of March 31, it appears that Breckenridge was actually under arrest for having reported the misdeeds of Quartermaster William Jay Smith, who would eventually replace Hurst as regimental commander. Smith and Hurst were very close and Breckenridge was the outsider. The offending officer here was Smith, whose postwar biographical sketches portray him as a patriotic and fervent Unionist. However, Breckenridge depicts him in a far different light, that of an opportunistic thief who is far more preoccupied with stealing from citizens than soldiering. This entry on Smith is only a prelude to Breckenridge's descriptions of him and his crimes.

Smith's Compiled Service Record reflects that he was "in arrest" in March 1863, thus confirming Breckenridge's March 31 journal entry.[32] Regardless, Hurst saw fit at the same time to promote Smith to the rank of major.[33] This is likely a reaction by Hurst to counter Smith's arrest and subsequent court-martial. Given Hurst's pattern of apparent flagrant disrespect for Breckenridge's knowledge and efforts to lead the regiment, this promotion was likely meant to frustrate Breckenridge.

---

31. Hainz could refer to either William F. Hance, Co. D, U.S. Sixth Tennessee (First West Tennessee) Cavalry, or William M. Hannes, Co. E of the same regiment. William F. Hance was a saddler and was detailed to act as an orderly for a court martial in May 1863. See Compiled Service Record of William F. Hance. Compiled Service Records of Volunteer Union Soldiers Who Served in Organizations from the State of Tennessee. Series Number M395, Roll 0055. National Archives and Records Administration, Washington, D.C.

32. Compiled Service Record of William Jay Smith. Records of the AGO, 1780s–1917. Record Group 94, Series Number M395, Roll 0060. National Archives and Records Administration, Washington, D.C.

33. Ibid.

During this time, Breckenridge exchanged significant correspondence with General Mason Brayman. A native of Buffalo, New York, Brayman (1813–1895) had been a newspaper editor and an attorney before the war. He tried to settle the dispute between the Mormons and their neighbors in Nauvoo, Illinois. He enjoyed an illustrious career: editor of the Buffalo *Bulletin* and other newspapers, reporter for the St. Louis *Union*, and solicitor general of the newly-formed Illinois Central Railroad. When the war began, Brayman volunteered and was commissioned a major in the Nineteenth Illinois Infantry. He was promoted to colonel in April 1862, and subsequently to the rank of brigadier general of volunteers as of September 24, 1862. He saw action at the battles of Belmont, Fort Donelson, and Shiloh. He then commanded the post at Bolivar, Tennessee, until June 1863.[34] It was in this assignment that Brayman came into contact with Breckenridge.

Breckenridge was preoccupied by operations in the vicinity of the Tennessee River. His personal observations regarding both Union and Confederate activities provide first-hand knowledge of this area of operations never before published. Further, he discloses the problem faced by Union sympathizers in areas where Confederate guerillas often roamed. Making war on civilians was not only a Union on Confederate issue; it was a proverbial two-way street.

> Registered Letter
> Bolivar Tennessee March 31ˢᵗ 1863
> General Brayman
> Commanding Post
> Sir, Col. Hurst has ordered me under arrest and I have written to him for the charges and he sent me word by the adjutant that he would furnish them to me in 8 days. General, I do not think he has the right to arrest me without your approval and I wish for you to inform me whether he has the right or not as I don't think he has the right to arrest anyone if he has I wish to know by what authority he can do it.[35]

---

34. Warner, *Generals in Blue*, 43–44.

35. Breckenridge's military record reflects that in March 1863, he was present for duty but under arrest. Breckenridge Compiled Service Record.

Respectfully Yours
William K.M. Breckenridge
Lieut. Col. 1st West Tenn. Cavalry[36]

Brayman's response must not have pleased Breckenridge:

Head Quarters Post of Bolivar
Bolivar Tennessee April 1st 1863
It is competent for the commanding officer of a regiment to arrest any under his authority without Special authority from his superior being careful that it be for good cause being required to me for charges with in the proper time and responsible for any abuse of power.
M. Bra[y]man
Brig. General[37]

Having received his answer, Breckenridge sat at his journal and wrote a detailed history of William Jay Smith from his perspective. This account is significant. All that is known about Smith was written following the war. In no way does it reflect or resemble the account provided by Breckenridge, which was written as events were occurring. The war, Union victory, and Smith's subsequent political career whitewashed many blemishes from his character and reputation, as often happened during that era.

April 1st 1863[38]

April 1st I wish to give a small acct. of Q.M. [Quartermaster] Smith of the 1st W.T.C.[39] Smith by some means and don't know what got the appointment of Regimental Quarter Master about the first of Oct. 1862 and for a while got along fine and attended to his business as well as a man of his sense could but the chances for gain was so great that he

36. Breckenridge Daybook, 189.
37. Ibid.
38. Ibid.

39. Throughout his journal, Breckenridge refers to the regiment as the First (1st) West Tennessee Cavalry, the designation given it when first organized through June 1863.

thought he would try his hand so him and Col. F. Hurst of this 1st W.T.C. commenced by sending Negroes and horses and mules to their farms. Smith's farm was near Grand Junction Tennessee and so he managed to get sum 6 or 8 mules and 5 Negroes out of camp and sent them home to the farm and 2 fine horses and a lot of things and not being satisfied with all of that he got a scout and went down in that part of the country and went to citizens' farms and took mules, bedclothes and ladies' dressing and a side saddle and took them to his farm and left them there and not being still satisfied he went to the post commissary at the Junction and drew rations for his party and in place of giving them to the boys he left them with his family and took the men out in the country to forage off the citizens and when he got to camp he then thought that he had the right to command the regiment as there was none of the field officers in camp and him and sum of the — had a mess about rank he countered that as he was Q.M. (Quartermaster) so he ranked a chit and so they had to go to the general about it and the little man soon found that he didn't wear the brass collar and so he got in a great rage and told the officers that in a short time he would give them to understand that he would command the regiment that the Col. was a going to get the appointment of state auditor and he was a going to be Col. and then he would give them hell and learn them how to respect an officer but the Col. hasn't got to be auditor of the state nor Smith Col. yet though he has got the appointment of Major of the 1st Battalion though he can't keep that. Col Hurst and Q.M. Smith on another petticoat stealing trip to Mississippi and they make a big thing of it this time. They got 8 of Sol's [Solomon Street's] men and 11 Colt Revolvers, 10 Carbines, 5 horses and a whole 11 horse wagon load of petticoats and quilts and didn't give the boys no choice at all.[40] Smith has sent his share home and is now gone to Memphis with his wife[41] to lay out the money

---

40. Confederate guerrilla Solomon "Sol" Street was a constant source of trouble for General Brayman. See McCann, *Hurst's Wurst*, 27–30.

41. Mary Ann (Ross) Smith

he got for finery that she may go as fine as anyone else. It is to be hoped that he will lose all he has without he be harmed himself. Smith back and reports that he had another $300 for his family while in Memphis.

Smith got here yesterday evening and this morning he learns that Sol visited house last night and took everything out of his house and told Mrs. S[mith] that Mr. S[mith] went to his house and took all his wife's dressing and that when he, Smith, sent his wife's ward robe home that he, Street, would send Mrs. S[mith's] home to her, that he, Sol, didn't take them because he needed them but to learn Mr. S[mith] to let the ladies' petticoats alone without he wanted to dress his men in petticoats and if he did that he, Sol, would send in what he had and it has raised hell among the boys for they don't want to because of stealing and Smith's actions and so the boys turned out and was a going to hang him but I got them to stop and not get themselves in trouble about as mean a man as Smith and so they got up a petition to the general to have him moved out of the regiment and then they turned out and got up charges against him for stealing and so the aforesaid is in arrest with charges enough against him. If they're sustained to send him out of the regiment and disgrace him forever if stealing is a disgrace though he think it not from what I learn he met a negro with a bail of cotton on a wagon and he sent that to his farm and sold it for the greenbacks and so if it ain't no harm to steal cotton it ain't no harm to steal anything else. Smith is a making a big fuss now about a scout to go to ~~the river~~ his house and take as much from the Rebels as they took from him. I don't think they took anything but there own from him and if there weren't so many like him trying to make a fortune off the poor people in the country this war would soon stop but they are too big cowards to fight and they go around and steal from women and children and put to their own use and don't give a damn for the country, it is the money they are after and if a party goes to their house and takes anything there is hell to pay right off and then me and my men must turn out and hunt for the

Brevet Brig. Gen. William Jay Smith
Author's Collection

thieves and half starve and run down our horses and then along to show where to go and they are stealing all the time and abusing women and children and then some men make a hell of a fuss if the Rebels say a word to their families. I think it a damn bad rule that must work both ways and told Smith that men that lived in glass houses should not throw stones and have everything to suit him and his thieving gang. There is a man here that is called Lt. Tom Walker and another 5th Ohio Cavalry man by the name of T.K. Morris and an org. private that put them all together I think are about as bad as ever Murrell was in his time. They took a prisoner out of the guard house and hung him to make him tell where him and the band that he belonged to kept their money and he wouldn't tell and they sent him out and had him shot by some of their clan that call themselves Union men and live in Mississippi but are nothing but thieves and murderers and house burners and if I had my way I would hang the last one of the party. I don't blame the Rebels for prosecuting such men and if our regiment would hang all such I think that it would help the cause of our country more than all the armies that is here. Smith seems to think that he has a right to take anything and put it to his own use. I heard him say that he intended to take everything that he could find. He didn't give a damn if the men did call him a petticoat stealer, that for every dollar that they took from him, he intended to take and so that such he would keep some or a little ahead. Smith went to Memphis without permission and has just got back and has been put under arrest and is now undergoing his trial for stealing and all together and as soon as I can I will get a copy of the charges.[42] I am now under arrest for reporting him absent without proper authority and as soon as I can I shall give a history of the charges and the evidence.[43]

42. Breckenridge Daybook, 142–146.

43. This is one of many examples of Breckenridge being punished by Hurst for taking action against Smith and others like him in the regiment. It is clear from Breckenridge's journal that his honesty and determination to see other officers behave in a professional manner only earned him the ire of Colonel Hurst and his superiors.

Breckenridge never specially identifies Smith's full name in his journal. Of course, he was writing it for his own purposes and knew exactly about whom he was writing. He is very disdainful of Smith, a man who, over time, would serve in the regiment as a private, quartermaster, and eventually colonel. Smith's official military record documents his promotion to regimental quartermaster beginning October 5, 1862, appointed by Colonel Hurst himself.[44] Smith joined the regiment as a private on September 18, 1862, and his appointment to regimental quartermaster came about speedily, less than three weeks from his enlistment. Like Walker's appointment to the commissary, Smith's appointment was one that appears to have been made out of expediency. As quartermaster, Smith would be in a position to direct the distribution of rations, supplies, military stores, and related tasks. As documented in his journal, Breckenridge would expose the dangers of Smith occupying this position.

In this entry, Breckenridge alleges the use and misuse of property and the spoils of war. It is apparent that Hurst, Smith, and others regularly appropriated slaves, mules, horses, wagons, and other property from local Confederate citizens. Rather than free the slaves, they were allegedly sent to the farms of these Union Army officers to be used as their own laborers. Certainly, these actions seem in contradiction to normal Army procedures. It further appears that Hurst, Smith, and others used these spoils to enrich themselves. Breckenridge's language—"managed to get"—makes it appear that Smith's actions are indeed irregular as he is making every effort to get them out of camp to use on his farm.

Smith appears to have been quite a greedy individual. From Breckenridge's account, he regularly stole from citizens in the region and wasn't alone in this type of behavior. Smith was especially anxious to enrich himself during the course of the war. He was not at all satisfied with stealing property from citizens but also misappropriated Union Army rations intended to feed his soldiers and diverted them for his family's personal use. Afterwards, he sent his men—who now needed food and supplies—out in the countryside to take what they needed from the residents of the area. It was this type of behavior that led to such an inflammatory reputation for the First West Tennessee Cavalry.

In his journal, Breckenridge exposes the political and bureaucratic intrigue that at times permeated Army life during the Civil War. In

---

44. Smith Compiled Service Records.

this case, Smith apparently wanted to establish his claim for leadership in the event that Colonel Hurst was elevated to state office, in this case the office of state auditor. Tennessee was now under military rule and the governor's seat that had been vacated by Isham G. Harris was now occupied by Military Governor Andrew Johnson. Being a staunch Unionist, perhaps Hurst was actually being considered for the office by Governor Johnson, but it may also have been only a camp rumor circulated by Hurst or his subordinates. Certainly his detractors would have seen this possible appointment as a case of putting the proverbial "fox" in charge of the state's financial "henhouse."

It is quite interesting that the notorius guerrilla Sol Street visited Smith's plantation in Grand Junction and gave him a taste of the treatment to which he had subjected others. It is apparent that the matter is a personal one and Street intended to teach Smith a valuable lesson in looting and taking undue advantage of the civil turmoil in the countryside. His suggestion that Smith's soldiers could wear the petticoats that Smith was stealing adds further insult to both Smith and the regiment.

The soldiers were ostensibly quite angered by Smith's actions. A common thread throughout Breckenridge's journal is the sentiments and opinions of the men against the looting and theft committed by the higher command. Their strong disdain for the actions of Hurst and Smith does much to acquit the men of the First West Tennessee Cavalry of the historical burden of guilt they have carried since the war. Unfortunately, the enlisted men have equally carried the burden of the crimes of Hurst and Smith, an inequitable position given the men's true dedication to the Union cause. When they were discouraged from hanging Quartermaster William J. Smith, they took more official actions by petitioning the commanding general for his removal from the regiment.

Apparently, Smith made no distinction between white Confederates and the blacks of the region, the very race of people whose freedom became a focal point in the war. Blacks were vulnerable to the whims of those in more prominent positions. Breckenridge gives his own social commentary on the war and its participants. In this diatribe, he condemns the preying upon of poor people by his fellow Union officers who he feels are fighting for all of the wrong reasons. Breckenridge is sorely disappointed in Smith and others like him. He notes the hypocrisy of his fellow officers who couldn't take the same treatment they meted out to others. He compares Smith and company to the infamous John A. Murrell, the highwayman and outlaw who was notorious for robbery, murder, and slave stealing along the Natchez Trace.[45]

Smith overplayed his hand at some point and was arrested for his crimes. This arrest led to his court-marital. The subsequent arrest of Breckenridge is one of many examples of him being punished by Hurst for taking action against Smith and others like him in the regiment. It becomes clear from his journal that his honesty and determination to see other officers behave in a professional manner only earned him the ire of Colonel Hurst and his subordinates.

---

45. James A. Crutchfield, *The Natchez Trace: A Pictorial History* (Nashville TN: Rutledge Hill Press, 1985), 118.

4

TAKING CHARGE

April 1–20, 1863

Breckenridge was no longer under arrest by the end of the day on April 1, 1863.[1] The nature of his exoneration is not recorded. However, following his release, there was a barrage of special orders issued that appeared to be corrective in nature. They give the appearance that Breckenridge is getting to the bottom of the troubles he had encountered with William Jay Smith and his subordinates. It appears that Breckenridge's superiors realized the gravity of the internal strife amongst the officers and men of the regiment and stepped in to assist. Indeed, what might otherwise seem a rather mundane set of orders is, in fact, documentation of an extraordinary and monumental shift in the regimental power structure, at least temporarily. It becomes clear from a review of these special orders that a sense of law and order is being restored to the ranks of the First West Tennessee Cavalry.

Curiously, none of these orders appear in the *Official Records*. They are only recorded in Breckenridge's private journal. By the time of the

1. Breckenridge Daybook, 182.

publication, Breckenridge had been long dead and the men who were at the bottom of the regiment's troubles were now men in powerful positions. Whether the omission of such important orders was intentional is only speculative. Still, the existence of these special orders was unknown until Breckenridge's journal publicly surfaced in 2012. A review of those special orders makes it apparent that Breckenridge is attempting to correct matters he felt had gotten out of hand. The order of the documents gives an effective timeline of events.

The first special order appoints an orderly to assist Breckenridge. At this point, he seemed to enjoy no special benefits as an officer but now he will have an orderly to assist him in his day to day responsibilities. The order, dated April 1, 1863, and known as Special Order No. 3, detailed Private William A. Newsom of Company E to serve in this capacity and to report immediately to Breckenridge for duty.[2] Young Private William A. Newsom's appointment as orderly for Breckenridge is verified in Newsom's military record.[3] A month later, he would be captured in the vicinity of the Tennessee River but was apparently released rather quickly because he was acting as an orderly again by June 1863.[4] Eventually, Newsom would be promoted to the offices of ordnance clerk, quartermaster clerk, and second lieutenant.[5] Breckenridge would need an orderly with the work that faced him.

On April 2, the formal order releasing Breckenridge from custody was issued by Hurst himself. The order was short and succinct, directly to the point.

> Head Quarters 1st West Tenn. Cav.
> Bolivar Tenn. April 2nd 1863
>
> Regimental Order
> No. 26   Lieut. Col. W.K.M. Breckinridge 1st West Tennessee Cavalry you are hereby released from arrest and will report yourself at once for duty

2. Ibid.

3. Compiled Service Record of William A. Newsom. Compiled Service Records of Volunteer Union Soldiers Who Served in Organizations from the State of Tennessee. Record Group Title Records of the AGO, 1780s-1917. Record Group 94, Series Number M395, Roll 0057. National Archives and Records Administration, Washington, D.C.

4. Ibid.

5. Ibid.

> By order of
> Fielding Hurst, Col.
> Comg. Regiment
> S.L. Warren[6]

Breckenridge's release appears to have been proper under the circumstances just as his detention appears to have been unwarranted. Stanford L. Warren's name appears on Hurst's order. Warren was a prominent man, both in antebellum and postwar years. Former Confederate Brigadier General Marcus J. Wright published a biographical sketch of Stanford L. Warren in his 1882 work, *Reminiscences of the Early Settlement and Early Settlers of McNairy County, Tennessee*. Describing Warren's wartime and postwar service, that sketch reads in part:

> He was a decided Union man, and enlisted in the 6th Tennessee Union Cavalry in September, 1862. He was appointed 2d lieutenant and adjutant of his regiment on September 22, 1862. He held this position until October, 1863, when he was made a captain; on March 28, 1864, he was made a major of the regiment, and was honorably mustered out of service under orders from the War Department.[7]

Like many men of the First West Tennessee Cavalry, Warren was successful in the public arena. He served as a member of the Tennessee House of Representatives from 1865 to 1867, before being appointed by President Andrew Johnson to serve as U.S. Attorney for West Tennessee. He returned to the state house from 1869 to 1870. From 1871 to 1872 and again from 1873 to 1874, Warren served in the state senate for two terms.[8] During the war, he was accompanied by his servant, Anderson, a situation not unusual for a number of officers of the First West Tennessee Cavalry.[9] The abolition of slavery was not always a major concern, even to some Union officers.

6. Breckenridge Daybook, 182.
7. Wright, Talbott and McCann, eds., *Reminiscences*, 83.
8. Ibid.
9. Compiled Service Record of Stanford L. Warren. Compiled Service Records of Volunteer Union Soldiers Who Served in Organizations from the State of Tennessee. The National Archives

The events of April 3 as recorded in the *Official Records* occurred only a day after Breckenridge was released.[10] While Colonel Prince requested information pertaining to Hurst directly, none was given. Breckenridge was attempting to set forth the egregious behavior of both Hurst and Smith in his entry of April 1, stating that both men were actually with a raiding party down in Mississippi. Breckenridge had been placed under arrest prior to this raiding party leaving camp. He remained confined to his tent until April 2, some forty-eight hours or less after the return of Smith to camp on March 31.

In correspondence not found in the *Official Records*, Smith was ordered to make out his quartermaster's report and account for all merchandise in his possession. This coupled with Breckenridge's release and being given significant leadership duties leads to the assumption that he convinced his superiors that his contentions about Hurst and Smith were correct.

Prince wrote to General Kimball in an effort to determine exactly what Hurst was doing:

> La Grange, April 3, 1863.
>
> Brigadier General Kimball:
>
> Sir: Please state precisely your information in reference to 200 rebels having crossed the Hatchie; especially what command; which way they were going, by points of compass, from Hatchie; also whether Colonel Hurst is notified; if so, what road he is supposed to be upon; and if your information is reliable. Colonel Grierson and cavalry have returned, bringing a number of prisoners, among them Richardson's quartermaster [Wiggins] and clerk.
>
> Edward Prince,
> Colonel, in Charge of Cavalry

General Kimball's reply divulged his source of information:

---

and Records Administration, Publication Number: M395, National Archives Catalogue ID 300398, Record Group 94, Roll 0061.

10. Breckenridge's journal is of limited assistance in tracking his activities following his release April 3–19, 1863. Because there are printed numerals on each page, it is obvious there are pages missing. The *OR* have been used to provide this information.

> Col. E. Prince:
>
> My information as to 200 rebel cavalry crossing Hatchie is from General Dodge, Corinth. They crossed below Pocahontas; supposed to be making for railroad between Bolivar and Jackson. General Brayman, at Bolivar, has been informed. I notified General Smith, as they may make a turn in toward Grand Junction and La Grange.
>
> Nathan Kimball[11]

The pro-Confederate newspaper, the Memphis *Daily Appeal*, reported that "Our scouts report at Grenada, from West Point and the Mobile and Ohio railroad, that Hurst's renegade Tennessee regiment of Federal cavalry had fallen back from Palo Alto toward Corinth."[12] The village of Palo Alto, located in Clay County, Mississippi, is now considered a ghost town.

The middle of April 1863 found Hurst back in Purdy, burning the homes of Confederate sympathizers and exacting his own vengeance upon those who he considered his tormentors in 1861 and early 1862. On April 16, he burned several structures and did considerable damage to the town. These activities came to the attention of his superiors and on the same day, Colonel Elliot Warren Rice wrote to Major General Richard James Oglesby from Bethel, Tennessee:

> Col. Hurst, 1st Tenn. Cavalry from Bolivar is at Purdy for the purpose of destroying property, has ordered the furniture removed from some of the houses and threatens to burn them. The Col. passed through here this morning but did not report to my Head Quarters & I don't know by what authority he destroys the property.[13]

---

11. *OR, Series I, Volume 24, Part III*, 169-170.

12. Memphis *Daily Appeal*, April 30, 1863.

13. Letter from Colonel E.W. Rice to Major General Richard Oglesby, April 16, 1863, as found in Compiled Service Records of Volunteer Union Soldiers Who Served in Organizations from the State of Tennessee. Series Number M395, Roll 0055. National Archives and Records Administration (NARA), Washington, D.C.

Capt. Stanford L. Warren
Author's Collection

This communication between Rice and Oglesby demonstrates that Hurst's superiors in the Union Army were very concerned about his behavior and the origin of his orders. This was not the first time that Union command had to contend with Hurst's conduct. From all appearances, the First West Tennessee Cavalry seemed to be a regiment that was out of control. In the meantime, the efforts to rectify the situation continued with orders for Breckenridge to report to Union Headquarters in Bolivar on April 19.[14] The nature of this meeting was not revealed, but it is surmised that he was to report on the state of the unit. Subsequent orders were implemented to restore order that had been lacking since the fall of 1862 and into the spring of 1863.

One of the first steps taken was to force a change in the quartermaster's ranks. Breckenridge ordered William Jay Smith to issue his final reports and provide him with a full accounting of all property under his control.

> Head Qt. 1st W.T.C.
> Bolivar, Tenn.
>
> Regimental }   April 20th '63
> Order   }
>
> Qt. Master Smith will make out his last Qt. papers and hand them in to the office immediately giving a full acct. of all property received and in hand.
>
> By order of
> Wm. K.M. Breckenridge
> Lt. Col. Comd. Rg.[15]

This begs the question: What did Hurst think of all of these sudden corrective measures? It is not known with certainty. His attitude and opinion in this matter is not recorded. However, Smith was a close friend and ally. After promoting Smith from private to regimental quartermaster in less than three weeks, Hurst proceeded to elevate him to major on February 4, 1863.

One of the next steps taken was the arrest of Benjamin Thomas Walker, the already notorious arsonist and looter who had been doing

---

14. Breckenridge Daybook, 181. This correspondence is not contained in the *OR* but only in Breckenridge's journal.

15. Ibid, 155.

Smith's and Hurst's bidding. It appears that Breckenridge made every effort to get to the bottom of the regiment's problems. Walker had been acting with impunity under the cloak of his commissary sergeant's rank. Breckenridge's direct actions against Hurst's closest associates gives the appearance that he was establishing the responsibility and culpability of the parties involved. If so, Breckenridge was simply following his training as a seasoned Army officer to address the infractions that had occurred within the ranks.

> Head Qrt. 1st W.T.C.
> Bolivar, Tenn.
> April 20
>
> Regimental }
> Ord. No. }
> The Adgt. Will arrest Thomas Walker, Commissary of —— and take his sword and confine him to the limits of the camp.
> By Ord. of
> Wm. K.M. Breckenridge
> Lt. Col. Com.
> Reg.[16]

With Walker's arrest, a new commissary officer was needed to oversee the regiment's food stores and related supplies.

> Head Qrt. 1rst W.T.C.
> Bolivar, Tenn.
> April 20th '63
>
> Regimental }
> Ord. No. }
> Commissary Sergt. Thomas ACG[17] will take charge of all commissary stores in camp and will be respected and obeyed as much by ord. of
> Wm. K.M. Breckenridge
> Lt. Col. Comm. Regt[18]

16. Ibid.
17. ACG is the acronym for Assistant Commissary General.
18. Ibid.

There were other appointments as well.

> Head QT. 1rst W.T.C.
> April 20th 63
>
> Regimental }
> Ord. No.   }
>   E.M.V. Furgasen [Ferguson] of Co. E, 1st W.T.C. will be detached as Regimental Wagon master and will be respected and obeyed as such he will be report immediately for duty.
>   By ord. of
>
> Wm. K.M. Breckenridge
> Lt. Col. Comd.
> Reg.[19]

Since the fall of 1862, Hurst, Smith, and their faithful subordinates had been systematically pillaging and looting local residents of their goods and property, including livestock, furnishings, clothing, and slaves from surrounding farms and plantations. Certainly, there had been no accounting of this property. Breckenridge noted in his journal that some of these plundered goods and human beings were sent back to the farms of both Hurst and Smith. Now granted the authority by his superiors, Breckenridge called for an accounting of such property and the "spoils" of war to prevent such motivation for waging war on citizens by the regiment. No doubt such actions aggravated the existing animosity between himself, Smith, and Hurst even more.

> Head Qrt. 1rst W.T.C.
> Bolivar, Tenn.
> April 20th '63

---

19. Ibid, 156. Private Edmond M.V. Ferguson was later accused of desertion. That charge was removed from his record with the following notation: "He was while sick with his command on or about April 15, 1864, sent out to a farm in the vicinity of Memphis, Tenn. carried on by colored men by order of Regimental Commander for the benefit of his health, and to superintend until captured by the enemy, escaped and at once returned to his command June 1, 1864." Compiled Service Record of Private Edmond M.V. Ferguson. Compiled Service Records of Volunteer Union Soldiers Who Served in Organizations from the State of Tennessee. The National Archives and Records Administration, Publication Number M395, National Archives Catalogue ID 300398, Record Group: 94, Roll 0053.

Regimental }
Ord. No.   }

The Comd. Of Camp will report to these Head Qt. all horses, mules, wagons and negroes that have been captured by their co[mpanies].

By ord. of

Wm. K.M. Breckenridge
Lt. Col. Comd.
Reg.[20]

This subsequent order may have been intended to account for Army issued horses more than horses picked up along the way.

Head Qrt. 1rst W.T.C.
Bolivar, Tenn.
April 20th '63

Regimental }
Ord. No.   }

Camp Comd. Will report at once the no. of horses received and the no. on hand and show what has become of them whether lost or dead.

By ord. of

Wm. K.M. Breckenridge
Lt. Col. Comd.
Reg[21]

The following order by Breckenridge is significant for two reasons. First, the war for the Union also included a desire by the Federal Government to espouse a stance for freedom and equality—at least unofficially—prior to the formal call for emancipation. Second, for Union officers to "liberate" slaves only to send them to their own farms to work flew in the face of such a policy. In fact, Hurst's and Smith's actions of liberating slaves and confiscating horses, mules, and other personal property from Confederates only to make use of them on their own farms and plantations gave the appearance that their motives for fighting the war

20. Breckenridge Daybook, 156.
21. Ibid.

were less than admirable. The motives of both men are fairly questioned in light of Breckenridge's diary entries and criticism of them by Breckenridge and others since the war seems justified.

The fact that this order applies to contrabands and black women only is telling. As will be evidenced by some of Breckenridge's entries, a problem developed with the presence of "Negro whores" in the camp and his appall at such women fraternizing with white officers.

>Head Qrt. 1rst W.T.C.
>Bolivar, Tenn.
>April 20th '63
>
>Regimental }
>Ord. No.   }
>
>The Adgt. will see that all Contrabands in camp be regularly enrolled and that they are reported and that all Negro women in camp that has no husbands leave at once and those that have husbands and no employment must leave by ord. of
>
>Wm. K.M. Breckenridge
>Lt. Col. Comd.
>Reg.[22]

There are also more mundane issues in need of resolution. Some of Breckenridge's orders deal simply with concerns of discipline and order in the camp. One must keep in mind the importance of discipline and order in an Army camp, especially for an irregular unit like the First West Tennessee Cavalry in a war-torn region such as West Tennessee. The order below covers several important issues.

>Head Qrt. 1rst W.T.C.
>Bolivar, Tenn.
>April 20th '63
>
>Regimental }
>Ord. No.   }
>
>Hereafter the guard will be mounted at 8 A.M. and the Adgt. will see that every man detached for guard is on the parade ground at the sound of the bugle and all those that fail to be

22. Ibid, 157.

there, he will confine and he will have a camp guard of 1 non com officer 6 pvt [privates] and they will be held responsible for all government property in their charge and at guard —— the non Com. officer in charge of the said guard will turn over all public property to the new non com[23] of the day and each officer of the day will make out a report of his guard and hand it in to the officer by 9 o'clock A.M.
     By ord. of
          Wm. K.M. Breckenridge
            Lt. Col. Comd.
              Reg.[24]

Breckenridge noticed a lack of discipline with men failing to be at their posts and problems with soldiers and officers—both commissioned and noncommissioned—failing to turn over confiscated property taken from civilians in the region. There was a continued concern over the fate of government property as is evidenced by the regimental order below.

         Head Qrt. 1rst W.T.C.
           Bolivar, Tenn.
            April 20th '63

Regimental }
Ord. No.   }
 Co. Commanders will have their Qt.M (Quartermaster) Report made out at once stating the amount of government property received by them and the amount on hand
By ord. of
         Wm. K.M. Breckenridge
           Lt. Col. Comd.
             Reg.[25]

The sheer number of these regimental orders issued by Breckenridge is a testament to the apparent state of disorder and lack of discipline throughout the First West Tennessee Cavalry on so many different fronts.

23. "Non com" refers to a noncommissioned officer.
24. Ibid.
25. Ibid, 158.

Apparently, soldiers had been roaming at will, whether on unofficial "foraging" expeditions or simply personal expeditions. Using their horses for such ventures constituted a misappropriation of government property.

Head Qrt. 1rst W.T.C.
Bolivar, Tenn.
April 20th '63

Regimental }
Ord. No.   }

No enlisted man will be allowed to take his horse out of camp without a proper pass, the habit of the men getting on their horses and running them all over the country must be stopped and any violation of this ord. the Co. commanders will be responsible for

By ord. of

Wm. K.M.B.
Lt. Col. Com'd
Reg.[26]

The condition of regimental horses was also an issue to be addressed.

H. Qt. 1rst W.T.C.
Bolivar, Tenn.
April 20th 63

Regimental }
Order No.   }

Hereafter at stable call[27] of a morning and evening the Co[mpany] Commanders will see that every horse is watered and well groomed.

W.K.M.B.
Lt. Col. Comd.
Regt.[28]

---

26. Ibid.

27. "Stable call" referred to the prescribed signal (a bugle call) for troops to feed and water their horses.

28. Ibid, 159.

The final order concerning organization and discipline pertains to appearances.

> H. Qt. 1rst W.T.C.
> Bolivar, Tenn.
> April 20th 63
>
> Regimental }
> Order No.   }
>   Co. Commanders will see that their picket lines and parade grounds are well policed every morning by drill and that the men keep themselves clear and their tents in good order and that all their men have good clothes.
> By order of W.K.M. Breck.
> Lt. Col. Com'd.
> Regt.[29]

The month of April 1863 found the two leaders of the First West Tennessee Cavalry at odds as to purpose and intent. While Breckenridge was hard at work straightening out the disorder and lawlessness of his regiment, his immediate superior, Hurst, was in his hometown burning, looting, and wreaking havoc amongst his neighbors and adversaries. The diametric positions of these two men were never more clear.

29. Ibid.

5

On the MOVE

April 21–July 11, 1863

Beginning with his groundless arrest by Fielding Hurst in late March 1863, Breckenridge had begun keeping a record of events. Perhaps it was for his own benefit and for his own protection should higher ranking Federal authorities intervene and take control of a regiment that appeared to be a rogue unit. In any event, Breckenridge resumed making regular entries in his journal the day after the multiple regimental orders were issued. From late April until his death in October 1863, the entries were largely consistent. By April 21, he had implemented measures to bring the situation under control. Now the business of the regiment could continue, although during these extraordinary times, there was no true business as usual for the First West Tennessee Cavalry or anyone else for that matter.

On April 21, Breckenridge wrote from his camp at Bolivar:

> This morning brings an order for our forces to march to Corinth and the boys are all very glad of it. Some very much

excited not having horses go to the wagon yard and get mules or anything that can carry them out of this place and all are getting ready to start what was not armed for anything they could some with shotguns and some with muskets we mounted and all are starting. We left about 9 o'clock A.M. and got to Corinth the 23rd of April, nothing of much interest in the way. A great many went home on the way and seen their families and then returned back to their companies.[1]

Interestingly, Breckenridge's description of the arms being carried by his regiment sounds more like those being carried by their Confederate counterparts. This entry also illustrates the state of the regiment and the very reasons that pressed Breckenridge to push the Army bureaucracy for armaments, munitions, and other supplies and equipment back in the late summer of 1862. He empathized with the soldiers under his command. Often he referred to their homesickness. He did not mention whether or not passes and written leaves were used. Interestingly, Breckenridge penned this portion into the entry sometime afterwards, possibly on April 23, 1863. It was not unusual when times were busy that he would use downtime to catch up on his journal entries. What appeared to be an interim entry above adds to our knowledge of the regiment's southward march.

On April 21, the regiment returned to Purdy to forage. It also gave Hurst an opportunity to visit his home. That day, Breckenridge wrote:

> The Reg[iment] left Bolivar for Cor[inth] at 8 A.M. and marched to Col. Hurst['s] farm and stopped for the night in the neighborhood and had to forage for supplies in the neighborhood.[2]

Breckenridge often refers to the foraging activities of his troops. It may seem strange that a Union cavalry regiment would have need to forage in the areas through which they traveled. However, time and again, he reveals that his troops were forced to forage in the neighborhoods around West Tennessee. It is possible that some of these activities included looting. Breckenridge took a strong stand against theft, arson, and other

1. Breckenridge Daybook, 160.
2. Ibid, 161.

activities tantamount to war crimes. We know from Breckenridge that William J. Smith sent government issued rations home to his plantation in Hardeman County, Tennessee, thus the regiment may have been short on rations. Such a situation would have required a regiment to forage.

On the same date that Breckenridge makes the journal entry above, General Oglesby reported on the general situation in the area, recording the account of a gentleman by the name of Mr. Wright. This refugee provided valuable information pertaining to arms and munitions manufacturing capabilities in Alabama as well as troop strengths and the general military situation in Mississippi.

>Corinth, Miss., April 21, 1863
Lieut. Col. Henry Binmore,
Asst. Adjt. Gen., Sixteenth Army Corp, Memphis, Tenn.

Herewith I inclose [sic] written statement of Mr. Wright, a refugee, containing some important information, which may be of interest at this time. I believe the statement to be true.

It is almost useless for me to state that I have found everything at this command in good condition. The supplies seem to be abundant, and troops in good state of discipline, with much spirit and good health. I have retained the forces at outposts of Chewalla, Camp Davis, Glendale, and Bethel unchanged, except at Bethel, where I called in one regiment (Forty-third Ohio) to move with Fuller to support of Dodge. These posts and distances the general is doubtless familiar with.

In order to communicate with Dodge at Hamburg, I have brought down a small squadron from Jackson, say 60 men, to be used, as soon as Hurst arrives, as vedettes and scouts, beyond the lines of pickets. At present I have no cavalry for this purpose. I communicate with Dodge by messenger and escort to Hamburg, thence to Eastport, thence 15 miles to his camp on Bear Creek. Sent him to-day ambulance, with ammunition for carbines, and mail, for the division escort of 75 men, under captain Third Michigan Cavalry. Hope we shall have no further trouble with guerrillas. To avoid all risk, however, Mr. Fuller has telegraphed he will send me cipher operator for this station, and I shall send this one to Dodge, to put all dispatches in cipher.

In regard to General Dodge and the forces under his command, I can say but little more than you are already informed of by dispatches. I think he feels confident of driving the enemy from Tuscumbia on Friday, and believes himself able to hold it until Streight can make his trip, as already agreed upon. Of Streight's success, he feels evidently less sanguine. He is master of his position, and clearly realizes the enemy can be strongly re-enforced before he will be able to attack. He has been kept by no indolence or neglect of his own. If the thing succeeds now, it will, to say the least, be a very fortunate result. He is well supplied with rations, forage, and ammunition, and is not annoyed by sickness or convalescents. As to any further aid from here, I think my forces too weak to be further reduced. Bethel is weak; Jackson and Bolivar sufficiently so. I must hold my outposts to the last. Can draw none from there. Dodge has taken his staff of scouts with him, and I am compelled to look to my own cavalry and outposts to look around Corinth. Shall send all important information as soon as received.

Most respectfully, your obedient servant,
R. J. Oglesby.

(Inclosure) [sic]

Statement of Wright, a refugee.

Corinth, Miss., _____, 1863

General Ruggles and staff came north from Columbus to Verona. An engineer came north with Wright, making maps of all the roads as far as Cotton-gin Port, at which place I got away from engineer, by taking the cut-off, piloted by a boy. Don't know what force is at Verona. All troops moved from Columbus with Ruggles. Some came up from Mobile, via Tombigbee River, to Columbus, on the Cherokee and Warrior. I left Selma 9th of April. Left Columbus on 16th. Parted with engineer Wednesday P.M., 16th. It was cavalry which came from Mobile. No troops to speak of at Selma, the largest arsenal in the South, except one in Georgia (Atlanta). No troops at Meridian. No troops on that road, except at Verona, I think, but I came across the country from Columbus. I came through Fulton Tuesday, 17th. Stopped that night 10 miles this side. Came through Bay Springs. Came through Burnsville Saturday. Saw no soldiers, but heard of some passing through Burnsville, going east. Heard of none moving till then. The talk was that General Ruggles was to occupy Verona, to protect people making crops. The talk is that Vicksburg is safe, and will be held anyhow. The negro who brought me owns his own team and carriage. His master lives in Columbus; he is a Union man (miller). Don't know what Ruggles' force is, but think it over 1,000 or 2,000. Can't say that Verona is his permanent headquarters. Saw no soldiers except at Smithville, and a few 10 miles south of Fulton. Heard no news of Charleston later. The talk is that they can hold it. Mobile, people think, may be easily taken. Three gunboats were launched at Selma February or March, two for harbor defense of Mobile. The third (Tennessee) is a sea-going, formidable craft.

Making all sorts of ammunition at Selma, but have made no guns. They are now sinking a pit for making guns of a large caliber; they have very large furnaces; hot-air furnaces, too, for brass pieces. Have any amount of iron; it comes from Montevallo, Talladega, and other places on Alabama and Tennessee Railroad. No powder-mill at Selma now in operation. They are making niter all along that railroad. Don't manufacture small-arms at Selma, but are repairing many. Are doing nothing in way of manufacture at Columbus; only a sort of barracks. Heard of no movements toward Tennessee now.

These reports are important in that they provide a relatively concise but clear idea on the circumstances in many of the areas in which the First West Tennessee Cavalry would find itself.

As Breckenridge and his men moved through the territory, they came across the effects of Hurst's activities. In his journal entry of April

22, Breckenridge referred to a house burned by Hurst. Homes were burned by Hurst and his subordinates in at least three locations: between Bethel Station and Purdy, Purdy itself, and Stantonville. On the 22nd, Breckenridge wrote that he and his men marched to Purdy, "the late scene of Col. Hurst['s] house burning there."[3] Breckenridge left Purdy at 2:00 P.M. with the companies of Captain Elijah Roberts and Captain David J. Dickerson and rode to Stantonville, where they foraged for the night.[4] He mentions going to the home of Thomas Carrs and taking supper before scouting and going to "General Mixes."[5] Likely the Thomas Carr or Thomas Car referred to is indeed Thomas Baker Kerr (1818–1895), who lived in the Stantonville community and is buried in Clear Creek Cemetery. Breckenridge often spelled proper names phonetically.

Breckenridge also mentioned General John H. Meeks, who lived quietly at his home in Stantonville when the war broke out. Meeks was born in Lincoln County, Tennessee, on September 27, 1814, and moved with his maternal grandfather, Captain John Henderson, to McNairy County in 1830. The family settled on Oxford's Creek, where Captain Henderson died on February 20, 1840. Meeks was elected major of the Second Battalion of the 108th Regiment of the Tennessee Militia. Later, he attained the rank of Colonel and afterwards brigadier general. Meeks served many roles in the county including deputy U.S. marshal and state representative. He was a Democrat and his sons served the Confederate Army. According to Marcus J. Wright's *Reminiscences*, Meeks was subjected to "many annoyances and losses, and would have lost his life but for the interference of Gen. Grant."[6] According to Judge John A. Pitts, his farm was raided by Fielding Hurst's scouts who carried off some of his livestock.[7] Meeks appealed directly to Grant:

> General Grant received him kindly, and they talked familiarly for perhaps an hour, General Meeks told me; and at the close of the interview, General Grant wrote out with his own hand, on a slip of paper, and gave to General Meeks what

3. Breckenridge Daybook, 161.
4. Ibid.
5. Ibid.
6. Wright, Talbott and McCann, eds., *Reminiscences*, 66.
7. Pitts, *Reminiscences of an Old Lawyer*, 189.

he what he called a "safeguard," which in substance ordered Hurst to return to General Meeks his livestock, and forbade any Federal soldier thereafter from molesting him or his property. This paper having been made known to Hurst, General Meeks' livestock was promptly returned to him, and thereafter to the end of the war, no Federal soldier disturbed him or his property, although he was most of the time within the Federal lines.[8]

Certainly, Grant proved helpful to the aged General Meeks, a man with strong ties to the Confederate cause.

The last week of April 1863 was a very busy one for Breckenridge. He and his men covered significant territory. The morning of April 23 found him in Corinth, Mississippi, riding toward McNairy County and back to familiar territory. He left Corinth at 6:00 A.M. and rode toward the site of a burned house place near General Meek's home to meet Hurst.[9]

The next morning, April 24, found Breckenridge riding towards Hamburg, a settlement along the banks of the Tennessee River. Hamburg was a small village some ten miles south down the river from Savannah. It had about one hundred residents, two stores, a grocery store, a post office, and a church by 1874.[10] Here along the river, Breckenridge encountered and reported in his journal a number of interesting events, none of which were recorded in the *Official Records*. At 2:00 P.M., Company B of the First West Tennessee rode towards Glendale, Mississippi, with fifty men providing an escort for an ordnance train to Hamburg.[11] Breckenridge arrived there at 8:00 P.M., found no gunboats or transport boats, and reconnoitered instead. As the evening ended, he took his supper at a Mrs. Dickerson's.[12]

The next day, Breckenridge expressed his frustration with Hurst. This entry and others in his journal make it difficult for Hurst's apologists to deny responsibility for the arson that plagued the village of Purdy. This contemporary account of Hurst's activities is recorded confirmation of

8. Ibid, 190.
9. Breckenridge Daybook, 161.
10. Killebrew and Stafford, *Resources of Tennessee*, 1093.
11. Breckenridge Daybook, 161.
12. Ibid.

JOHN H. MEEKS
Author's Collection

JOHN H. MEEKS HOME
Author's Collection

that portion of local oral history alleging Hurst to be an arsonist during the war. However, there is a more insidious fact seeping through the surface of history here as well. This entry reinforces the stark contrast between the respective activities of Breckenridge and Hurst during the same period of time. Breckenridge is present for action and leading his men; Hurst is busy pursuing personal vendettas.

On that morning of the 25th, Breckenridge and his men crossed the Tennessee River at Hamburg and made their way up Horse Creek. The valley along Horse Creek was made up of rich soil. The creek derived its name from the number of horses found there in the days of Hardin County's earliest settlers, as well as for the alleged horse thieves that could be found along it.[13] Scouting for the enemy as they made their way up Horse Creek, they finally reached the small settlement known as Lowryville (also known as Loweryville). It was named for a Dr. Lowery, who also built one of the first brick homes in Hardin County.[14] Breckenridge's ride to Lowryville was almost eleven miles due east from Hamburg. Apparently, he and his party didn't stay long as they rode directly back to Hamburg, another eleven mile ride.

> No boats come until 4 P.M. No feed for horses, have to bring it across the river in a canoe from G. Moors. Took breakfast at Mrs. Dickerson's and in the evening crossed the river with my Command and scouted the Horse Creek as far as Lowryville and then back to Hamburg and fed and rested and took dinner with Capt. Landes of the gunboat and left Hamburg for Corinth about 8 P.M. and it rained very hard all the way getting to camp at 9 P.M. Men and horses nearly worn out and we had only 3 meals on the trip and 2 feeds for the horses and made a march of over 100 miles in the time Col. H[urst] has gone to Purdy again with a party to burn more houses. I suppose though I can't tell what his business is.[15]

---

13. B.G. Brazelton, *A History of Hardin County, Tennessee* (Nashville TN: Cumberland Presbyterian Publishing House, 1885), 85. P.M. Harbert, *Early History of Hardin County* (Memphis TN: Tri-State Printing and Binding Co., 1968), 63.

14. Harbert, *Hardin County*, 48–49.

15. Breckenridge Daybook, 161–162.

Breckenridge's notation of Hurst's arson activities in Purdy on April 25 is significant for a number of reasons. This wanton destruction would leave a permanent impact on the town and create feelings among locals that no amount of time would ever wash away. In fact, Purdy would never recover from the effects of the war. According to Killebrew's *Introduction to the Resources of Tennessee* in 1874, it "was almost totally destroyed during the war and has never been entirely rebuilt."[16]

On the 26th, Breckenridge had a moment of enjoyment despite all of his diligent work. He rode to Corinth, Mississippi, and spent the evening with a Captain Weir of Steward's Battalion, visiting with a Mr. Graves.[17] The next day, while still in Corinth, Breckenridge documented the injuries incurred to some of his men, including Sergeant Calvin Roberts of Company E.[18] Roberts enrolled in the First West Tennessee Cavalry at Bethel Station on September 18, 1862.[19] He was officially mustered into service at Bolivar on November 13, 1862.[20] On April 27, 1863, Breckenridge wrote:

> In camps all day and Sergt. Roberts got shot on picket accidently and his leg broke all to pieces. 4 men of the 10 men shot on picket. It seems that there is something here to interest the boys in place of attending to their business.[21]

According to Roberts' military service record, he was "wounded in left leg on Picket Post accidentally at Corinth, Mississippi[,] where he was left in Post Hospital.[22] Discharged for amputation of left leg Aug. 16/63 by order of Maj. Gen. Hurlbut."[23] According to his Certificate

16. Killebrew and Stafford, *Resources of Tennessee*, 1147.
17. Breckenridge Daybook, 162.
18. Ibid.
19. Compiled Service Record of Calvin Roberts. Compiled Service Records of Volunteer Union Soldiers Who Served in Organizations from the State of Tennessee. Record Group Title Records of the AGO, 1780s–1917. National Archives Catalogue ID 300398, Record Group 94, Series Number M395, Roll 0059. National Archives and Records Administration; Washington, D.C.
20. Ibid.
21. Breckenridge Daybook, 162.
22. Ibid.
23. Ibid.

of Disability for Discharge dated August 3, 1863, his accidental injury was to his left knee by the "accidental discharge of a gun in the hands of a comrade (Apr. 28th 1863) so extensively injuring the knee and lower portion of femur as to make amputation necessary at the juncture of the lower and middle third" rendering Roberts totally disabled for either "field garrison or invalid corps."[24] Interestingly, there is a small discrepancy between the Breckenridge account and the actual official record.[25]

On April 30, the two commanders, Hurst and Breckenridge, who often feuded and seldom got along, went together to discuss regimental difficulties with General Richard James "Uncle Dick" Oglesby. The men of the First West Tennessee Cavalry had not been paid and had been serving up to this time on a promise of pay. Breckenridge himself surely knew that his men, after all they had endured and witnessed, might not continue to serve if they did not soon receive their wages. It must have been an interesting occasion for Breckenridge and Hurst to join together to address a mutual concern. It seems to have brought Breckenridge great satisfaction that Hurst could not leave the regiment to travel to Nashville, even if the stated purpose was to inquire about officers' commissions, an issue of contention for Breckenridge for some time.[26]

On the same day, April 30, Breckenridge wrote that Generals Dodge, Brayman, and Lawler have lauded both Breckenridge and his men, stating that his men were the most efficient men they had under their command. This was either an overstated compliment by Breckenridge's superiors or a reference to the men under his practical command who were rendering constructive service under their lieutenant colonel's guidance. After all, the Union command had been critical at other times of Hurst and the regiment.

In May, Breckenridge found himself busy with operations along the Tennessee River. His journal is silent during the entire month except for his correspondence, which is vital to our larger understanding of his role in the affairs of the regiment during that time. Once again, the correspondence and reports contained in the *Official Records* and communications

---

24. Ibid.

25. Breckenridge records the event as having occurred on April 27, 1863. Roberts' military records document it as having occurred the following day. If it occurred late on the evening of April 27, such a discrepancy is easily explained. It may not have been reported until after midnight.

26. Breckenridge Daybook, 164.

recorded by Breckenridge himself give an account of events that would otherwise be lost.

On May 14, Lieutenant Commander Seth Ledyard Phelps reported by telegraph on an action against Linden, Tennessee, in Perry County, led by Breckenridge.[27] That telegraph was forwarded directly to Lincoln's Secretary of the Navy, Gideon Welles. On the night of the 12th, Phelps took Breckenridge and fifty-five men and horses on his gunboats, ferried them over the Tennessee River, and landed them on the east bank of the river. He then dispatched his gunboats to cover the landings above and below where the men disembarked. From there, Breckenridge "dashed across the country to Linden" where he surprised Rebel forces twice his number. His action that night resulted in considerable success. He burned the Perry County Courthouse, which was being used as a Rebel arsenal, along with considerable arms and supplies.[28] Incidentally, Southern courthouses were often used as supply depots and makeshift hospitals. During the raid, three Confederates were killed and one captain, one surgeon, four lieutenants, thirty soldiers, 10 conscripts, and Lieutenant Colonel William Frierson were captured.[29] The First West Tennessee also took 50 horses, two wagons, and various arms.[30] When it was over, Breckenridge and his detachment returned to the safety of the gunboats without the loss of a single man.[31]

This was a bold action. It was the type of operation Breckenridge most assuredly envisioned for his regiment, not as a group of marauders making war on civilians for personal gain. Prisoners captured during this mission were sent to a prison camp at Cairo, Illinois, and no retribution

27. *OR*, Series 1, Volume 24, Part I, 316. Ibid, Part 3, 331. This correspondence as written in Breckenridge's journal varies slightly from the version found in the *OR*.

28. Ibid.

29. Ibid. Lieutenant Colonel Frierson was a member of the field staff of the Twenty-Seventh Tennessee Infantry, CSA. He enlisted as a private at Camp Trousdale in November 1861 and was promoted directly to lieutenant colonel on May 12, 1862, quite a jump in rank in one promotion. He had been wounded at the Battle of Perryville, Kentucky. There is some confusion as to his fate after his capture. War Department records indicate he was sent to the Military Prison at Alton, Illinois, then paroled on June 12, 1863, and sent to City Point, Virginia, for exchange. However, his records also reflect that he was paroled at Johnson's Island, Ohio, a Union prison exclusively for Confederate officers, and sent to Point Lookout, Maryland, for exchange on February 20, 1865.

30. Ibid.

31. Ibid.

or crude vigilante "justice" was extracted against them. Interestingly, Breckenridge made no journal entry or record or duplicated a letter detailing his exploits at Linden. Such may be an indication of his humility.

Four days later, on May 18, Breckenridge reported to Colonel Elliot Warren Rice intelligence that scouts had acquired along the Tennessee River. He mentioned Chalk Bluff, a river bluff located in Hardin County in a bend of the river north of Coffee Bottom. The bluff overlooks the river itself and draws its name from nearby Chalk Creek. Breckenridge referred to Lieutenant William C. Webb, who rose from private to first lieutenant in February 1863.[32] Webb was a native of Perry County and more familiar with the territory east of the Tennessee River. He would rise to the rank of captain before the war was over. Breckenridge wrote to Colonel Rice:

> Registered Letter
> Adamsville, Tennessee
> May 18th 1863
>
> Colonel Rice[33]
> Commanding Post Bethel
>
> I have information from the Harrison scouts that there is a small force opposite Hamburg & Pittsburg and that the enemy is a moving down the River. Mr. H. Harrison reports to me that with his glass from the top of Chalk Bluff that he saw some several hundred Cavalry pass down in the direction of Saltillo and Clifton. I will order another Co. to Saltillo to reinforce Lieut. Webb and scout as low as Clifton and report in the morning.[34]
>
> Yours very Respectfully,
> Wm. K.M. Breckenridge
> Lieut. Col. 1st W.T.C. Comg. De.[35]

---

32. Compiled Service Record of William C. Webb. Compiled Service Records of Volunteer Union Soldiers Who Served in Organizations from the State of Tennessee. Record Group Title Records of the AGO, 1780s–1917. Record Group 94, Series Number M395, Roll 0062. National Archives and Records Administration, Washington, D.C.

33. Colonel E.W. Rice was the post commander at Bethel Station, Tennessee.

34. Lieutenant William C. Webb of Company G was promoted to Captain of Company E on March 28, 1865.

35. Breckenridge Daybook, 196.

Breckenridge's next letter is to a Captain Kevold. He instructs Kevold:

> Adamsville, Tennessee
> May 18th 1863
>
> Captain Kevold
> Yours of the 6 P.M. has come to hand. The Major has gone to Bethel and I would like for you to go to Saltillo to reinforce Lieut. Webb of my command who is there and report to me in the morning all important news and have Lieut. Webb to send scouts to Clifton and Perryville and report as soon as they cannot spare horses.
>
> Yours very Respectfully
> Wm. K.M. Breckenridge
> Lieut. Col. 1st W.T.C. Comg. De[36]

Breckenridge had been invited by General Oglesby to receive both his officer's commission and his backpay, each long-standing issues of contention for him. However, in a demonstration of his dedication to duty, he chose to forgo the opportunity in order to remain on the Tennessee River. He was evidently very apprehensive about the stability of the situation there.

He had received reports from scouts that several hundred Confederate cavalry troops were traveling down the river toward Saltillo and Clifton. He had received a dispatch from Captain Joseph G. Berry with Company H of his regiment. It was possible that some of them belonged to commands under Biffle, Cox, and Dibbrel. The Second Tennessee Cavalry Battalion was also known as Biffle's Battalion and Cox's Battalion. Locally, Colonel Nicholas N. Cox made quite the stir the previous autumn when his battalion attacked Henderson Station, Tennessee, on October 25, 1862, killing one Union soldier and capturing three officers and 33 enlisted men, all of the 49th Illinois Infantry. Cox's Battalion burned the railroad station, the railroad bridge, and destroyed the tracks of the Mobile and Ohio Railroad and Union Army supplies. This was known as Cox's Raid.[37]

36. Ibid.

37. Cathy Tudor Forester, ed. *Tennessee Historical Markers* (Nashville: Tennessee Historical Commission, 1996), 282.

Registered Report
Adamsville, Tennessee
May 18th 1863

Colonel Rice
Commanding Post Bethel

I have just received an order to report to General Oglesby[38] at Jackson to be commissioned and paid and the boys to remain until we see how times are here on the river and you will please telegraph to General Oglesby for permission for me and my men to remain on the river until we learn what the Rebels are a going to do I will be very much obliged to you and in the mean time I will get the men together and be ready to move as soon as you think my services are not required here I shall go to the river this evening. I have no news from there and I suppose all is quiet there. The Rebels burned 22 bales of cotton for Mr. Cherry last night. Since writing the above I have received a dispatch from Captain Berry, he reports that there was some of the Rebels across the River last night and them and his pickets had some skirmishing but they have crossed back this morning and from the noise they made during the night he thinks they are a fixing to cross. They have a band and he thinks there is a larger force there some of Biffle Coxes and a part of Dibberels command.[39]

---

38. General Richard James "Uncle Dick" Oglesby (1824–1899) was a Kentucky native with a meager and humble background. He studied law and passed the bar exam, served in the Mexican War, and was elected to the Illinois Senate in 1860 just prior to the outbreak of the Civil War. Oglesby accepted a commission as colonel of the Eighth Illinois Infantry. He was promoted to brigadier general on March 22, 1862, and served in the Battle of Corinth, where he was severely injured. His injuries were so severe that he was unable to serve again until April 1863. At the time of this dispatch between Rice and Breckenridge, Oglesby had been promoted to major general. Warner, *Generals in Blue*, 346–347.

39. Brigadier George Gibbs Dibrell (1822–1888) was colonel of the Eighth Tennessee Cavalry, CSA, before rising to brigadier general. He served first with General Nathan Bedford Forrest before transferring to General Joseph E. Johnston. He achieved brigade command in 1863, but did not receive his generalship until January 28, 1865, to rank from July 26, 1864. When Richmond fell and the Confederate government fled, Dibrell was placed in charge of the Confederate archives. Ibid, 72–73.

>Wm. K.M. Breckenridge
>Lieut. Col. 1st West Tenn. Cav.
>Commanding Detach.[40]

Two days later, Breckenridge wrote to Colonel Rice again.

>Saltillo, Tennessee
>May 20th 1863
>
>Colonel Rice
>Commanding Post Bethel
>
>I have a dispatch from Lieut. Webb at Decaturville he reports that one Gunboat was as high as Perryville on Monday morning but returned immediately to the mouth of Duck River and he also reports that Col. Woodard with his Regiment is at the mouth of the Duck River but no sign of crossing as he could learn. There was 30 Rebels at East Perryville yesterday scouts reported 300 of the Michigan Cavalry opposite Clifton today at 11 O'clock P.M. and others at Swallow Bluff, Shannonsville and Matthewses and I will go up to Chalk Bluff to night and to Adamsville in the morning if any boats come up I will dispatch to you immediately.
>
>Yours very respectfully
>Wm. K.M. Breckenridge
>Lieut. Col. 1st W.T.C.
>Commanding Detach.[41]

On May 20, Breckenridge wrote to Lieutenant William C. Webb disclosing the issues still plaguing the regiment. Drunkenness was a common problem for many regimental leaders. Troops became bored and when action was lacking and alcohol was available, it led to trouble. The last thing Breckenridge wanted was for cooperative citizens in areas where he was operating to suffer undue hardship because his soldiers

---

40. Breckenridge Daybook, 194.
41. Ibid, 194–195.

became drunk and disorderly. This attitude offers a stark contrast to that of Hurst and Smith.

Saltillo, Tennessee
May 20th 1863

Lieut. Webb

Yours of this morning has just come to hand. It is now 3 ½ past 3 P.M. I am sorry that the boats went back. They will be more up soon. My understanding is that they left Paducah on Monday morning. Keep a good lookout and if you can't keep the men from drinking and cutting up you had better destroy all the whiskey that is in the country and stop the stills and then you can get along with them but as long as they can get the whiskey you will have trouble and I want the men to behave in Decaturville for the citizens have treated us too well to be mistreated by the boys. So you had better spill the stuff and then they can't get it. I will leave here for Adamsville this morning and as soon as I learn what we have to do or when I get different orders I will let you know. Keep me informed of all the movements of the enemy I think I will be there soon.

Yours very Respectfully,
Wm. K.M. Breckenridge, Lieut. Col.[42]

On May 25, Breckenridge drafted a lengthy dispatch to Third Division Headquarters reporting on his activities along the Tennessee River. He was very detailed about his whereabouts and activities. Among other events he disclosed, he mentioned what transpired at the tanyards he visited, including the threat of a conflict at Hassle's Tannery. The mission was quite successful and he was able to report great gains from his efforts.

Head Qt., 3rd Division _____ Corps
Jackson, Tenn. May 25th [18]63

In pursuance to
  Special Order No. 32
    I left Jackson Tenn., 8 o clock P.M. and marched to Cotton Grove and camped for the night and during the night Lt.

42. Ibid, 195–196.

DeFord with 30 men I sent him to Hamburg to see if boats was there and to let them know that I wished to cross at Perryville and also another party to Saltillo and another to Perryville for the same purpose and the men rested and fed and at 4 A.M. I resumed the march and camped the night of the 26 at Decaturville and kept pickets on the river to hail the boats and sent scouts across the River to see what the enemy was a doing and on the 29th my scouts reported about a hundred men a crossing at Matthias Nichols and Cotam's ferry in shifts and [...] and I went down to check them but they had re-crossed the river before I got there and I had my trip for nothing. On the 30th my men had a skirmish and took 2 men and horses and at night 2 of my men fell in with 3 of the enemy and killed one and got his horse and repeater and one of my men was wounded in the shoulder slightly. On the evening of the 31st the gunboats came down and set me across the river and I started at once to Mr. Sutton's tan yard 7 miles from the River and Moss creek and got 3 wagon loads of leather, 3 mules, a shot gun and rifle, the guns I left on gunboats with the leather. While at Suttons a scout come in and reported 300 rebels camped 4 miles farther up the creek but none showed themselves after putting the leather on the boats. I started for Hassles tan yard and Spring Creek and loaded and come back to the river that night, there was no wagons in the country to press and so I had to make out with the 3 wagons I had. Along after I left the tannery that night there was a party of the enemy went to the house and told Mrs. Hassle that if I come there the next day after leather that I would go up for they had a 1100 men close by and when I went back she told me and wanted me to leave for fear of a fight but I staid all day and kept the wagons a running and never saw one. the next morning I went to another tannery of Mr. H[assle]'s on Lick Creek that way and was only 3 miles from the river and worked all day and saw but one of the enemy and he out run my men and in the evening my scouts reported that at the tannery where I was to go the next day there was 800 camped and it being 2 miles from the river I thought it best to not go as my men and horses was all tired and the men had had but 5 meals of bacon and corn bread from Sunday dinner up to this time Thursday 2 P.M. they got breakfast at the gunboats. I then marched to Decaturville and rested some till Saturday and then left for Lexington and camped there for the night a waiting for Capt. Kemp and he did not come Sunday morning. I learnt that he had gone to Purdy and I then started for Jackson and got there at 9 P.M. and reported to Col. Misener, Chief of Cav., and was ordered to Lagrange. Captured 12 head of horses and mules on the trip and a wagon and yoke of cattle and 26 wagon loads of leather and 31 conscripts and administered the oath to them and let them go and at Lexington, arrested Deberry and turned him over at Jackson.

Wm. K. M. Breckenridge
Lt. Col. 1rst WTC[43]

This particular correspondence provides details of the activities of both Breckenridge and his men. He records his efforts at procuring leather, an important resource to a cavalry regiment. The significant difference between the way Breckenridge acquired needed resources for the regiment and the manner in which others—especially William J. Smith—scoured the countryside for their own benefit is evident.

One of the character traits of Breckenridge that emerges from the pages of his journal is his sense of decency and humanity in a time of war. Recorded is a letter from the wife of a captured Confederate soldier to her husband. Apparently, Breckenridge had agreed to be a go-between for the couple. This gesture demonstrates his integrity and the kindnesses he was willing to extend to the enemy. Despite the often wholesale characterization of the officers and men of the First West Tennessee Cavalry as brutes, his courtesy shows otherwise.

---

43. Ibid, 165.

Decaturville, Tennessee

May 31st 1863

My dear Husband

This being the first opportunity I have of writing or rather sending a letter. Believe me I embrace it with the greatest pleasure. I have regretted so often I did not start to Perryville immediately after hearing of your arrival at that place but circumstances being such at that time I did not deem it prudent but imagine my feeling when I ascertained I could have gone with the greatest safety. But alas, at too late an hour for when I received this information you were far down the River. Col. Breckenridge handed me your letter the evening of your departure and I was happy indeed to hear from you, that you were well and had been taken by such perfect Gentlemen as I now believe them to be. I was perfectly satisfied after hearing of you being taken, but felt some anxiety about your destination. I was fearful Alton, Ill. would be your fate for heart-rendering it must be to anyone to have their relations or friends sent to that place. Awful and horrid as it has been represented. I would like so much for you to take the "Oath" and come home and stay if agreeable with your feelings. But if you do not feel so disposed I must content myself with the anticipation of you soon being exchanged and one consoling thought finds refuge in my bosom though in prison and deprived of many liberties far from home and loved one you are not exposed to bullets and the many trials incident to a soldier's life. For hard indeed must be a soldier's life at best Beset with the many temptations attending a camp life at every turn deprived of the luxury of home and counsel of kind Friends. How can we wonder so many have been led astray perhaps never to reform. But may I not hope. May I well hope that you have been enabled to resist every temptation. Oh how I hope and at an early period too that the Goddess Peace may spread her wings o'er our once happy and prosperous country. That we may be permitted to live and see tranquility restored to our land and a permanent peace established. Oh that the leaders of this horrid war would look to their country's good instead of pursuing the Glittering bubble of fame but little do they know, little do they consider the desolations brought on their land and the many thousands happy homes & firesides by war begot in pride and luxury. The child of malice and revengeful hate but let them have one look at the battle field where death may be seen in its most shocking and revolting form where naught is heard. But the shrieks of the wounded and dying. The bubbling groans as the blood oozes from the death wound and the mournful wailing note of pain, what kind of pain such as is caused by arms torn from their sockets, eyes put out by the bayonets thrust, hearts torn from the yet living bodies and the wounded trampled beneath by the iron shod hoofs of the war horse. I can give but a faint description for what pencil snatches from the hands of a friend could paint it in sufficiently horrible colors I say could they have one gaze and imagine loved ones a participant in such misery. I cannot but think they would stop And reflect in their wild career. But enough of this. Your Pa has just returned from Columbia where he was sent after Mr. Ledbetter a citizen arrested on the other side of the river. He had him released after some little difficulty. Aunt Lizzie has been quite sick the past few weeks but is now somewhat recovered. I am fearful the summer season will be more than she can beare. The children are in fine health. Leland has had the sore eyes but they are now well. Uncle William & his family, Grand Father & Grand Mother are all very well. Gennia J. says give Tom her love also Venia. Gennia has quite a nice beau (a soldier) from her description of him. She calls him her beau though she says she is afraid she cannot captivate him – His heart is invulnerable to Cupids darts But she will not despair but make good the old proverb "Live in hopes & —."

Evalina and the family sends love to you. Leland says "Yankees got Pa and gone Chargo" [Chicago] I know you think this is an uninteresting letter for I have seen the day this would be only a beginning. I will close hoping to see you very soon.

Write the first opportunity without fail. May the good one ever guide and protect you will be my prayer until death.

Affectionately your wife

M.E. Scott[44]

Breckenridge noted in his journal following his transcription of the letter: "This letter was wrote [*sic*] by Mrs. Scott to her husband a prisoner."

Beginning in June 1863, Breckenridge's activities increased along with the regiment's cooperation with other units. On the 2nd, Captain Eagleton Carmichael of the Fifteenth Illinois Cavalry reported on his joint activities with Breckenridge and certain men of the First West Tennessee Cavalry under his command. This report demonstrates a certain degree of the "slash and burn" tactics often necessary to neutralize the enemy's ability to sustain the war. Such actions resulted in long-term animosities that long survived the war itself. It also provides important details about operations along the Tennessee River in 1863 that were significant but long overshadowed by larger battles such as Shiloh and Corinth.

Brig. Gen. Grenville M. Dodge, Comdg. District of Corinth[45]

No. 2

Report of Capt. Eagleton Carmichael,
Fifteenth Illinois Cavalry

Hdqrs. 1ST Battalion 15TH Illinois Cavalry,
Corinth, Miss., June 2, 1863

Sir: After leaving the main command, we camped on the Waynesborough and Florence road, 5 miles north of Lowryville.[46]

On the morning of the 29th, moved on the Waynesborough road to Indian Creek, near Martin's Mills. Learning there that the enemy were on our left, we moved in that direction, traveling a road leading to Gerald's, on the Pinhook and Savannah road, where they had camped the previous night, but

---

44. Ibid, 197–199.

45. *OR*, Series 1, Volume 23, Part 1, 352–353.

46. Lowryville, Tennessee, was a small settlement located just south of Horse Creek in Hardin County, Tennessee and south of the current Cherry Chapel Road. It is also mentioned in Breckenridge's journal entry of April 25, 1863.

did not come up with them. Distance from Savannah, 12 miles. From thence we went to Oldtown, on the Savannah and Waynesborough road, the first place we found enough forage for our stock, and from thence to Savannah.

On the morning of the 29th, after ferrying our ambulances and pack train over the river, we left Savannah about 7.30 o'clock, and moved out on the Clifton road, expecting to form a junction with Colonel Breckenridge, of the First Tennessee Cavalry, it being necessary to have a larger force, to operate successfully in that direction, I having learned that [J.B.] Biffle was in that vicinity with his own regiment, a part of Cox's, and all the guerillas he could collect. This he did so effectually that we found no men at home, except very old ones, and no blacks, except the women and children. We struck Indian Creek 8 miles above its mouth, and went up it, burning corn on both sides of the creek to the amount of 30,000 bushels, and captured nearly 100 horses and mules. That valley we found to be very rich, every foot of arable land being under cultivation, mostly in wheat and corn, but very little cotton. After going 12 miles, I learned that a portion of Biffle's command was within a mile of us, and, turning to the right, I went across the hills, striking the Waynesborough and Savannah road 1½ miles from Oldtown. I there found that a part of the enemy's column was in my front and a part in my rear. Had a slight skirmish with a small squad. They skedaddled. I then turned to the left in the direction of Pinhook, up Turkey Creek. Night coming on, and being compelled to travel over a very rough road, I lost nearly all the stock that was captured that day. I struck the Savannah and Hamburg road, 8 miles from Savannah, at 1 A.M., having traveled nearly 55 miles.

On the morning of the 30th, the enemy appeared on the Hamburg road, and were driven back by the pickets after a small skirmish. They soon made their appearance on all sides of the town in small squads, but were driven back at all points. At 10 o'clock Colonel Biffle sent a flag of truce, demanding an immediate surrender of the force under my command. I replied, "If Colonel Biffle wants us, he must come and take us, if he can." After the return of the flag of truce, they made no demonstration except on the left, which was repulsed by a squadron which was in position on that flank.

The following is the number of officers and men under my command:

Commissioned officer—field and staff, 1; Company A, 1; Company B, 2; Company C, 2; Company D, 1; Company G, 2; total, 9. Enlisted men—sergeant-major, 1; Company A, 20; Company B, 35; Company C, 25; Company D, 24; Company G, 26; total, 131. Aggregate, 140.

Number of horses and mules confiscated and brought in, and in possession of the regimental quartermaster, 17 mules and 5 horses. We took 4 prisoners during the expedition, two on this side of the river and two on the other side.

The above is very respectfully submitted.

E. CARMICHAEL,
Capt. Company B, Comdg. Detachment of Fifteenth Illinois Cav.
Lieut. J.F. Young,
    Acting Assistant Adjutant-General.

The leather that Breckenridge mentioned in his correspondence on May 25 is referenced in General Oglesby's report, which amounted to easily more than ten thousand pounds.

Report of Maj. Gen. Richard J. Oglesby, U.S. Army
Colonel: Lieutenant-Colonel Breckenridge, First West Tennessee Cavalry, just returned to Jackson from expedition across Tennessee River. Destroyed a large amount of property; secured and put on gunboats three thousand sides of leather, and re-crossed without any loss, except stragglers.

Scout in to-day reports Chalmers at Panola week ago, with 1,800 infantry and one battery. Enemy all withdrawn from Mississippi swamps and encamped 14 miles below Yazoo City. On the 26th of May, Johnston had around Jackson 25,000. Re-enforcements constantly arriving.

> Three deserters confirm reports that but one brigade is at Port Hudson.
>
> R.J. OGLESBY,
Major General
>
> Lieutenant-Colonel Binmore,
> Assistant Adjutant-General[47]

Beginning on June 12, Breckenridge made routine journal entries that would continue until a few days before his death. These have proven vital to understanding the activities and revealing the truth—and untruth—of many allegations surrounding the First West Tennessee Cavalry. On June 12, Breckenridge wrote:

> The sun has shone out today for the 1st time in 3 days and it is very warm. The grounds a drying up fine. Capt. Roberts and Lt. Webb and party has not arrived yet and I am afraid they are prisoners for I learn there are some 600 of Jackson's and Richardson's cavalry[48] at Bolivar this morning and the Rebels tore up the track between here and Memphis this morning but didn't stop the train only about 4 hours and between here and Corinth. The pickets had some fighting and on the Bolivar Road. The pickets saw some of the enemy and had a fired shots. No damages done on our side. I am very sick this evening.[49]

Breckenridge was concerned that certain men led by Captain Elijah Roberts and Lieutenant William C. Webb might have been captured by an irregular cavalry group. He mentioned Jackson and Richardson. Colonel Robert V. Richardson commanded the 12th (Richardson's/Green's) Tennessee Cavalry Regiment, also known as the 1st (or 12th) Tennessee Partisan Ranger Regiment. This was a partisan group viewed very negatively by the Union authorities. In 1863, Major General Stephen Augustus Hurlbut commanded the 16th Army Corps garrisoned at Memphis. He wrote of Richardson's command:

47. *O.R.*, Series 1, Volume 24, Part 2, 445.
48. See *Tennesseans in the Civil War, Part 1*, 80.
49. Breckenridge Daybook, 167.

I am assured by high Confederate authority that they act without, and against orders, and are simply robbers, to be treated as such. The organization must be exterminated, and the sooner the better.[50]

At one point, Confederate Lieutenant General John C. Pemberton ordered Richardson's arrest. Richardson was wounded at Bolivar and Colonel John Uriah Green was captured in April 1863. Richardson escaped across the Mississippi River in a canoe. Eventually, the problems in the command were resolved and Richardson was placed back in command. He remained a thorn in the side of the Union Army like Hurst was in the side of Confederate partisans.

Just as the actual field action that Breckenridge experienced was not dull, neither was camp life in the First West Tennessee Cavalry. Keeping in mind that the men who comprised the unit were themselves diverse, so were their morals and characters. On June 13, having already stated he was very sick, Breckenridge revealed the source of his complaints as the "piles," what is now called hemorrhoids. Cavalrymen often suffered from a number of ailments resulting from sitting in the saddle for long periods of time. These included hemorrhoids, testicular pain, and back problems. As Breckenridge lay on his cot, he heard the goings on in camp. To anyone other than a seasoned and disciplined officer, it might seem like a humorous clamor. But Breckinridge was not amused.

> Last night I suffered more than I ever did in my life with the piles and not much better today.[51] Been in bed all day. There is a good many troops a leaving here today. Tonight as I lay on my bed I can hear preaching and praying, swearing, vulgar songs, card players a making about their game, fiddling and dancing and a fuss with a Capt. of our command and a sergeant about a whore that the Sergt. brought into camp and the Cpt. wants to take her himself and I lay here and studied about what I could hear, all they a have a going on in hearing of my tent. The whore I sent out of camp. Drunk is the Col.

50. *OR*, Series 1, Volume 24, Part 3, 111.

51. The piles were a common term in that day for hemorrhoids. *Webster's Encyclopedic Unabridged Dictionary of the English Language* (New York: Portland House, 1989), 1092.

> and I listened until they got tired and went to bed and then I thought I would give one right in the 1st W.T.C. at Lagrange. What will be next I can't tell. Though I hope something better and if the Col. will send all the whores out of camp I think it would be the best thing he could do.[52]

Breckenridge gave a thorough description of the types of vices regularly seen in army camps during the Civil War mixed humorously with more righteous activities. Prostitution was a common issue. The presence of such women caused significant trouble for men who were far away from home and very lonely. Breckenridge mentioned a conflict between an officer and a non-commissioned officer over a prostitute. Ribald behavior was not uncommon either with the introduction of these women into the camp.

To understand why Breckenridge might be so indignant, aside from his own personal views, is the fact that the regiment is encamped at LaGrange, Tennessee. It was a quiet yet prosperous antebellum village whose population was Southern in their allegiances. According to Eastin Morris in 1834, LaGrange was "a thriving post town in the south east corner of Fayette county, on Wolf river. In 1828, LaGrange contained sixty houses, 240 inhabitants, four stores, two taverns, and a dozen mechanics. In 1831 it was incorporated, and it bids fair to be one of the most interesting villages in that section of the state."[53] Following the war in 1874, J.B. Killebrew wrote of the town:

> LaGrange was once called LaBelle Village, and had a population of some 2,500; not more than half of which remains. "Owing to the war" is the explanatory legend that may be written over many such. Grant had his headquarters here for some time, with 60,000 men. This was the wealthiest section of Fayette county, and much of the refinement and elegance of those days remain. The trade of the village, like that of the other towns in the county, is simply local, consisting mainly in plantation supplies. A fine female academy is located here.[54]

52. Breckenridge Daybook, 168.
53. Morris, *Tennessee Gazetteer*, 189.
54. Killebrew and Safford, *Resources of Tennessee*, 1063.

LaGrange, Tennessee, during the Civil War

Indeed, LaGrange was a cultured and refined Southern village. One can only imagine the influence of tens of thousands of Union soldiers suddenly flooding into the community and then the citizens witnessing white Union officers and soldiers cavorting with black women openly. Breckenridge himself seems disapproving.

His professionalism as a career soldier and officer shines through at this juncture. Knowing his place in the chain of formal command, he defers to the judgment of Colonel Hurst to solve the problems which appear prevalent in the regimental camps. On June 14, Breckenridge addressed a situation that may have bothered him on more than one level. First, there remained the difficulty of keeping prostitutes in the camp, a practice he knows is problematic. He also touched upon a subject that would have been taboo for the day: interracial sexual relations. Given that he was accused of being a secessionist at the outset of the war, one can speculate about his feelings on the subject. It cannot be known with certainty if his background or simply the social mores of the day dictated his disapproval of white men keeping black prostitutes. Regardless, it must have occurred to him—and most likely is a partial reason for his concern—that the Southern sympathizing residents of LaGrange would not approve of such public flaunting "...of white men engaging Negro prostitutes." Breckenridge's comment about "officers keep them publicly" makes it readily apparent that he disapproves of such behavior. He wrote:

> June 14th [18]63
>
> The whores or at best all the white whores have left camp though there is some negroes in the camp and white men and officers keep them publicly.⁵⁵

The subject of pay for the troops of the First West Tennessee Cavalry was a recurring issue. Despite the fact that the U.S. Government had regular and recurring resources to arm, supply, and pay its troops, this regiment seemed neglected by the military bureaucracy. This could have resulted from any number of factors and assigning any one factor would be conjecture. On June 19, Breckenridge groused privately that his men had as much duty or more than any other regiment with which they operated and that all other troops but his had been paid. He hoped that his men would be paid in the coming days.⁵⁶

On June 20, Breckenridge again confronts the saga of William Jay Smith. As had become the custom, the talents of Benjamin Thomas Walker were employed to extract from local citizens the plunder Smith desired. Smith employed tactics of retaliation, taking from local people certain goods and possessions sufficient to repay him for what he alleged the Mississippi guerilla Solomon G. "Sol" Street previously took from him. Apparently, he deemed these people in sympathy with Street and the regiment was camped at LaGrange, the seat of many beautiful plantation homes and significant wealth. Being a resident of nearby Grand Junction, Smith was familiar with the affluence that abounded in LaGrange. His contention that General Hurlbut issued an order allowing him to engage in such activities is not supported by proof. Indeed, Breckenridge held little faith in the prospect. Further, Breckenridge's reference to his men's losses and those of his own father again gives the impression that he viewed Smith's actions as those of a man seeking personal gain from a national conflict.

Breckenridge expressed his frustration with Smith and his cohorts. It was a major point of contention between the two men. He writes on June 20, 1863:

---

55. Breckenridge Daybook, 168.
56. Ibid, 169.

> This morning Major Smith got up a detail of about 20 men to go with Thomas Walker out in the country and take sixty dollars' worth of property from each citizen until they collect one Thousand Eight hundred Dollars to pay the Major for what Sol Street taken from him. He said he had an order from General Hurlbut but if he did he could not show it. There is plenty of men in my Regiment that have had more taken from them than Major Smith ever had taken from him and they can't get no such orders. My Father has had nearly everything taken from him by the Guerillas and a great many others that belongs to the Service and they cannot get such orders to go and take it from other Citizens.[57]

Service records reveal that among Walker's accomplices in June 1863 was Private Stephen J. Thomas of Company B.[58] Many of the looters were assigned to his company, which was under the direct command of Captain Horry Hodges. In fact, Thomas was recruited by Hodges.[59] In January 1863, Thomas was appointed to the rank of corporal. Five months later, he was on "detached service by order of Col. Hurst with Lt. Walker." His record would be marred by his confinement in military prison.[60]

Breckenridge directly addressed the methods by which Smith engaged in the plundering of the local population. By paying a grossly undervalued price for the items stolen, Smith could boast that he paid a local woman rather than simply "requisitioning" her property. He could argue that he had a right to do so. However, paying her roughly ten percent of what she alleged the property was worth again gave Smith the license to say he had purchased the woman's finery. Again, the plundered items find a place at Smith's Grand Junction home. Breckenridge reported the incident on June 21:

---

57. Ibid.

58. Compiled Service Record of Stephen J. Thomas. Compiled Service Records of Volunteer Union Soldiers Who Served in Organizations from the State of Tennessee. Publication Number M395, National Archives Catalogue ID 300398, Record Group 94, Roll 0061. National Archives and Records Administration, Washington, D.C.

59. Ibid.

60. Ibid.

> It is a fine nice day. Everything seems to getting along fine until evening when Thomas Walker came in camp with a wagon loaded with house furniture and fine clothing for Major Smith, among the things was a fine Piano & bed Stead that they had taken from an old Lady in the country. She said it cost her five hundred Dollars. And Major Smith valued it at 40 dollars and the bed Stead and fine clothes they valued at 20 Dollars and all this taken from an old Lady and put in Major Smith's house.[61]

The next day, Breckenridge recorded a far more insidious fact about Walker and Hurst's direct involvement in Smith's activities.

> This morning Tom Walker starts out again a stealing from the citizens. Some of the men would not go. Col. Hurst had them tied to an apple tree for not going. The whole Regiment is in an uproar, the men all mad about this stealing business. And they Swear by all that is good and bad if they don't quit it they will leave the Regiment. Tom Walker come in this evening with some more Property that he had taken and sent it out to Major Smith.[62]

Breckenridge directly implicates Hurst for complicity with Smith's activities. Indeed, these actions seem to go beyond complicity. Breckenridge once again credits the regiment as a whole for being opposed to them. Hurst's order to tie the protesting men to an apple tree gives further evidence of how the regiment, fairly or unfairly, came to be tarnished as thieves and outlaws. Failure to engage in Smith's and Hurst's sanctioned activities could lead to public castigation for an enlisted man. It is quite a telling indictment of Colonel Hurst that he would punish a man for standing by his morals. These types of actions could easily cause the reputation he has attained as a renegade Union officer.

Throughout their professional relationship, there is ample evidence of the ill will between Breckenridge and Hurst. Breckenridge documented instances in which it seems very clear that Hurst was doing all he could

61. Breckenridge Daybook, 170.
62. Ibid.

to antagonize Breckenridge and make his duties all the more difficult to fulfill. It is quite clear from Breckenridge's early involvement in the regiment that such treatment as working to keep him from advancing could be intentional on the part of Hurst.

On June 23, Breckenridge laid out a long list of his grievances with Hurst. Two are recurring themes: Hurst is not willing to share in his men's privations but instead uses every excuse to enjoy the comforts of home back in Purdy. It falls upon Breckenridge to keep the men from leaving the regiment in disgust over Hurst's actions and complicity with those of others. Breckenridge was quite vocal in his criticism of Hurst, which prompted Hurst on occasion to attempt to arrest him, efforts that were never successful long-term. Breckenridge's journal entries for June 23–24 show the men may have had more allegiance and loyalty to Breckenridge than to Hurst. In any event, the two men were forced to contend with one another, for better or for worse, and usually worse.

> Today every officer in the Regiment got a commission but three, two of the Lieutenants and myself never got any. Col. Hurst said he did not know that we wanted any commission and did not send them. He has often said that he did not intend to give me any commission. I have done all I could towards getting up the Regt. and have done the most of the scouting and him at home with his wife. I have kept the men together and done all I could for them and now he treats me with contempt. He has tried to arrest me several times and could not do it according to regulations and that makes me mad. He wants to arrest me for talking about his way of getting along but he can't make it.[63]

On the 24th, Breckenridge complained that Hurst continued to thwart him from getting his commission, which also deprived him of his pay.[64] He reiterated that the men were not happy about the way he was being treated. This is an interesting observation. For one thing, Breckenridge records certain situations in which he had to convince them not to desert over their disgust at the actions of Hurst, Smith, and their subordinates.

63. Ibid, 171.
64. Ibid.

It seems Breckenridge was well respected by his men. Captain Elijah James Hodges, Company B, brought home from the war a small *carte de visite* of Breckenridge, which remains with his descendants even today. Breckenridge worked to maintain his men's courage and faith as best he could. On June 24, 1863, he wrote:

> This morning everything seems to be a little more quiet but the men are all mad because Col. Hurst never sent for my commission. But I have done all I could to keep the men contented and to get them to wait and see what would be done. Some of them run away this evening and said they would not stand the way they have been treated. But I have persuaded them and done all I could to keep them from leaving that I thought it would not be long until things would come up a little better.[65]

In his journal entries of June 25 and 26, Breckenridge again referred to the activities of Benjamin Thomas Walker. Regardless of the tumult it created within the regiment, Smith and his faithful subordinate continued their endeavors to make Smith wealthier by theft. Apparently, only rain could hinder their efforts.[66] Certainly, Breckenridge's observations of these men call for a complete reevaluation of Smith. The regularity, scope, and intensity of his activities place them beyond the limits of impulsive behavior displayed in a heated moment. According to Breckenridge, they are very calculated and ongoing.

Breckenridge also recorded that a gift of one thousand dollars was being presented to the men, which in itself causes doubt and concern. It appears that the men simply wanted equity and fairness in the way they were to be paid as they expected upon enlisting. This sharing of funds may have been done in the same manner as others within the regiment, along the lines of favoritism and cronyism. The thousand dollar gift from "the General" (whom he did not identify, though it would likely be General Stephen Hurlbut) was a present for the "most needy men." This made

---

65. Ibid.

66. Ibid, 172. Breckenridge recorded on June 25, 1863, that Tom Walker could not make his mission to steal that day because of the rain.

VETERANS OF THE FIRST WEST TENNESSEE CAVALRY
(LATER RENAMED THE SIXTH TENNESSEE CAVALRY)

them angry and they responded that "if they will not pay them what is coming to them that they will not have any."[67]

By the morning of June 26, it had become apparent that continued thievery and related types of behavior would no longer be tolerated by the enlisted men. Breckenridge was in his tent writing in his journal with the wind blowing so hard that he thought his tent might be carried away.[68] The First West Tennessee was cooperating with the Second Iowa Cavalry and the Seventh Illinois,[69] whose men were operating as scouts while Breckenridge's men served as pickets during their absence.[70] It is evident that he believes his men are being underused and given less prestigious assignments than befit them.

67. Ibid.
68. Ibid.
69. Breckenridge does not specify whether the Seventh Illinois was cavalry or infantry. During this period, detachments of the Seventh Illinois Cavalry were in northwest Mississippi, Middle Tennessee, and Louisiana. The Seventh Illinois Infantry was "mounted June 18 and engaged in scout and patrol duty through West Tennessee till October…" Frederick H. Dyer, *A Compendium of the War of the Rebellion* (New York: Thomas Yoseloff, 1959), 3:1026, 1046.
70. Breckenridge Daybook, 172.

The next day, Breckenridge clearly had his hands full trying to keep his men from deserting over issues of pay and theft by their comrades and superiors. It can be argued that these objections vindicate the men of the First West Tennessee Cavalry, who were collectively accused of such behavior. His efforts to calm their anger were apparently successful. He wrote, "the men are getting along some better. I have got them to wait and see what will be done and not to run away yet and wait and see if they won't pay them."[71]

On June 28, Breckenridge refers in his journal to the "Refugees." These were Confederates from West Tennessee whose existence has been upended by the war since the fall of Forts Henry and Donelson and the Southern defeat at Shiloh. These refugees included the families of many prominent people including planters, businessmen, merchants, politicians, and old families with strong ties. Many of those from Hurst's own McNairy County ended up in Madison County, Tennessee. Once again, General Hurlbut is credited with authorizing the collection of funds from citizens, this time from Confederate refugees. Breckenridge wrote:

> This morning is cloudy and looks like it will rain. The thousand dollars that the General sent to us on the 25th Inst. was distributed among the men that had none. The General said that it was a present he intended for them, that it was collected at Jackson from the Refugees and when they left Jackson he brought it with him and said he had no use for it and he wanted the men to have it and he would have them paid off as soon as he could. This morning we had to send 100 men on Picket.[72]

After months of uncertainty, the legal status of the First West Tennessee Cavalry was finally resolved by the payment of the men and their proper mustering into Union service. It was a day that Breckenridge and his men had long awaited. He wrote on June 30:

> Today we mustered for pay and the mustering Officer came down and told the men that they had not been mustered in to

71. Ibid, 173.
72. Ibid.

service by legal authority and that he was sent here to muster them in to service so as they could get their pay and the most the men were satisfied and said they were willing to be mustered in to service again And then they thought they would get pay and they talked to the others and got them in the notion to be mustered.[73]

He also recorded that 175 men were sent out on picket duty to relieve others who had stood the same duty since the previous day.[74]

As the month of July 1863 began, Breckenridge noted that regiments other than his own were returning to camp with captured goods and chattels.[75] Certainly, the First West Tennessee was not alone in such activities. One must question if the cattle came from civilians or guerillas as stated. It may very well be that he understood the property to have come from guerillas, whether or not it actually did.

On July 1, Companies A, B, C, and D of the regiment were mustered into service formally.[76] All four of these companies were composed of men from McNairy County.[77] The next ten days were relatively quiet in terms of military activities. There were, however, moments of celebration. Breckenridge recorded the observance of the Fourth of July in camp. It certainly was a loud celebration with a thirty-four gun salute from the various regimental artilleries.

At that moment, the men did not know of the events occurring in other theaters of the war. They could not have known at that moment of the Confederate loss at Gettysburg, Pennsylvania, or the fall of Vicksburg, Mississippi, to Union forces under General Grant. Both events would be historically significant. The fall of Vicksburg opened the Mississippi River to navigation by the Union Navy and cut the Confederacy in half. General Robert E. Lee's loss to General George Meade at Gettysburg became the "high watermark" for the Confederacy. The Southern armies would never again invade the Union that far north. The three-day battle forever enshrined the small Pennsylvania town into the national memory,

73. Ibid.
74. Ibid.
75. Ibid, 174.
76. Ibid.
77. *Tennesseans in the Civil War, Part I*, 333.

as would President Abraham Lincoln's address at the Gettysburg cemetery later that year.

On July 2, some men of the First West Tennessee still had not been mustered properly and the paymaster had not yet arrived. Breckenridge recorded that the men needed their pay for the benefit of their families.[78] Things were quiet the next day as they cleaned the camp and prepared for the Fourth of July celebrations.[79] The kind of order that Breckenridge sought for the regiment appeared to have finally been achieved. On the 4th, a momentous day for the Union, he made the following observations in his journal:

> This morning is a beautiful one. Nothing of much interest passing this morning, the men are all set free from duty today because this is the day our independence was gained by Washington. The soldiers were marched out in line with the Artillery and thirty-four shots fired with the cannons. One shot for every state in union. And then the men rallied 'round the flag and gave three loud cheers for the Union and the Stripes and Stars and then with a band of Music broke up.[80]

Breckenridge and the men learned of the victory at Vicksburg on July 5.

> Nothing of much importance passing this morning, everything seems to be quiet this morning. The news came that Vicksburg was ours and that General Grant was in the place and had the stars and stripes waving over Vicksburg and there is a terrible excitement up about it. The men are so much better. They are going to have a fine affair.[81]

The next day, the men fired a fifteen-gun salute to this momentous Union victory. They were yelling continually with joy over the news.[82] In

78. Breckenridge Daybook, 174.
79. Ibid, 175.
80. Ibid.
81. Ibid, 175.
82. Ibid, 176.

the midst of the celebration, Breckenridge received a report that Rebels had been seen about ten miles from the camp. He dispatched fifteen men to scout for information on their presence, but they learned nothing. On July 7, he spent part of his day riding across the countryside looking for a better campsite where decent water would be found. The current campsite was swampy on one side and plagued with "large washed places on the other" and no room for tents for the newest recruits. Ultimately, Breckenridge didn't find a more suitable location.[83]

The morning of July 8 dawned with heavy dark clouds rising in the northwest and thunder that threatened rain. Breckenridge stayed in camp and didn't venture out looking for a new campsite until the afternoon. He rode to headquarters where he was instructed to make do with the site he currently occupied. Once his men received sufficient arms, they would be sent to the Tennessee River for further operations. Afterwards, he returned back to camp.[84]

On July 9–10, all the men of the First West Tennessee finally saw their long labors rewarded with pay from the Federal Government. They had been without pay for the entirety of their service to date. Breckenridge himself celebrated at the equity his men received. Given the frustration he felt seeing their deprivations, his own words best express the moment appropriately.

> [July] 9th [1863]
> This morning everything is quiet in Camp. The Paymaster telegraphed from Memphis that he would be up on the first train and for Col. Hurst to have an ambulance at the Depot to bring him to camp. He arrived at camp at ½ after one O'clock P.M. and commenced getting up the Rolls to pay the men. He paid off three Companies this morning and stayed for the evening to commence at 8 O'clock tomorrow Morning.[85]

> [July] 10th [1863]
> This morning the men are all well pleased. The pay Master paid all of the Regiment from the time they enlisted up to

83. Ibid.
84. Ibid.
85. Ibid, 177.

the 1st of this month, nearly ten months pay all at one time and the men were all well pleased. A portion of the field and Staff did not get any pay on account of the pay Master not having enough with him. He went to Memphis this evening after more and said he would return by the fifteenth instant and pay the balance.[86]

On July 11, with the men paid and their frustrations pacified, Breckenridge ordered the camp to be policed and tidied. He noted that they "all had their money and did not have any duty to do and they are as happy as any set of men can be."[87] Things seemed calm and at peace.

This moment had been long in coming. Breckenridge had struggled to lead in a positive and professional manner while building a regiment that would be seen as legitimate by the Union command. His men had now been paid and were apparently content. The wartime activities of the First West Tennessee Cavalry were finally gaining legitimacy and respect. Yet things were not always what they seemed. The capacity for trouble still lay ahead.

86. Ibid.
87. Ibid, 178.

6

THREE PIVOTAL DAYS *and the* MILE MARKER MURDERS

July 12–23, 1863

Despite the progress made, the month of July 1863 would haunt the men and the reputation of the First West Tennessee Cavalry for the next century and a half. Over the next two weeks, their involvement in operations in southwest Tennessee would intensify. In fact, it may have been the regiment's most active month since its formation.

On the morning of July 12, Breckenridge was ordered to have all of his armed men mounted and ready to march by four o'clock in the afternoon.[1] He and his men saddled their horses and began their march to Jackson, Tennessee.[2] They traveled through Bolivar and rode out into the country, stopping for the night at Medon Station without encountering any Confederate forces.[3]

---

1. Breckenridge Daybook, 178.
2. Ibid.
3. Ibid. In 1863, the railroad running through Medon Station, Tennessee, was the Mississippi Central Railroad. See Emma Inman Williams, *Historical Madison: The Story of Jackson and*

The next morning, Breckenridge and his troops left Medon Station at 8:00 A.M. and arrived in Jackson at 2:00 P.M.[4] According to Breckenridge, he found the enemy strength there to be some 2,500 strong and attacked them as he found them. The fight lasted about two-and-a-half hours before they routed the Confederate forces, chasing them out of town for about three miles. Following the pursuit, Breckenridge and his men turned back and returned to town. The rest of the Union force continued their pursuit of the Confederates but ultimately could not catch them. According to Breckenridge, two companies were captured as were about 300 stands of arms. All of this was accomplished by Union forces of about eight hundred men comprised roughly of 200 men from U.S. Seventh Tennessee Cavalry, 200 from the Sixth Illinois Cavalry, 200 of the Second Iowa, and 200 from the First West Tennessee Cavalry.[5]

THE JACKSON ENGAGEMENT

Breckenridge only gives a scant account of the battle at Jackson, but other diarists add to the detail and certainly give an alternative spin on the event. Cannonading and skirmishing occurred around Campbell's Bridge and other area bridges and some Confederate soldiers passed up Main Street in a rush as if being pursued, which is likely the rout and pursuit of which Breckenridge spoke.[6] Madison County resident and ardent Southern supporter Robert H. Cartmell made the following entries into his diary concerning the events of July 13 and July 14:

> 13th...Soon heavy firing began north of town[,] a short distance from & south of the Episcopal Parsonage. here was the heaviest & severest fighting...The fight north of town lasted some half hour. [W]hen the Rebels retreated, The Federals had 4 or 6 six pounders. The loss so far as I could ascertain was about the same. [O]ne Confederate was killed near Mrs. Hale's. [O]ne was at the City Hotel[,] one at the Methodist

Madison County, Tennessee, From the Prehistoric Moundbuilders to 1917 (Jackson TN: McCowat-Mercer Press, Inc., 1972), 145.

4. Breckenridge Daybook, 178–179.
5. Ibid.
6. Williams, *Historic Madison*, 170.

parsonage. (died since the fight)...The stores in Jackson were broken open, and Such destruction I never saw. [A]t John Miller's a fire was built in the middle of the street & Thousands of dollars worth of goods burned...a Thousand dollars worth of fine bolting cloths, at least a Thousand dollars worth of Indian rubber belting[,] a large quantity of Jeans &c goods Thrown all over the floors[,] tramped upon, torn, broken, bent, &c &c – his safe was bursted into atoms, money taken, books[,] accounts &c &c – Same Thing done at Murrell's, Wolholms, Tollivers[.] also I understood, Mrs. Newman, a widow lady, Kept a Millenary [sic] store, was litterally [sic] ruined[.] Uncle Jho [Joseph Cannon Sharp][7] had a large quantity of Tobacco, some domestics, shoes &c, all destroyed...'twas sickening to look at such wholesale & wanton destruction.[8]

14[th]...The last (Hursts reg[imen]t) left about 2.o.clock This Evening. The federals left some of Their wounded here...Hurst went to the hospital before leaving to parole The wounded. took some exceptions to a remark made by a young lady, made to Dr. Still. Saying That it was directed to him (Hurst) He became furious – called the Lady a d____d slut & told her if she did not get out he would Kick her out – as quick as he would kick any damned proud slut. There were other Ladies present, & Several Physicians. I heard Those present repeat his language, and worse Than I have written it. This is truly a war upon private Citizens & private property. They pass Thro' The Country, burn & rob.[9]

Cartmell complained of looting and random unnecessary destruction, activities like those of William Jay Smith, Tom Walker, Isaac McIntyre, and Stephen J. Thomas. Further, Hurst's behavior toward a woman is chronicled by Cartmell, behavior less than gentlemanly

---

7. Joseph Cannon Sharp owned a grocery store in Jackson.
8. Robert H. Cartmell Diary, 3:26. Tennessee State Library and Archives website. https://cdm15138.contentdm.oclc.org/customizations/global/pages/collections/cartmell/cartmell.html.
9. Ibid, 27.

though Breckenridge makes no mention of it. Assuredly, he would have documented it had he known.[10]

Breckenridge's account differs with Cartmell's version of the events of July 14. Breckenridge alludes to the capture of "government property" whereas Cartmell laments the attacks on "private citizens and private property."[11] Breckenridge later gave his report of what occurred at Jackson, but it would not be written until September 28. In the meantime, he and the regiment left Jackson and rode toward Purdy, arriving there on the night of July 14 at about 9:00 P.M. They camped there for the night.[12]

Breckenridge and his men mounted up the following morning and rode to Camden, a village in McNairy County now known as Rose Creek. In the period of the Civil War, the thriving village of Camden was ten miles west of Purdy on the Bolivar and Purdy Road. Its principal citizen was Fountain P. Duke, a merchant and farmer who had acquired a sizable fortune by 1861. Perhaps in an effort to avoid the destruction of the pending conflict, Duke moved west in the spring of 1861, settling on the White River in Arkansas.[13] In any event, after resting in Camden a while, Breckenridge and his men continued west in the direction of Bolivar. Eleven miles away, they learned that the Hatchie Bridge had been burned and turned back toward Camden.[14] Along the way, they captured three guerillas and camped at Camden for the night.[15]

The burned bridge mentioned by Breckenridge was confirmed by Hurst in his report to Col. Edward Hatch, commander of the Second Cavalry Brigade, dated July 20, 1863. Their accounts differ regarding the

---

10. An account published in the Nashville *Republican Banner* on June 25, 1867, describes another instance when Hurst insulted women in public. Disrupting a speech made by Congressman Henry Emerson Ethridge in Purdy, Hurst allegedly shouted severe obscenities to the audience:

"God d—n the law. If anybody said he perjured himself, he told a d—d lie. God d—n the Church; d—n the preachers – all were a d—d set of canting hypocritical rebels. God d—n the rebels…God d—m the women. They are all rebel b—h-s; worse than men; ought all to be sent to h–ll. I would like to kick their God d—d—. God d—n their souls."

Hurst established a widespread reputation for inflammatory and crude public speech, both during and following the war. Nashville *Republican Banner*, June 25, 1867.

11. Breckenridge Daybook, 179.

12. Ibid, July 14, 1863 (page ???).

13. Wright, Talbott and McCann, eds., *Reminiscences*, 37–38.

14. Breckenridge Daybook, 179.

15. Ibid.

JACKSON, TENNESSEE, DURING THE CIVIL WAR

action that took place, however. Hurst claimed it was a skirmish and reported a huge force in the vicinity. He and his men captured about 20 prisoners, eight of which were paroled, seven brought back, and five or six escaped. Breckenridge, on the other hand, reported only coming across three guerillas. Either Breckenridge is very understated in the matter or Hurst is exaggerating the circumstances. Either scenario is entirely possible. Breckenridge is a seasoned officer by 1863, having seen action in the Mexican War and in the western and Indian territories. He may not have been overly impressed by the show of force against him, thus being quite understated in his journal entries. On the other hand, it is possible that Breckenridge and his detachment captured only three men and Hurst and his men captured far more.

Nonetheless, Hurst's official report does give information that Breckenridge either failed to report in his journal or saw no need to record for his own purposes.

> LA GRANGE TENN., July 20, 1863
> SIR: I have the honor of submitting the following report:
> In compliance with your order bearing date Jackson, Tenn., July 15, 1863, I proceeded with the regiment to Montezuma; thence to Purdy and Camden, where I ascertained the bridge across Big Hatchie River, near Bolivar, was destroyed. I then moved to this place, by way of Pocahontas. On leaving Jackson I marched up the Forked Deer 8 miles, and found the trail of 1,500 to 1,800 rebels, under Biffle, Forrest, and Newsom. They fled before us in great haste, destroying all the bridges they crossed on, giving me such difficulty in crossing streams in 40 miles travel that I found myself 10 or 12 miles in their rear without any hope of overtaking them this side of our lines.
> We took about 20 prisoners; paroled 8 and brought in 7. Some 5 or 6 fell back and made their escape, my rear guard being worn out with fatigue from hard marching and crossing streams by fording, swimming, & c.
> I beg leave to state it as my belief that the entire rebel force which we met at Jackson fled by way of Shiloh in a badly torn up and demoralized condition, and could have been easily captured by a small force if thrown out from Corinth.

The prisoners all concur in stating that they were out of ammunition and low-spirited.

I am, sir, your very obedient servant,

FIELDING HURST,
Colonel, Commanding Regiment

Col. EDWARD HATCH,
Commanding Second Cavalry Brigade.[16]

Hurst reports that this large Rebel force is ahead of him and has made catching up very difficult. Breckenridge records in his journal that three guerillas were captured but gives no indication that these men were part of any larger force. Giving them the designation of "guerilla" implies that they were not part of the regular Confederate Army. Note the statement from Hurst's report that "*Some 5 or 6 fell back and made their escape…*" This may be one of the most important and yet overlooked statements that ever flowed from the pen of Fielding Hurst.

THE MILE MARKER MURDERS: FACT OR FICTION?

On July 23, 1863, Purdy native and Confederate Colonel Dew M. Wisdom wrote to Colonel Philip Dale Roddey regarding an allegation that Hurst and the First West Tennessee Cavalry were guilty of murderous activity that would later be characterized as the "Mile Marker Murders."

While such sensational allegations make for wonderfully sinister folklore, one must be careful in perpetuating what are indeed only allegations. It is wise to take an almost legalistic mindset to determine the veracity of these claims. Several questions must be asked. First, what proof exists to verify the claim that Hurst and his men committed the murder of Confederate soldiers on the Pocahontas-Purdy Road? Second, is that information—if it exists—of a firsthand nature or second or even thirdhand that would otherwise be considered the rankest form of hearsay? Third, if there exists such a firsthand account, was it recorded in or about July 1863? Fourth, are there firsthand sources that either contradict these claims of atrocity or report facts contrary to the allegations?

In the case of the so-called "Mile Marker Murders," not only could they have been grossly exaggerated, but they may not in fact have occurred.

16. *OR*, Series 1, Vol. 24, Part 2, 682.

Murder is a strong word in any case and the climate of war-torn McNairy County in 1863 was filled with guerilla warfare. Many unsavory events took place. Using a legal rationale, the veracity of the claims can be determined. Over the years and especially into the latter half of the twentieth century, many individuals have maintained or embellished the story of these alleged "murders." The only evidence that could be produced were the oral tradition of the Locke family and a single letter written by Colonel Dew Moore Wisdom to Colonel (later Brigadier General) Philip Dale Roddey. The Wisdom-Roddey letter was also the subject of correspondence between James A. Seddon, the Confederate Secretary of War, and Major General Braxton Bragg.

First, let us address the issue of the Locke family oral tradition. Reliance upon oral tradition is risky at best. These traditions often have variations in the stories as they are passed from generation to generation. Seldom is a story told verbally the exact way twice. Oral traditions are highly unreliable, especially where emotions run high or passions run deep. In the case of the American Civil War, they have proven dubious owing to the bitter enmity that has left the nation divided for more than a century and a half afterwards. Further, the Locke family tradition was recorded in writing only in the late twentieth century, some one hundred thirty years after the alleged events. For purposes of historical documentation, this folklore offers little more than a limited explanation of the injuries and death of a single individual, Thomas W.S. Morgan, whose tombstone along the Pocahontas-Purdy Road alleges that he was murdered. Even that may be attenuated and highly inaccurate. Nonetheless, we shall return to Thomas W.S. Morgan again further in this discussion.

In regards to the Wisdom-Roddey letter and subsequent correspondence between Confederate Secretary of War Seddon and Major General Bragg, these are the only contemporary sources that exist to establish the possibility of the alleged murders. This claim found its roots first in the letter from Colonel Wisdom in which he reported allegations of the capture and murder of Confederate Captain John Ambrose Wharton and at least four other men by order of Colonel Fielding Hurst. According to Wisdom, the four men were George Brown, Dr. Hugh Hollis, Thomas W.S. Morgan, and Thomas Starks.[17]

17. Dew M. Wisdom to Col. Philip D. Roddey, July 23, 1863. NARA M474, RG 109, Reel 88, Frames 167–169, National Archives and Records Administration, Washington, D.C.

It behooves the reader to carefully read and analyze this letter. First, it should be noted that Wisdom does not cite or identify his source, but only states that it was entitled to "the highest credit." However, how can such credit be extended to an otherwise anonymous source? Put simply, it cannot. The question that is more interesting is how would Wisdom's source have firsthand information about the alleged encounter between Hurst and Wharton? Was his informant a Union soldier, a member of Hurst's own regiment? That is highly doubtful. Was it a citizen who secretly saw the alleged incidents? If so, why not disclose it to his superiors? After all, during wartime, this correspondence is not going to be widely shared with others outside of the Confederate government or army. Indeed, it only appears again with the publication of the Federal government's official record of the war known as *The War of the Rebellion: A Compilation of the Official Records of the Union and Confederate Armies*. With no actual source cited or identified by Wisdom, his information would constitute the rankest form of inflammatory hearsay.

Wisdom also employs very provocative language by labeling the First West Tennessee Cavalry in such terms as "Hurst's Renegade Regt." Such verbiage could be very effective in wartime. Further, Wisdom provides direct quotes—almost what he purports to be verbatim quotes—between Hurst and Wharton. Such quotes are themselves inflammatory and again it must be asked: who would have been close enough to hear them and gotten away to tell if Hurst and his men were so savage and brutal? They certainly would not have allowed a witness to recount these allegedly brutal actions to anyone. It is inconsistent to give Hurst credit for such cruelty and then to allege he was unaware of a witness close enough to hear all.

Wisdom goes on to offer great credit to Dock Wharton as a soldier and that may well have been true. With the others, he describes Wharton as a good man, in peace and war. Yet many of the purveyors of the "Mile Marker Murders" have always described Dock Wharton as a Confederate guerilla, a crafty and resourceful irregular Confederate fighter. It seems Wisdom and believers of the legend are in dispute on the character of Dock Wharton. If Wharton was a regular officer and soldier of the Confederacy and not a guerilla as Wisdom claims, then what makes him such a target for Hurst? Why would a "murderous arm" be extended to him, when the record is plain that other guerillas captured by Hurst were safely turned over to Federal authorities? Again, the inconsistencies are glaring.

Wisdom's letter is even more interesting as it continues. He almost provokes his superiors into taking action, literally goading them. As this commentary continues, we see that Wisdom very well may have had his own motives for seeking Hurst's elimination. Immediately after requesting that Hurst receive retaliation, Wisdom denies that Wharton is a guerilla, which is interesting. Why make the denial? Had there been credible charges that Wharton was indeed a guerilla? To rephrase Queen Gertrude in Shakespeare's *Hamlet*, "The gentleman doth protest too much." As he closes his letter, Wisdom attempts to rouse his government to the cause of eliminating Hurst. That wasn't particularly unusual, but one does have to question his motives. Now, let us review the only two pieces of correspondence or documentation to establish this alleged war crime and then review the subsequently discovered evidence to refute its occurrence.

Colonel Dew Moore Wisdom's July 23, 1863, letter to Colonel Phillip Dale Roddey reads as follows:

Head Qrs Forrest Regt
July 23rd 1863

Col. Roddy:

I have just learned from a source entitled to the highest credit that a few days ago, Capt. Dock Wharton of Col. Wilson's Regt. had a skirmish with a portion of Col. Hurst's Renegade Regt. In the skirmish Capt. Wharton was wounded & he and 4 of his men captured. When brought into Col. Hurst's presence, he told Wharton that he should be killed. Wharton replied if you kill me 10 of your men will go up for me. Hurst was true to his word for on the road leading from Purdy to Pocahontas, Hurst had Capt. Wharton & his 4 men shot. The names of the men were as follows: Thos. Starks, George Brown, Doctor Hugh Hollis & Morgan. I was acquainted well with every man shot except Morgan and know them to have been good & true men, in peace, as well as in war. Capt. Wharton served under me one year in the 13th Tenn. Regt. and a braver man had not perished in this unholy war. He received a severe wound on the field of Shiloh, and still fought on, when his very life blood was fast ebbing away and before he recovered from his wound I know that he was again at the post of duty and honor. Against his character as a private citizen there never was a breath of suspicion. But he dared to fight like a true knight for his home and friends and on this account a murderous arm has deprived him of this life. Cannot his words be verified and 10 men be slain for him. Is it not a case for retaliation – Should not our authorities demand that Hurst be given up to justice?

It is proper, perhaps, to state that Hurst said Capt. Wharton was a guerilla, and had been seeking his life. You know the falsity of the charge, if not, I would state that Capt. Wharton had a company regularly enlisted into Capt. Wilson's Regt, and his authority you have seen. I hope you will pardon the length of this communication but justice to the gallant dead required that I should not say less. The fate of Wharton and his comrades should evoke a storm of indignation from the entire Army, and rouse every Southern heart to "Strike! Till the last armed foe expires!"

Respectfully,
D.M. Wisdom

Respectfully forwarded to Gen'l Bragg, the truth of the statements made vouched for by me.

P.D. Roddey, Col. Commdg.[18]

Wisdom's complaints to Colonel Roddey resulted in Secretary of War James Seddon writing to General Braxton Bragg as follows:

> Confederate States of America, War Department
>   Richmond, August 14, 1863
> General Braxton Bragg,
>   Commanding Department of Tennessee:
>   General: A letter of D.M. Wisdom addressed to Colonel Roddey, of the 23d ultimo, was referred from your headquarters to this Department and has been submitted to the President. The letter contained a narrative of the capture of Captain

18. Ibid.

Wharton and a portion of his men by Colonel Hurst, of the U.S. Army, and the murder of the captured party on the road from Purdy to Pocahontas. The President directs that you will inquire into the accuracy of the statement of Mr. Wisdom, and that when you are satisfied on that subject you will adopt such retaliatory measures as are authorized by the usages of war, without awaiting specific instructions or making any reference to this Department. And this course will be adopted not only in this case, but whenever such instances of enormity and wickedness in violation of the laws of war shall come to your knowledge. The subject is placed under your control as a military commander, and you are expected to exercise a wise discretion in reference to it. The enemy have, in their military Order, No. 100, declaring the laws and usages of war, allowed to their subordinate commanders every latitude for cruelty and injustice that they can desire, and we hear from every quarter that they are not slow in using and abusing the authority given. To repress this abuse a corresponding power must sometimes be exerted by our own officers.

Very respectfully,
James A. Seddon
Secretary of War.[19]

The implications of Seddon's letter are significant. First, we learn this matter reached the desk of President Jefferson Davis in Richmond, attesting to its importance to Confederate authorities if proven to be true. Second, it is important to note that neither Secretary Seddon nor President Davis blindly accepted the allegations as fact but directed that they be investigated. Finally, Seddon issued a broad and sweeping, almost carte blanche, authority to General Bragg to exercise whatever measures necessary—but still acceptable to the rules of warfare—to retaliate. Interestingly, we have no further proof of an investigation of this matter. What follow-up was actually taken is uncertain. No records exist that these allegations received any further verification or acceptance or that Bragg ever took action on this matter. No documentation has come to light.

19. Ibid.

Col. Dew Moore Wisdom
Author's Collection

Still, enough facts are provided by Wisdom to allow for an independent investigation of Wharton's death. But what of the other four men alleged to have also been murdered? Did anyone bother to track down their military records or determine what became of them? They are identified as George Brown, Doctor Hugh Hollis, Thomas W.S. Morgan, and Thomas Starks. These men were said to be under the command of Captain John Ambrose "Dock" Wharton and all five were alleged to be serving in Wilson's Cavalry. Rigorous investigation into these men will cast doubt upon Wisdom's statement that these men were not guerillas and were serving in a regular military capacity.

A review of each man's military service record is warranted to verify Wisdom's claim that they were members of Wilson's Cavalry. The issue of Wharton's service on behalf of the Confederacy will be addressed in the latter part of this commentary. First, it is appropriate to address the enlisted men themselves: Hollis, Starks, Morgan, and Brown.

Private Hugh Hollis was a member of Lieutenant G.W. Churchwell's Company of the Thirteenth Regiment of Tennessee Volunteers, CSA.[20] He enlisted in the Confederate Army at Jackson, Tennessee, on May 31, 1861, being recruited by W.H. Carroll.[21] Interestingly, Colonel Wisdom, who stated that he personally knew Hollis and claimed he had been murdered by Hurst or members of the First West Tennessee Cavalry, enlisted on the same day, at the same place, and was recruited by the same officer. Hollis was discharged from the service that September and there is no further record of any subsequent enlistment. His official record with the Confederate Army ends in September 1861.[22] Incidentally, there is no record of any other Hugh Hollis in any Confederate unit comprised of Tennesseans.

Private Thomas Starks, also known as Thomas Stark, was a member of Captain John Wesley Eldridge's Artillery Company, which was organized on October 15, 1861.[23] He was recruited by a Lieutenant Jones

---

20. Compiled Service Record of Hugh Hollis. Compiled Service Records of Confederate Soldiers Who Served in Organizations from the State of Tennessee. Series Number M268, Roll 170. National Archives and Records Administration, Washington, D.C.

21. Ibid.

22. Ibid.

23. Compiled Service Record of Thomas Stark. Compiled Service Records of Confederate Soldiers Who Served in Organizations from the State of Tennessee. Series Number M268, Roll

and enlisted in McNairy County on October 15, 1861, for a period of twelve months.[24] He never served his full term, however. Starks was discharged on January 16, 1862, in Bowling Green, Kentucky.[25] There exists no further record of any subsequent enlistment and his official record with the Confederate authorities ends in January 1862. As with Hollis, there is no record of any other Thomas Starks in any Confederate unit comprised of Tennesseans.

Thomas W.S. Morgan enlisted in Company H of the 154th Senior Tennessee Infantry, CSA. Company H was made up of men from McNairy County and commanded by Alphonso Cross, C.R. Wharton, and Christopher Sherwin.[26] An analysis of the records of other young men named Thomas Morgan or any combination of the name thereof was made and their records were examined. These young men belonged to Confederate Army groups including the Fifth Tennessee Cavalry, Eighth Tennessee Cavalry, Twelfth Cavalry Battalion, Tenth Tennessee Infantry, Twenty-Fourth Tennessee Infantry, and the One Hundred Fifty-Fourth Senior Tennessee Infantry. The only potential fit was the Thomas S. Morgan who enlisted in the 154th Senior Tennessee Infantry in 1861.

There are two George Browns who appear in Confederate service records in this part of West Tennessee. One George Brown enlisted as a private in Company F of Newsom's Cavalry.[27] He enlisted in McNairy County, the only such George Brown to do so. It should be recalled that Colonel Wisdom himself stated he knew this man well.[28] Brown was enlisted by Captain Damron but that was not until September 1, 1863, a month-and-a-half after the alleged event.[29] That George Brown's service record further noted that he was absent without leave as of April 13, 1864, and there is no other record of enlistment for this man, but

96, National Archives and Records Administration (NARA), Washington, D.C.

24. Ibid.

25. Ibid.

26. *Tennesseans in the Civil War, Part I*, 333.

27. Compiled Service Record of George Brown. Compiled Service Records of Confederate Soldiers Who Served in Organizations from the State of Tennessee. National Archives Publication No. M268, NARA, Catalogue No. 586957, Record Group 109, Tennessee, Roll 0065. National Archives and Records Administration, Washington, D.C.

28. Ibid.

29. Ibid.

still indicating that he was alive in April of 1864.³⁰ The only other local Brown for whom a Confederate service record existed was W.G. Brown, a member of Wilson's Cavalry, the 21st Tennessee Cavalry, the successor unit to which Wisdom referred.³¹ However, this W.G. Brown also did not enlist until September 1, 1863, and that was at Centerpoint, Tennessee.³² Again, this occurred *after* the alleged war crime along the Pocahontas-Purdy Road.

With the exception of this W.G. Brown, when the rolls of the Twenty-First Tennessee Cavalry (also known as Wilson's Cavalry) were examined, there was no record of any of the other men referenced—Hollis, Starks, or Morgan—having ever served. Therefore, Wisdom's contention that all of these men were part of Wilson's Cavalry lacks credibility entirely. An examination of the rolls of the two units that were known as Wilson's Cavalry do not include any of the four men identified by Wisdom as serving under Captain John A. "Dock" Wharton and W.G. Brown is never referred to specifically as George Brown. If these four men were serving with Wharton in any capacity, it was not official and must have been as guerilla forces, not protected under the normal usages and rules of war. Guerillas would be, in fact, serving at their own peril entirely. However, regardless of the capacity in which these four men were allegedly acting, there are still other facts to be considered and scrutinized.

Before examining the lives of the men alleged to have been murdered and their ultimate fates, a discussion of the events of July 1863 and their relation to Hurst and the First West Tennessee Cavalry is warranted. For example, more of this historical puzzle is known today from the Union perspective thanks to Breckenridge's journal. From all indications, the alleged murders took place in and around July 1863 sometime just prior to July 23. Breckenridge's journal documents the month of July in some detail and helps account for the activities and whereabouts of both Hurst and the regiment. From July 1 through July 12, neither were in the vicinity of Pocahontas, Tennessee, or appear to have been near or on the

30. Ibid.

31. Compiled Service Record of W.G. Brown. Compiled Service Records of Confederate Soldiers Who Served in Organizations from the State of Tennessee. National Archives Publication No. M268, NARA, Catalogue No. 586957, Record Group 109, Tennessee, Roll 0073. National Archives and Records Administration, Washington, D.C.

32. Ibid.

Pocahontas-Purdy Road during that time. The incident has always been alleged to have occurred following the battle of Jackson, Tennessee.

Breckenridge records the events surrounding the battle of Jackson in his journal for July 13–14. According to him, the regiment left Jackson for Purdy on July 14. They left Purdy the next day and went to Camden (now Rose Creek) toward Bolivar, but turned back to Camden because a bridge over the Hatchie River had been burned. In his report to Colonel Hatch on July 20, Hurst reported that upon leaving Jackson, he and his men pursued some 1,500 to 1,800 Rebels under the command of Biffle, Forrest, and Newsom. His men captured about twenty prisoners. From that number, eight were paroled, seven taken into custody, and some five or six fell back and escaped.

The fact that Fielding Hurst himself, on July 15, 1863, reported to Colonel Edward Hatch that five or six captured guerillas fell back and made their escape is significant. There were five men allegedly murdered on the Pocahontas-Purdy Road. According to Wisdom, these five men were Wharton, Hollis, Starks, Brown and Morgan. However, it is also possible that these five men were among the five or six men referenced by Hurst and did make their escape during which one of them, Thomas W.S. Morgan, was mortally wounded. Despite the subsequent folklore that these men were brutally murdered, dismembered, and their heads and/or bodies used for mile markers, such allegations were not even made by even Wisdom. In fact, Wisdom only accused Hurst of having the men shot while in captivity.[33] He made absolutely no claims of brutality upon the bodies of these men.

Again, let us review Breckenridge's words to see if they shed any light on the incident. His journal entry for July 15 makes no mention of Hurst but records only his own encounters with three guerillas.[34] Further, when it comes to subsequent days, on July 16, Breckenridge noted that the regiment left Camden for Pocahontas, arrived there at about 3:30 P.M., and camped for the night.[35] They remained in Pocahontas for approximately twenty-four hours and left at about 3:00 P.M. on July 17 and arrived at LaGrange at 6:00 P.M. Breckenridge recorded that July 18–19 were passed

33. Dew M. Wisdom to Col. Philip D. Roddey, July 23, 1863. NARA M474, RG 109, Reel 88, Frames 167-169, National Archives and Records Administration, Washington, D.C.

34. Breckenridge Daybook, 179.

35. Ibid, 201.

quietly in LaGrange.[36] On the 20th, it was raining and quiet in camp. It was from LaGrange that Hurst made his report to Colonel Hatch.[37] The regiment stayed in camp through July 21–22 and Breckenridge reported nothing of note.[38]

On July 23, Breckenridge was given a leave of absence to go to Memphis.[39] He had business to attend to there for the regiment. He recorded in his journal for that day that when he arrived in Memphis, he learned that Hurst had headed to Whiteville, Tennessee, with a body of approximately 100 troops.[40] Taken together, this is interesting because Breckenridge reported no incident in his journal in July or afterwards about such an event or even hinted at such. Given his penchant for recording and commenting on the transgressions of Hurst and others in the regiment, it is almost certain he would have documented at least some minimal information or hint pertaining to the alleged events, if not a full account of such.

Thus, the question becomes what—if anything—*did* happen on the Pocahontas-Purdy Road in July 1863? There are no Federal records, memoirs, statements, or other memoranda that mention, document, or even hint at such an event. What Federal records exist pertaining to the month of July 1863 reveal Fielding Hurst's activities in some significant detail as well as the presence and activities of the First West Tennessee Cavalry. Such an event would almost certainly have been taken very seriously by the Federal authorities, including Hurst's immediate superiors all the way up to General Ulysses S. Grant. The reader must keep in mind that as early as October 1862, Grant considered disbanding the First West Tennessee Cavalry over horse thievery. It would have been very hard to imagine the Federal command tolerating or turning a blind eye to such horrendous atrocities and carnage as alleged on the Pocahontas-Purdy Road. Further, there is little doubt that the Confederate authorities in Richmond would have retaliated and perhaps even reached out to Washington, D.C., to address the wrongs of the Federal troops under Hurst's command had such an event actually occurred.

36. Ibid, 201–202.
37. Ibid, 202.
38. Ibid, 202–203.
39. Ibid, 203.
40. Ibid.

In point of fact, only one grave may be found to exist along the Pocahontas-Purdy Road, even today. If others existed, they have been long hidden and no monuments, rocks, markers, or other memorials have been placed to mark their locations. Some second or thirdhand, if not more extenuated, sources claim that as many as two additional graves exist, but none can be located and marked. The only grave that does exist is that of Thomas W.S. Morgan, a twenty-four year old man whose tombstone states that he "was murdered." That is all it tells us. There is no military stone to commemorate his service in a unit of the Confederate Army. He is identified by Colonel Wisdom in his letter to Roddey as a participant in the skirmish between Wharton's men and Hurst's men. For more than a century and a half, many have simply and readily accepted that Wisdom's word, itself based upon hearsay, was sufficient to establish Hurst and men of the First West Tennessee Cavalry as the alleged killers of Wharton and company.

Private Thomas W.S. Morgan is an interesting case. The popular and adamant legend and lore pertaining to this alleged incident asserts that Morgan was from Alabama, that he was mortally injured but lingered, that his family arrived too late from Alabama to retrieve him, and that he died along the road. The legend also maintains that the Locke family could do nothing to alleviate the poor man's suffering and could not take him into their home because of the fear that Hurst's men would burn their home or otherwise retaliate against them.

Unfortunately, none of that stands up to research and critical review. In fact, Morgan was from McNairy County, not Alabama. According to his gravestone, he died in 1863 at the age of 24 and was the son of J.R. and L. Morgan. Those facts, carved in stone, may be the only truth related to him that has remained since July 1863. In point of fact, Morgan was born in Virginia in 1838 to John R. Morgan and wife Lucinda Debell Morgan.[41] His parents were married in Frederick County, Virginia, on February 28, 1828.[42] By 1850, the family was living in McNairy County, Tennessee, in the Third Civil District, in the village of Montezuma,

---

41. Eighth Census of the United States, 1860. District 14, McNairy County, Tennessee, page 508. Family History Library Film 805262, National Archives and Records Administration, Washington, D.C.

42. Jordan R. Dodd, et al. *Early American Marriages: Virginia to 1850* (Bountiful UT: Precision Indexing Publishers, 1990).

now located in Chester County.[43] The Morgans resided there with their children William (age 22), Ann (age 20), Mary (age 18), John (age 14), Thomas W.S. (12), Franklin (10), and Henry Abel (age 6).[44] By 1860, the Morgans and four of their children were still living in McNairy County in District Fourteen.[45] Those four children were John E. (age 24), Thomas W.S. (age 22), James F. (age 20), and Abel Henry (age 16).[46] Ultimately, it is quite possible that Thomas W.S. Morgan died at the hands of Hurst's First West Tennessee Cavalry, but that possibility will be discussed further in this commentary.

One of the alleged victims, Doctor Hugh Hollis, had many connections to members of the First West Tennessee Cavalry and to Thomas W.S. Morgan. Hugh Lawson White Hollis was the son of James C. Hollis and wife Elizabeth Hollis.[47] He was born in 1839 and raised in the village of Montezuma in what was then north McNairy County.[48] Another verification of his birthplace is found on the death certificate of James Wilson Hollis, which identifies that his father, Dr. Hugh Hollis, who was born in McNairy County, Tennessee.[49]

Hollis graduated from the University of Louisiana in 1861.[50] On May 31, he enlisted in Company F of the Thirteenth Infantry, a company known as the Wright Boys and led by Captain Dew Moore Wisdom.

---

43. Seventh Census of the United States, 1850. District 3, McNairy County, Tennessee. Roll 888, page 73A. Records of the Bureau of Census. Record Group 29. National Archives and Records Administration, Washington, D.C.

44. Ibid.

45. Eighth Census of the United States, 1860. District 14, McNairy County, Tennessee, page 508. Family History Library Film 805262. National Archives and Records Administration, Washington, D.C.

46. Ibid.

47. Tenth Census of the United States, 1880. District 4, McNairy County, Tennessee, page 394. Family History Library Film 805262. National Archives and Records Administration, Washington, D.C.

48. *College Student Lists* (Worchester MA: American Antiquarian Society). The fact that Dr. Hugh Hollis was raised in Montezuma, Tennessee, is substantiated by a number of records, including the Federal Census rolls and the burial sites of his parents and other family.

49. Tennessee Death Records, 1908–1958. Roll Number 9. Tennessee State Library and Archives, Nashville, Tennessee.

50. *College Student Lists*.

He was twenty-two years old and had been recruited by W.H. Carroll.[51] Hollis was discharged in September 1861 after being sick on furlough.[52] There are no subsequent records that he ever reenlisted. Interestingly, he signed a promissory note payable to his father, James C. Hollis, a merchant in Montezuma, on January 1, 1864, some five months after his alleged murder.[53]

By 1866, Hollis had moved to Arkadelphia, Arkansas, where he married Sallie W. "Mamie" Wilson and was a merchant and a physician.[54] He was still living and practicing medicine there as late as 1871.[55] Reconstruction had practically ended in Tennessee in 1869 with the defeat of radical Republicans in legislative races across the state.[56] This made it more feasible and far safer for exiled Confederates to return home. Dr. Hollis was living at Jack's Creek in Henderson County by 1873, where he had been appointed postmaster.[57] His father had years before opened a branch of his mercantile business in Jack's Creek.[58] He was identified as a druggist and a physician in 1876 as well as the postmaster of Jack's Creek, having been reappointed the previous year.[59] In 1880, Dr. Hollis,

---

51. Compiled Service Record of Hugh Hollis. Compiled Service Records of Confederate Soldiers Who Served in Organizations from the State of Tennessee. Series Number M268, Roll 170. National Archives and Records Administration, Washington, D.C.

52. Ibid.

53. Papers of Hollis & Cason as found in Nancy Wardlow Kennedy, ed. *Hollis & Cason Merchant's Accounts, ca. 1857–1861* (Selmer TN: Self-published, 2005), 6.

54. Records of the Internal Revenue Service. Record Group 58. National Archives and Records Administration, Washington, D.C. Jordan Dodd, Liahona Research, comp. *Arkansas Marriages, 1851–1900*.

55. Ibid, for tax years 1866, 1868, and 1869. *College Student Lists*.

56. Robert E. Corlew, *Tennessee: A Short History*, 2nd ed. (Knoxville: The University of Tennessee Press, 1990), 343–345.

57. "U.S. City Directories, 1822–1995" (database online). Ancestry.com. Record of Appointment of Postmasters, 1832–1971. NARA Microfilm Publication M841, 145 rolls. Records of the Post Office Department, Record Group Number 28. National Archives and Records Administration, Washington, D.C.

58. Kennedy, *Hollis & Cason*, 1.

59. Ancestry.com. U.S. City Directories, 1822–1995 (database online). Provo, UT: Ancestry.com Operations, Inc. 2011. Record of Appointment of Postmasters, 1832–1971. NARA Microfilm Publication, M841, 145 rolls. Records of the Post Office Department, Record Group Number 28. National Archives and Records Administration, Washington, D.C.

his wife Mamie, and his son James Wilson Hollis were living with the Enos Foster family in Jack's Creek.[60]

Dr. Hollis attended at least two Confederate reunions in Henderson, Tennessee, held in 1880 and on August 11, 1893.[61] He had died by the time of the reunion at Horner, Tennessee, on August 8, 1894.[62] Notations on the original attendance sheets reflect that he died sometime between the 1893 and 1894 events.[63]

With the knowledge that Hollis was not murdered by Fielding Hurst and soldiers of the First West Tennessee Cavalry but instead survived the war, the allegations warrant an explanation. The whole story may never be known, but pieces of the puzzle can be scrutinized. One possible answer to explain matters lies in the business ledgers of Hollis & Cason, the mercantile business in Montezuma owned by Dr. Hollis' father, James C. Hollis, and his partner C.M. Cason. Hollis & Cason was quite busy in the years leading up to the Civil War. It is important to understand that both Hollis and Cason were staunchly pro-Confederate in their views.[64]

Cason was a former Confederate officer in 1863, having served as a lieutenant colonel in the Thirty-First (A.H. Bradford's) Tennessee Infantry Regiment.[65] According his service record, he enlisted at Trenton, Tennessee, on September 12, 1861, for a period of twelve months. He

---

60. Tenth Census of the United States, 1880. District 5, Henderson County, Tennessee. Roll 1262, page 337A, Enumeration District 056. National Archives and Records Administration, Washington, D.C.

61. 1880 Confederate Veterans' Reunion Attendance Rolls, Henderson, Tennessee. Joanne Talley Van Cleave private papers, unpublished.

62. 1893 Confederate Veterans' Reunion Attendance Rolls, Henderson, Tennessee. Joanne Talley Van Cleave private papers, unpublished.

63. 1894 Confederate Veterans' Reunion Attendance Rolls, Horner, Tennessee. Joanne Talley Van Cleave private papers, unpublished.

64. Cason enlisted as a captain in the Thirty-First Regiment, Tennessee Infantry, CSA, under Colonel Bradford of Brownsville, Tennessee. According to *Goodspeed*, he "remained in active duty for some time, but, on account of ill health was obliged to leave the service" and returned home in 1863. See *History of Tennessee: From The Earliest Time to the Present; Together with an Historical and a Biographical Sketch of the Counties of Henderson, Chester, Decatur, McNairy and Hardin, Besides a Valuable Fund of Notes, Original Observations, Reminiscences, Etc., Etc., Illustrated.* (Nashville TN: The Goodspeed Publishing Co., 1887), 863.

65. *Tennesseans in the Civil War, Part I*, 240.

was recruited by A.M. Johnson.⁶⁶ Originally enlisting as a captain in Company C, Cason was elected Lieutenant Colonel on October 12, 1861. He left the service on May 11, 1862, the notation on his record only stating he was "dropped."⁶⁷ Interestingly, Dr. Hollis' brother, W.T. Hollis, served in Company C of the Thirty-First Tennessee Infantry with Cason's younger brother, T.K. Cason.⁶⁸ The younger Cason enlisted as a Second Lieutenant on September 12, 1861, but died on Christmas Eve that year.⁶⁹ His replacement was W.T. Hollis.⁷⁰ W.T. Hollis originally enlisted as a Third Lieutenant in the same regiment on September 12, 1861, for a period of twelve months. By early 1863, he had "left out in amalgamation, gone home."⁷¹

An examination of the extant records for Hollis & Cason confirms that James C. Hollis and C.M. Cason held pre-war promissory notes and open accounts for many notable individuals either enlisted in or affiliated with the First West Tennessee Cavalry.⁷² Those notes were still unsatisfied after the war began.⁷³ At the time of the alleged executions, feelings were running extremely high in McNairy County and Hollis and Cason had taken action against many of their alleged debtors who were now supporters of the Union. Some of those individuals affiliated with the First West Tennessee Cavalry included: C.B. Covey, Elijah J. Hodges, Horry Hodges, W.C. McIntyre, R.T. McIntyre, R.M. Thompson, John Coleman, Thomas M. Clayton, E.M.R. Hodges, W.L. Gattis, Elza

66. Compiled Service Record of C.M. Cason. Records Showing Military Service of Soldiers Who Fought in Confederate Organizations, compiled 1903–1927, documenting the period 1861–1865. National Archives Catalogue ID 586957, Record Group 109, NARA M268, Tennessee, Roll 0245. National Archives and Records Administration, Washington, D.C.

67. Ibid.

68. Compiled Service Record of T.K. Cason. Records Showing Military Service of Soldiers Who Fought in Confederate Organizations, compiled 1903–1927, documenting the period 1861–1865. National Archives Catalogue ID 586957, Record Group 109, NARA M268, Tennessee, Roll 0245. National Archives and Records Administration, Washington, D.C.

69. Ibid.

70. Service Record of W.T. Hollis. Records Showing Military Service of Soldiers Who Fought in Confederate Organizations, compiled 1903–1927, documenting the period 1861–1865. National Archives Catalogue ID 586957, Record Group 109, NARA M268, Tennessee, Roll 0246. National Archives and Records Administration, Washington, D.C.

71. Ibid.

72. Kennedy, *Hollis & Cason*.

73. Ibid.

Hurst, W.D. Holloway, James Holloway, Long B. Ivy, John Jackson, James Bryant, Francis M. Rankin, Alfred Sipes, William C. Walker, and Achabod Brown.[74]

Of these twenty debtors to Hollis & Cason, fifteen had enlisted in the First West Tennessee Cavalry. The other five were close relatives or associates of other soldiers in the regiment. One was R.T. McIntyre, the father of Isaac T. McIntyre, who had already made himself a bad reputation among area Confederates. Another was Elza Hurst, the younger brother of Fielding Hurst. Hollis and Cason were actively involved in the pursuit of debts through the courts prior to and during the war. With the collapse of the Confederate controlled government in McNairy County and Federal authority reestablished in the state, the firm of Hollis & Cason had no real recourse against their debtors. This set of circumstances begs the question: Did they actively participate in a ruse to arouse Confederate military authorities to eliminate Fielding Hurst and target members of the First West Tennessee Cavalry? Facing the reality of sustained Union occupation and great financial loss, did they seek to "exact their pound of flesh?" Simply put, we cannot know. However, we know one thing now. Dr. Hugh Hollis was not executed along the Pocahontas-Purdy Road in July 1863. This is another glaring incorrect assertion by Colonel Wisdom in his letter to Roddey.

George Brown is another enigmatic individual about whom little is known. A few facts have surfaced through research. It is known that one of the two possible Browns of whom Wisdom is referring, George Brown of Newsom's Cavalry, did not enlist in the Confederate service until well after the executions allegedly occurred. The second issue is that W.G. Brown, the other possible Brown, survived the war and attended Confederate reunions, including one held in Henderson, Tennessee, in 1880.[75] This W.G. Brown completed a pension application filed on October 18, 1899. It states that he was injured "near Ripley, Miss., 10th of March, 1865, was on scout duty, were charged upon by the Federals and in trying to escape over a deep ravine horse fell on me and I was

---

74. Ibid.

75. 1880 Confederate Veterans' Reunion Attendance Rolls, Henderson, Tennessee.

made prisoner."⁷⁶ Dr. John B. Hardeman found Brown to be suffering with the following disability:

> A chronic sore leg caused by a severe bruise received while in the Confederate service also enlargement of one testicle caused by injury by horn of saddle while in service which gives him considerable trouble. Said leg has been a running sore & pieces of bone have been working out from time to time along rendering him unable to unable to perform manual labor more than half his time.⁷⁷

Regardless which Brown is the individual to which Wisdom refers, it matters little. It would have been difficult for either one to enlist in either September 1863 or in 1864 had death befallen him in July 1863.

Another of the alleged victims was Thomas Starks. He was born in Tennessee about 1828 according to the 1860 Census for McNairy County.⁷⁸ When the war broke out, Starks was married to Lucinda Hill, the daughter of Abraham and Martha Hill. The couple had one surviving son, Elijah Starks, though others died before the war.⁷⁹ There was another son, whose name is not known, born on July 19, 1854, and died October 18, 1855. There was also a daughter, Nancy W. Starks, whose birth date is unknown. Both children are buried in the Rose Hill Cemetery in McNairy County.⁸⁰

We know nothing further about Thomas Starks himself. However, some important information is known about his family. His date of death cannot be found, but Lucinda Starks remarried to William R. Ferguson on August 26, 1867.⁸¹ James Hill filed a petition to the Commissioner of Claims in 1873 regarding his inhumane treatment by Confederates

76. Tennessee Confederate Applications, Soldiers and Widows, 1891–1965, filed by soldier, Nos. 2193–2241. Tennessee State Library and Archives, Nashville, Tennessee.

77. Ibid.

78. Eighth Census of the United States, 1860. McNairy County, Tennessee. NARA microfilm publication M653. National Archives and Records Administration, Washington, D.C.

79. Ibid.

80. Nancy Starks' grave has been previously documented in various cemetery records. It has also been photographed and listed in the Rose Hill Cemetery census on the website www.findagrave.com. The author was unable to find the broken tombstone during a recent search of the cemetery.

81. Tennessee State Marriages, 1780–2002. Microfilm, Tennessee State Library and Archives.

and his loss of certain items, including corn, fodder, and livestock to the Union Army.[82] He claimed absolute loyalty as a Unionist and sought the supporting testimony of others loyal to the Union.[83] Among his witnesses were Lucinda Ferguson, the presumed widow of Thomas Starks (if he had indeed died by 1867) and her son Elijah W. Starks. According to Elijah Starks' own statement: "I was a Union man and Mr. Hill always regarded me as a Union man."[84] Lucinda Ferguson was also mentioned as a witness to the loyalty of James Hill.[85]

It would seem very strange for either Lucinda (Starks) Ferguson or Elijah W. Starks to be willing to testify to the loyalist qualities of a Union sympathizer if their husband and father, respectively, had been the victim of a heinous murder by the Union Army. Further, both were cooperating with Hill's attorney, Robert M. Thompson, who himself had been an officer serving under Colonel Fielding Hurst. It is hard to imagine a situation where Starks' family would assist anyone so directly if he had been executed in such a brutal fashion along the Pocahontas-Purdy Road just ten years before.

Finally, there is the case of Captain John Ambrose "Dock" Wharton. Tradition and folklore insist that Wharton was executed by Hurst in July 1863 while leading the four men referenced in Wisdom's letter. Once again, careful research debunks and corrects such tradition and folklore. The case of Dock Wharton's fate must be submitted to the same rigors of research to which the lives and fates of Hollis, Brown, Starks, and Morgan were examined. First, no specific document exists to substantiate that Wharton died in July 1863 other than Wisdom's letter. That document has already proven inaccurate pertaining to the fates of Hollis, Brown, and possibly Stark. Further, it has already been proven inaccurate as to the status of the men as soldiers of Wilson's Cavalry, which they were not.

There are facts that refute Wharton's death date—and thus his manner of death at the hands of Hurst and the First West Tennessee Cavalry.

---

82. Barred and Disallowed Case Files of the Southern Claims Commission, 1871–1880. Records of the U.S. House of Representatives, 1789–2015. Record Group Number 233, Series M1407. National Archives and Records Administration, Washington, D.C.

83. Ibid.

84. Ibid.

85. Ibid.

THREE PIVOTAL DAYS AND THE MILE MARKER MURDERS 159

Wharton was born in McNairy County in 1836.[86] He was living with his parents John and Polly Wharton, his seven siblings, and his maternal grandmother, Harrietta Hightower, in 1850.[87] Ten years later, he was married and living with his wife Martha in the Seventh Civil District of McNairy County with their children John J. (age 3) and Mary E. (age 2), where he worked as a tenant farmer.[88] At the age of twenty-five, Wharton enlisted in the Thirteenth Tennessee Infantry at Jackson on May 23, 1861.[89] As a second sergeant in Company F, he was directly under the command of Captain Dew Moore Wisdom, the very man who alleged his execution two years later.[90] Wharton was discharged because of physical disability in August 1862 at Tupelo, Mississippi, presumably from the effects of a grievous wound suffered at the Battle of Shiloh.[91]

Between 1914 and 1915, questionnaires were sent to all known surviving veterans of the Civil War in Tennessee. Joe C. Brooks of Michie was among those who completed it.[92] A Confederate veteran, he had served in Company I of the 154th Senior Tennessee Infantry, which consolidated with the Thirteenth Tennessee Infantry in March 1863.[93] According to Brooks' rather lengthy and thorough questionnaire, he served with the four Wharton brothers—Charley Wharton, Bill Wharton, Caleb Wharton, and Dock Wharton.[94] Although he acknowledged Dock Wharton,

---

86. Compiled Service Record of John Ambrose Wharton. Compiled Service Records of Confederate Soldiers Who Served in Organizations from the State of Tennessee. Record Group 109, Series Number M268, Roll 172. National Archives and Records Administration, Washington, D.C.

87. Seventh Census of the United States, 1850. McNairy County, Tennessee. National Archives Microfilm Publication M432. Records of the Bureau of the Census. Record Group 29. National Archives and Records Administration, Washington, D.C.

88. Eighth Census of the United States, 1860. McNairy County, Tennessee. National Archives Microfilm Publication M653. Records of the Bureau of the Census. National Archives and Records Administration, Washington, D.C.

89. Wharton's enlistment officer was W.H. Carroll. Compiled Service Record of John Ambrose Wharton.

90. Ibid.

91. Ibid.

92. Gustavus W. Dyer and John Trotwood Moore, *The Tennessee Civil War Veterans Questionnaires. Federal Soldiers (Accuff-Wood) Confederate Soldiers (Abbott-Byrne)* (Easley SC: Southern Historical Press, Inc., 1985), 1:384

93. Ibid.

94. Ibid, 385. Brooks refers to the Wharton brothers by their nicknames rather than their given names. There is an apparent transcription error as to Dock Wharton, which is transcribed

Brooks gave no particulars about him or the manner of his death. While not unusual, given the legends pertaining to Wharton's death, it seems strange that he would not offer it some attention. Still, this omission is by no means conclusive of anything, but just another factor to consider.

There is no further record of John A. Wharton re-enlisting in the Confederate Army. Some have pointed to the existing record establishing that one A.J. Wharton served in Wilson's Twenty-First Cavalry to demonstrate that Wisdom was truthful in his claim that John Ambrose "Dock" Wharton had served in Wilson's Cavalry. But Wisdom alleged that Wharton died in July 1863. Though he enlisted in McNairy County, this A.J. Wharton—who may very well be John Ambrose Wharton—did not enlist in Wilson's Twenty-First Cavalry until June 15, 1863. He had been recruited by a Captain Wharton.[95] This A.J. Wharton was alive on May 6, 1864, when he deserted from the Confederate Army.[96] With this possibility refuted, one might instead believe that Captain Wharton, who had recruited A.J. Wharton, was Dock Wharton himself. However, the records of the Confederate Army do not substantiate this belief. Instead, they partially disprove the veracity of Wisdom's story.

There is additional information that further discredits the July 1863 murder allegation. The 1870 Census for McNairy County lists Martha Wharton as a widow living with her four children: John J. (age 13), Mary A. (age 13), William A. (age 7), and Kenneth M. (age 4).[97] Though enumerated as Horton, this is simple misspelling by the census taker. The youngest of the Wharton children was Kenneth McIntire Wharton, born in Purdy, Tennessee, on September 13, 1865.[98] There is no indication, even in Wharton family records, that Kenneth McIntire Wharton belonged to anyone other than John Ambrose Wharton. In fact, according

as "Dick." The brothers were Charles R. "Charley" Wharton, William "Bill" Wharton, Caleb F. Wharton, and John Ambrose "Dock" Wharton.

95. Compiled Service Record of A.J. Wharton. Compiled Service Records of Confederate Soldiers Who Served in Organizations from the State of Tennessee. Record Group 109, Series Number M268, Roll 74. National Archives and Records Administration, Washington, D.C.

96. Ibid.

97. Ninth Census of the United States, 1870. McNairy County, Tennessee. U.S. Census Population Schedules. NARA Microfilm Publication M593, National Archives and Records Administration, Washington, D.C.

98. Photograph of gravestone of Kenneth McIntire Wharton, www.findagrave.com. The 1880 and 1910 Census establish Wharton's birth year as late as 1867 and 1866, respectively.

to family records, Wharton died in Purdy in April of 1865 and was buried in the Mars Hill Cemetery in what eventually became the Leapwood community.[99] It would seem that the descendants of Dock Wharton do not believe that he perished on the Pocahontas-Purdy Road in July 1863. Obviously, he and Martha could not have conceived Kenneth McIntire "Kit" Wharton had he not survived.[100]

Another indicator that Wharton died after the war is the fact that his widow opened his estate on or about October 2, 1865.[101] Letters of Administration were not issued to Martha (Wilkerson) Wharton until December 3, 1866, with her bond being assured by D.N. Huddleston and J.A.L. Alexander.[102] This legal document is another potentially important indication against the alleged killing of Wharton and the other four men by Hurst and the First West Tennessee Cavalry. David N. Huddleston, one of Wharton's bondsmen, was an in-law to Fielding Hurst. This association would seem highly unlikely if Hurst had been directly responsible for Wharton's death.

Martha Wharton remarried to R.M. McCann in McNairy County on December 9, 1876.[103] She and her son William Wharton were living with him in the Fourth Civil District in 1880.[104] McCann had remarried by 1896, suggesting that Martha had died by that time. She was buried with her first husband, Dock Wharton, at Mars Hill Cemetery. Their son William A. Wharton (1864–1917) is buried within yards of Martha. Their youngest child, Kenneth McIntire "Kit" Wharton, moved to Jonesboro, Arkansas, where he lived out his life. His obituary, published after his death on March 27, 1934, related that he had been born in McNairy County, Tennessee, and moved to Craighead County, Arkansas, in 1887.

99. Family information sheets/charts documented on https://www.familysearch.org/tree/pedigree/landscape/K81N-7L8.

100. Ibid. This website documents the date of Dock Wharton's death as April 1865.

101. McNairy County, Tennessee, Inventories, 1865–1890, Volume E. Tennessee Probate Court Books, 1795–1927. www.familysearch.org. The files of the McNairy County, Tennessee Archives, Selmer, Tennessee.

102. Ibid.

103. Tennessee State Marriages, 1780–2002. Tennessee State Library and Archives, Nashville, Tennessee.

104. Tenth Census of the United States, 1880. McNairy County, Tennessee, page 394. Family History Library Film 805262. National Archives and Records Administration, Washington, D.C.

Interestingly, there was no other mention of his Tennessee background or relatives but for his own wife and children.[105]

Drawing this discussion of the alleged Mile Marker murders to a conclusion, it is appropriate to recap what has been discovered and add a few final integral points. First, despite the allegations made by Colonel Dew Moore Wisdom that Captain John Ambrose "Dock" Wharton, Dr. Hugh Hollis, George Brown, Thomas Stark, and Thomas W.S. Morgan all were executed along the Pocahontas-Purdy Road in July 1863, conclusive proof substantiates that neither Hollis nor Brown died that day and that both survived decades after the war. More evidence exists to substantiate that Wharton died at the end of the war in April 1865 than proves he died in July 1863. These facts, along with the incorrect assertion that all of these men were serving together under Wharton's command in Wilson's Cavalry, are enough by themselves to render the letter and the accusations void for lack of credibility. However, there are still other factors to be considered as well. The Locke oral tradition—that Thomas W.S. Morgan of Alabama was cared for by the Locke family and died from his wounds before his family could reach him—may also be discounted. No one today can know the timeline pertaining to Morgan's death, but he did not come from Alabama. He and his family both lived in McNairy County.

The motives of Wisdom and those of the alleged victims and their families, as noted with the Hollis family, should also be explored. Dew Moore Wisdom made this accusation on July 23, 1863. Given all the facts uncovered, it is more than fair to question what might have possessed him to make the allegations or to be so willing to believe them if his information came from another individual.

In fact, Dew Wisdom may well have had his own ax to grind. Just three months prior, Hurst had been back to Purdy, Tennessee, where both men lived, and a place which Wisdom held in near reverence. Angry over the alleged theft of two of his horses, Hurst determined to burn the homes of a number of local secessionists and Confederate sympathizers. He ordered them to remove their furnishings and belongings before he burned their homes.[106] Hurst intended to set fire to the brick mansion home of William S. Wisdom, the father of Dew Wisdom, but through

---

105. Jonesboro AR *Evening Sun*, March 27, 1934.
106. McCann, *Hurst's Wurst*, 36.

the intercession of Fielding Hurst's own wife, who received an appeal from Celia (Shull) Wisdom, the Wisdom home was spared.[107] The elder Wisdom had returned to the town and found it on fire, the citizens under the threat of harm by Hurst's men if they reacted or resisted.[108] These events may well have spurred Wisdom to take drastic action to stop Hurst. Accusing him of the systematic execution and slaughter of Confederate soldiers would certainly make Hurst a target. The very wording of Wisdom's letter to Roddey makes it clear that Wisdom is seeking to have Hurst and his regiment treated as guerillas.

In the final analysis, it is evident that the burden of proof has long since turned against the legend of the Mile Marker Murders. No contemporary reports or correspondence in any Southern newspaper can be found pertaining to these allegations. Had they been proven true and accurate, one can be assured that much propaganda use would have been made of the events. Further, it cannot be ignored that no proof exists that the Confederate authorities ever revisited the issue. Anti-radical and "unreconstructed" post-war Southern newspapers often published highly negative reports and accounts about Fielding Hurst. Those newspaper accounts referred to Hurst as blasphemous, infamous, vile, savage, demonical, disgraceful, base, a reprobate, cruel, unscrupulous, an extortionist, a bloated countenance, and as a commander of the notorious robbing, burning, and pillaging 6th Tennessee Cavalry (first known as the First West Tennessee Cavalry).[109] Despite referring to all of Hurst's worst characteristics and his many past crimes—both true and alleged—none ever repeated the allegations made by Wisdom in July 1863.

Finally, three of Purdy's most prominent Confederate military figures—Dew Moore Wisdom himself, General Marcus J. Wright, and Colonel John Vines Wright—spent the next decades writing and speaking about their beloved Purdy and McNairy County on many occasions. These alleged murders appear to have never been raised or otherwise referenced again, at least in writing. No other historian or contemporary of Hurst or his Confederate foes ever appear to have raised this issue again. In fact, it was not raised in writing until 1946 when Emma

107. Ibid.
108. Ibid.

109. Nashville *Republican Banner*, June 23, 1867; June 25, 1867; June 27, 1867; December 21, 1867; July 3, 1868; July 8, 1868. Jackson TN *West Tennessee Whig*, December 2, 1865.

Inman Williams published her book *Historic Madison: The Story of Jackson and Madison County, Tennessee from Mound Builders to World War I*. She recounted briefly the mile marker legend and cited Wisdom's letter, even though her citation was misleading and incorrect as Wisdom never claimed that Hurst or his soldiers used the dead men for mile markers.[110] Further, Ms. Williams wrote that six of Wharton's men were killed, one every mile, once again a flawed interpretation of Wisdom's letter.[111] She went on to state as fact that Hurst's regiment also captured and killed seven of Colonel John Newsome's command and pinned their bodies to a tree near the roadside. No single source was given for this story.[112] Nathan Bedford Forrest himself did make the allegations pertaining to the killing of Newsome's men, but they have never been substantiated or independently investigated.

Ultimately, it is the opinion of the author that an objective review of the existing evidence and records renders Colonel Wisdom's accusations groundless and the exaggerated version of his accusations even more incredible and ridiculous. All evidence taken together over the period of 1862 through 1865 may indeed prove Hurst an arsonist, a looter, an opportunist, and a petty individual. But no evidence actually exists to validate him a cold-blooded murderer guilty of systematic and illegal executions of prisoners. All such allegations over the years have been purely anecdotal in nature.

110. Williams, *Historic Madison*, 178.
111. Ibid.
112. Ibid.

WILLIAM S. WISDOM (*above*) AND CELIA (SHULL) WISDOM (*below*)

RIDING *toward* a LEGACY

July 16–August 31, 1863

On the morning of July 16, 1863, Breckenridge and his troops left Camden for Pocahontas, a distance of approximately twelve miles.[1] Camden was still considered a village as late as 1874 with a population of about fifty people.[2] They arrived at Pocahontas at 3:30 P.M. and camped there for the night. The week of July 16–22 passed rather uneventfully. Breckenridge made no mention of anything controversial, including the execution of Confederates— whether regular soldiers or guerillas—along the Pocahontas-Purdy Road.

The next morning, Breckenridge ordered his men to mount and start for their camps at LaGrange, arriving at about 3:00 P.M. They rested for a few hours, then began cleaning their camp as well as their guns and sabers.[3] For the next three days, the regiment endured heavy rains and a

---

1. Breckenridge Daybook, 201.
2. Killebrew, *Resources of Tennessee*, 1147.
3. Breckenridge Daybook, 201.

very muddy camp but were able to get much-needed rest.[4] On July 20, the patrol guard came into camp with five new prisoners and Breckenridge sent them to the guardhouse and their charges to the Provost Marshal.[5] On the 21st, he noted that his men were pleased at the news that they would be receiving arms that morning.[6] Breckenridge himself applied for a three-day leave in Memphis to pick up new clothing and arms for himself and his fellow officers.[7] He sent out a scout the next morning but heard nothing of Rebels in the territory.[8]

On July 23, Breckenridge received his much-needed leave of absence, apparently for the purpose of rest. It had been an eventful year organizing the First West Tennessee Cavalry. Despite being on leave, it is apparent that he felt the need to stay in touch and keep abreast of the comings and goings of the regiment, perhaps a wise decision. Prior to leaving, he issued an order that is found only in his journal.

> Head Qrt. 1st W.T.C.
> Lagrange, Tenn.
> July 23 [1863]
>
> Reg. Ord.
> No.
> Co[mpany]. Commanders will have 3 men and 1 non-Com[missioned] officer detached each day to act as stable guards and see that there is no nuisance committed about their tents and that the horses air [sic] kept tied up and each Co. will have a sink dug and bushes put around them.[9]
>
> By Ord[er]. of
> Wm. K.M. Breckenridge
> Lt. Col. 1st W.T.C.[10]

---

4. Ibid, 201–202.
5. Ibid, 202.
6. Ibid.
7. Ibid.
8. Ibid, 203.
9. The term "sink" is likely used here to refer to a latrine or place for human waste and raw sewage. It is not difficult to see how disease became a leading cause of death during the war.
10. Breckenridge Daybook, 200.

On July 23, Breckenridge mentions catching the train at the LaGrange Depot. The railroad depot at LaGrange was a station for the old Memphis & Charleston Railroad Company, chartered in Tennessee in 1846. By 1863, it had acquired the old LaGrange & Memphis Railroad Company which had also been chartered in 1846. This line ran through a number of stations, including LaGrange, Moscow, Rossville, Collierville, Forest Hill, and Germantown.[11] Breckenridge arrived in Memphis at 3:30 P.M. and received news that Hurst had gone out on a scout in the direction of Whiteville, Tennessee, with approximately one hundred men.[12]

One can only imagine Breckenridge walking the streets of Memphis while on leave, taking in the sights, sounds and smells of this river town. It was a hub of activity during the war and probably a welcome diversion after months spent in camp, on the trail of Confederate guerillas and irregulars and dealing with the frustrating behaviors of Hurst, Smith, and company. On July 24, he hears Federal soldiers referring to the open and free navigation of the Mississippi River now serving as a Union controlled river highway running right through the heart of the Southern Confederacy.

> [July] 24th [1863]
> This morning a transport boat arrived at the landing at Memphis just from New Orleans with a great many prisoners carrying them north from New Orleans the troops yelling for joy everywhere that they could go through the Southern Confederacy and never see a Rebel. I went out in the middle part of city to a uniform clothing store and from there to the provost marshal's office to get a pass to come to Camp but they were closed up and I have to wait until tomorrow.[13]

The following day, Breckenridge is summoned by Brigadier General Jeremiah Cutler Sullivan.[14] A native of Madison, Indiana, Sullivan (1830–1890) had served in the U.S. Navy from 1848 until 1854. He studied law afterward. When the war broke out, he assisted in recruiting and

11. Sulzer, *Ghost Railroads of Tennessee*, 177.
12. Breckenridge Daybook, 203.
13. Ibid.
14. Ibid, 204.

organizing the Sixth Indiana Volunteers with the rank of captain. After fighting at the battle of Philippi, Virginia, Sullivan became colonel of the 13th Indiana, seeing action at Rich Mountain. He served in the Shenandoah Valley campaign of 1862 and was commissioned a brigadier general before being sent west to command a brigade in Brigadier General William S. Rosecrans' Army of the Mississippi, where he led his troops at the battles of Iuka and Corinth.[15]

While meeting with General Sullivan, Breckenridge received an order for 75 pistols.[16] He went back to town and was given his pass for leave for the next day and picked up what he needed. Afterwards, he returned to his hotel and stayed there until the next morning.[17] It is likely that he needed this period of rest desperately. He had been constantly on duty since September 1862 and under very challenging circumstances. Still, even on leave, he was serving the needs of his regiment.

On July 26, Breckenridge left Memphis only to return to LaGrange and learn that his colleague and nemesis, Hurst, had been captured. Up to this point, Breckenridge had made no mention in his journal of the execution or murder of enemy combatants along the Pocahontas-Purdy Road. It is reasonable to speculate why enraged Confederate soldiers and their superiors—given this opportunity for immediate justice—would not have executed the captured Hurst as might be expected. The alleged acts would have been very fresh in their minds. This dramatic series of events and the erroneous news of Hurst's death must have had a sensational effect on his comrades in the 1st West Tennessee Cavalry. Indeed, his capture brought about some commotion.

> [July] 26th [1863]
> This morning I left Memphis at 8 o'clock A.M. for Lagrange where my men is camped and I arrived at Lagrange at ½ after 11 o'clock A.M. and had my things carried down to camp and when I got to camp I found out that Col. Hurst was captured and I went to Head Quarters and tried to get a scout to go and recapture him. But they would not let me have a Scout

---

15. Warner, *Generals in Blue*, 487–488. Biographical information for General Sullivan is taken from this work.

16. Breckenridge Daybook, 204.

17. Ibid.

then. They said wait until morning and see what report they would get from the Scout.

[July] 27th [1863]
This morning the report came that the Rebs had killed Col. Hurst and I went up to Head Quarters to see what they had learned about it there but they had not heard a word from him since his capture and then I came back to camp and had not been there long until I heard the boys yelling and I ran out of my tent and seen the Col. and all of his men coming. They had captured him back by the loss of one man; he got shot through the head and killed.[18]

Others wrote of this exciting event as well. The partisan Unionist newspaper, the Memphis *Bulletin*, reported on Hurst's capture for the first time on July 31, 1863.[19]

SAFETY OF COL. HURST—We are pleased to learn that Col. Hurst of the 1st Tennessee regiment of (Union) cavalry has made his escape from the guerillas, who it was reported had shot him. Col. Hurst is yet in the land of the living, and will yet make the prowling bands of rebel bush whackers who have been annoying the citizens feel his prowess. We are the more pleased to make this announcement as we hope to hear of his finishing up the notorious horse-thief, Richardson.[20]

On August 4, 1863, a letter was published in the *Bulletin* from a writer identified himself as E.L.H. from LaGrange, Tennessee. The letter, dated July 30, read:

In your issue of to-day it is stated that Col. Fielding Hurst, of the 1st West Tennessee Federal cavalry, was captured by guerillas, and shot by them when they became satisfied they could not hold him. The statement—thanks to the gallant

---

18. Ibid.
19. Memphis *Bulletin*, July 31, 1863.
20. Ibid.

Lieutenant Deford, is incorrect. He was captured by some *cowardly sneaks in Federal uniform*, but thanks to God, the gallant Deford, and his boys, they did not long enjoy the fruits of their treachery.

Lieut. Deford and ten men got on their trail, pursued them five miles, and dashed on to the cowardly sneaks when they were within three hundred yards of their den of one hundred strong, and wrested Col. Hurst from their satanic grasp.

His captors no doubt thirsted for his blood, but their thirst is unappeased. He yet lives–the pride of his friends, the terror of his foes. A braver man than he never followed Napoleon Bonaparte to the field of carnage–a nobler or more generous-hearted neighbor never drew the breath of life – yet he is marked for destruction by the demons infesting the *dark ravines* of West Tennessee. These same *cowardly fiends* of hell loaded Col. Hurst with chains and thrust him into a dungeon as they did the noble Brownlow, because he would not bow down at the shrine of their immaculate Jeff! He yet lives and is worth a hundred thousand dollars, and intends to sacrifice the last dollar and the last drop of his blood, ere he succumbs. He bows to none, save God and the flag of the Union.[21]

It is clear from the above "letter" that pro-Union newspaper editors were just as guilty of spreading propaganda as their pro-secessionist counterparts. On August 5, the Memphis *Bulletin* published yet another letter from LaGrange, dated July 31, this one authored by a different anonymous source known as "A Friend to the First."[22] It provides a more factual—though still highly editorialized—version of events.

Having noticed in yesterday's issue of the BULLETIN an item headed "Outrageous," wherein the death of Col. Fielding Hurst, commanding 1st Regiment West Tennessee Vol. Cavalry, is described, and that officer being still in the land of the living, I presumed that you would like to have the facts of the case. Col. Hurst having gone on a scout, was captured

21. Ibid, August 4, 1863.
22. Ibid, August 5, 1863.

on the 25th of the present month, four miles south west of Somerville. Knowing that his men would make strenuous efforts to retake him, he insisted upon riding slowly, advising his captors to shoot him if they did not approve of his mode of progress. This they dared not do, so they placed him between them, and let him have his own way about traveling, inwardly consoling themselves, however, with thoughts of how they would repay him when he got into Richardson's hands. But, alas! for them, they were destined to see their glorious visions dissolve into thin air before their eager eyes. The column had gone on, and Col. Hurst had dismounted and was talking to a lady while waiting for some men, whom he had sent in another direction, to join him. Instead of doing this, however, they rode on and rejoined the command. Colonel H. seeing this, was just turning from the lady to remount, when he was captured. Being on foot, and unarmed, his pistols being in his holsters, he fell an easy prey. It was in consequence of the mode of his capture that his command did not miss him for some time. When his loss became known it was almost impossible to restrain the men. To think that their beloved commander, who had lived and suffered with them through the long years of this cruel war, was at last captured by the enemy from whom he had only escaped by "strategy" to join Uncle Sam's noble band of warriors, was too much for them. Led by Capt. Harry [sic] Hodges, of company B, they galloped back with all possible speed, and the one who rode the swiftest horse was the best man then. After pursuing them about seven miles, Lieutenant DeFord and a Negro belonging to Capt. Thompson, of the same regiment, out-stripped the others and dashed up to the Colonel just as the guerillas were kindly informing him that he should see Richardson in five more minutes. The Negro, to use his own expressive language, "fired four times, and would have fired anudder, but she would'nt go." The Colonel had of course been disarmed, so to save himself from "eleven balls," he, with extraordinary presence of mind laid down on his horse, and turned into the woods. Just then Capt. Hodges came up, who, handing him a revolver, they all started in pursuit of the whilom captors. When the guerillas saw them, they ran as fast as their horses could carry them, shouting to Col. Hurst to "come on." He obeyed, taking his eight men, who had by this time come up, with him, however. On they dashed until they came within a few hundred yards of the rebel camp, containing about sixty men, who, yelling like demons, started in pursuit of the colonel and command. Col. Hurst, not being one of those valiant men who run one day to fight another, and yet not being able to compete with them in the open road, drew his command up on the summit of a hill. He had now been joined by about twenty men. Just as the guerillas were meditating as to whether it would be safe to make a charge, seven or eight more men came up, and seeing their brave Colonel once more at the head of his men, cheered lustily, making so much noise that the rebels thought the whole regiment was coming to avenge their Colonel's wrongs. Thinking therefore that discretion was the better part of valor, they precipitately retreated. The Colonel returned to camp uninjured. It was an occasion of rejoicing. Pleasure reigned supreme. There was but one thought – one great cause for their extravagant demonstrations of joy: "Our Colonel has returned."

Having read both Breckenridge's brief account and the editorialized accounts of the Memphis *Bulletin*, let us now examine other accounts of the incident. James T. Wolverton, a veteran of the First West Tennessee Cavalry, mentioned in an 1922 letter attached to his veteran's questionnaire that he possessed much information pertaining to the capture of Colonel Fielding Hurst and his rescue if he only had the time to write about it.[23] Whether or not he ever did record his account of this incident is not known. Historian Kevin D. McCann detailed this incident and the involvement of Captain Horry Hodges of Company B in the incident. Colonel Hurst allowed himself to be captured by two Confederate soldiers, a story which was related as well by seventy-three year old former Confederate soldier, Dr. Christopher Wood Robertson in 1922. Dr. Robertson opens the story:

23. Dyer and Moore, *Questionnaires*, 145.

> ...at one time, Hurst was passing south of Somerville and stopped to talk with Mrs. Lewis a widow and her daughter standing at their front gate. His command passed on and were met by C.A.S. Shaw and Hugh Nelson of my company [Company H, Fourteenth Tennessee Cavalry, C.S.A.], who were coming home to Somerville to get new horses, clothes, etc....they saw the Yankees first and dodged into the bushes until they passed and then coming on saw Hurst talking to the ladies...[Shaw and Nelson] dismounted and slipped up behind Hurst...he (Hurst) laughed and said no two rebels could take him...just as he said it Shaw and Nelson said surrender and Shaw took Hurst's pistols and buckled them on... made Hurst mount and started off with him...[24]

The factual, non-editorialized portions of the July 31, 1863, letter to the Memphis *Bulletin* do provide what seem to be accepted facts about the incident.

Upon his return, Hurst directed Breckenridge to continue his measures improving ongoing issues with the regiment. This seems like an unusual request from Hurst and Breckenridge gives no reasons for this turnabout in his journal. However, from his subsequent journal entries, it appears that drunkenness in the ranks had become a problem.

On July 28, Breckenridge noted in his journal that "the Col. has given me command of the Regiment to straighten it out."[25] Otherwise, he records a state of relative quiet on the 28th and 29th. Things changed on July 29 when the sutler brought whisky into camp and "several of the boys got tight." Breckenridge ordered him to stop selling the men so much whisky.[26] Many men were sick that morning and the sutler stopped selling whisky altogether.[27] Drunken soldiers could lead to a breakdown in order and discipline. Given the recent issue of prostitution in camp, Breckenridge wanted to move swiftly to eliminate any problems with drunkenness. The month ended peacefully on the 31st as the men cleaned

---

24. Ibid, 1865.
25. Breckenridge Daybook, 205.
26. Ibid.
27. Ibid.

up around camp and rubbed down their sabers and arms in case they are called upon to go on a scout.[28]

Things remained quiet for the regiment as the month of August began. Breckenridge reported that he had heard of no Rebels in their vicinity lately.[29] On August 2, the sutler returned to camp with whisky but he was ordered not to sell enough to make any man drunk.[30] The weather was wet and the men were laying up in their tents. Breckenridge likely feared another spell of drunkenness by his men resulting from idleness.[31] On August 3, Hurst received Special Order No. 66 requiring him to detail a "reliable and prudent" officer to ride toward the town of Spring Hill, Mississippi. The reliable and prudent officer he chose was Breckenridge.

>   Head Qrs. Chief of Cavalry
> Left Wing 16th Army Corps
> Lagrange, Tenn. Aug. 3rd 1863
>
> Special Order }
> No. 66   } IIII IIII – Col. Fielding Hurst
> Comdg. 1st West Tenn. Cavalry will detail a reliable and prudent officer with one hundred men well mounted to proceed at once to Spring Hill to watch the movements of a force reported to be advancing from Desoto and Ripley. They will give timely notice of any discovered movements of the Enemy and hold him in check until an arrangement may be made for his reception.
>   By Order of
>   J.K. Mizner
>   Chief of Cavalry
>   Thos. B. Weir
>   A.A.A.G.[32]

Breckenridge received his orders to ride with a detachment of men to Spring Hill on August 3. Though ordered to send one hundred men,

---

28. Ibid, 206.
29. Ibid.
30. Ibid.
31. Ibid.
32. Ibid, 206–207.

Hurst instead sent only half that number. The party does encounter Rebels, but it also meets a small party of women traveling to Memphis:

> This morning all is quiet, the sun is shining and everything looks beautiful But this evening it is cloudy and thundering, looks very much like we will have a storm. I received orders to take 50 men and go to Spring Hill near Ripley, Mississippi, And I got up my men and started and about to Grand Junction and stayed there a while and then we started out on the Spring Hill road and we had not went more than 15 miles when we met 7 of the Rebels but they got away and then we chased them about 1 mile but could not find them and I met 4 or 5 women with provisions, 5 days rations and after questioning them & some Union Citizens, I found out it was not intended for the Rebels for they was going to Memphis and was taking their Rations with them.[33]

The next day, Breckenridge records the capture of five Rebels on the road to Spring Hill. He also mentions the illness of Captain Elijah Roberts. Sickness plagued him that summer and he was given a twenty-day leave of absence. Shortly thereafter, the regimental surgeon, Thomas Williams, found him to be unfit for duty by reason of pneumonia. Roberts would be mustered out of the service on November 8, 1864, due to disability.[34]

The first ten days or so of the month were rainy, wet days for the men.[35] Things were quiet in the camp and they were expecting new arms and munitions to arrive any day.[36] Breckenridge himself awaited new "horse equipment" though he didn't mention what particular equipment. Up until August 10, the men had more to fear from battling rain and mud than the enemy. That day, Breckenridge put them to work cleaning camp

---

33. Ibid.

34. Compiled Service Record of Elijah Roberts. Compiled Service Records of Volunteer Union Soldiers Who Served in Organizations from the State of Tennessee. Records of the AGO, 1780s–1917. Record Group 94, Series Number M395, Roll 0059. National Archives and Records Administration, Washington, D.C.

35. Breckenridge Daybook, 206–208.

36. Ibid, 208.

and building sheds for their horses but also allowed them to indulge in a little peach brandy. By the 11th, the weather had become very hot and humid. The roads had dried up and were becoming dusty.[37]

On August 12, Breckenridge welcomed Lieutenant Webb back to camp from the hospital. He wrote that all the men were glad to see him feeling well and he had taken his company out on the drill field for the first time in two weeks. The regiment had its first excitement in many days when a man was arrested for trying to get out of the picket line by going around them. The patrol caught the man and put him in the guard house. The man's business was never disclosed. The weather had turned very dry and hot, a typical August in West Tennessee. The dust was raging and hot winds were stirring the dust up, making things more difficult and trying.[38]

By August 15, Breckenridge had been trying to get a scout out to the Tennessee River but his Chief of Cavalry wouldn't allow it until new arms arrived. The next day, Breckenridge reported that Captain Elijah Roberts had returned from the hospital and was not yet ready for duty. He felt a dress parade was in order and ordered one for 6:00 P.M. on August 17. All the men turned out; he noted that "if we all had arms we could make Rebs get out of our country in double quick."[39] Breckenridge made some interesting observations about citizens showing up in the camp August 18–19.

> [August] 18th [1863]
> Nothing of much importance going on in camp. It is cloudy and looks very much like raining. And the men are out drilling this morning. We had to furnish about 150 men for guards. I got 4 recruits today and there is several Citizens in camps but they will not volunteer and this morning orders was issued for all citizens to leave camp or volunteer in 24 hours.[40]

---

37. Ibid, 209.
38. Ibid.
39. Ibid, 201.
40. Ibid.

> Aug. 19th [1863]
>
> This morning the Citizens all leave camps. They left about 8 o'clock A.M. rather than volunteer. They all went out to lay in the woods from the Guerillas and let us fight for them.[41]

His observation is a keen one. He seemed to hold these citizens in disdain for not showing more courage.

On August 20, Breckenridge sent out foraging teams and put his men to drilling, ever remaining in a state of preparedness. His forage trains returned that evening with enough corn to last one day and night. He dispatched out more forage trains the next day. Colonel Mizner meanwhile left LaGrange traveling to Memphis to get permission to either stay at LaGrange or relocate to Corinth. The next three days, August 22–24, passed quietly. Breckenridge spent considerable time putting the men to keeping order in the camp and preparing their equipment in the event of action.[42] He also learned that the much-needed arms for his regiment were finally ready in Memphis. He made application to travel there and retrieve them, leaving on the noon train on the 24th. The weapons were drawn, inspected, and boxed up and he got his requisitions. According to Breckenridge, the city was quiet.[43]

On the morning of August 27, Breckenridge left Memphis on the 8:00 A.M. train for LaGrange and arrived at about 11:30. All was serene when he arrived, his men eagerly awaiting their arms. Outfitted better than they had been for some time, the next two days were peaceful. Breckenridge expected horses to arrive over land from Memphis.[44] On August 30–31, a group of ladies from Middle Tennessee arrived in the camp. They had been displaced by guerillas who plundered their possessions and those of other citizens. He arranged for them to stay at a boarding house in town.[45] Breckenridge's month ended without any apparent incident.

41. Ibid, 211.
42. Ibid, 211.
43. Ibid, 212.
44. Ibid.
45. Ibid, 213.

The LAST DUTY

September 1–October 15, 1863

The month of September 1863 found the First West Tennessee Cavalry encountering increased Rebel activity. In Breckenridge's journal entries, he used the term "Rebel" generally and did not differentiate between regular Confederate soldiers and Rebel guerillas. In any event, the regiment's activities picked up in September 1863 and Breckenridge recorded more consequential entries. Although the men did not always encounter the enemy, there were regular reports of them operating within the area. One concern that he had as the month began was the continued lack of sufficient arms for his men.

On September 1, the horses requested by Breckenridge finally arrived in camp and were issued to the men. However, the guns and arms had not yet arrived.[1] The next morning, news came that some thirty Rebels were out in the countryside near the Union camps, but his scouts could not find them.[2] Much time was being spent scouting for Rebel guerillas

1. Breckenridge Daybook, 213.
2. Ibid.

and Confederate troops as well as making themselves ready for any duty imposed upon them.

On September 4, Breckenridge recorded that a considerable force of some sixty Rebels were within about six miles of the camp.[3] He sent Major Thomas H. Boswell and about one hundred men out to find them. His orders were to follow these Rebels and take them if possible.[4] Boswell was a dark-complexioned young man of thirty years of age when he was sent on this scout. He was elected captain of Company D of the First West Tennessee Cavalry on August 9, 1862, and promoted to the rank of major on July 1, 1863.[5] According to Breckenridge, Rebels were encountered by Boswell's scout and chased.[6] However, the more important news of the day on September 5 may have been the delivery of firearms on the train from Memphis.[7] Breckenridge and the men had long awaited these much-needed arms. Given the many delays experienced by the regiment on a number of issues, the efficiency of the Army bureaucracy must be questioned.

On September 6, Breckenridge was ordered to send a detachment down to Salem, Mississippi, and Captain Horry Hodges was placed in command.[8] Hodges had served as captain of Company B since its organization in 1862. He played an integral part in rescuing Hurst from his Confederate captors back in July. Now he led some seventy-five men to Salem to determine Rebel positions in the area.[9]

Things were relatively quiet for the first half of September 1863. On the 13th, Breckenridge finally received his long-awaited commission.[10] He had waited more than a year to receive it. Though he made no men-

---

3. Ibid, 214.

4. Ibid.

5. Compiled Service Record of Thomas H. Boswell. Compiled Service Records of Volunteer Union Soldiers Who Served in Organizations from the State of Tennessee. Records of the AGO, 1780s–1917. Record Group 94, Series Number M395, Roll 0051. National Archives and Records Administration, Washington, D.C.

6. Breckenridge Daybook, 214.

7. Ibid.

8. Ibid.

9. Ibid.

10. Ibid, 197.

tion of it in his journal, he did record Hurst's letter of recommendation to Tennessee Military Governor Andrew Johnson.

> Head Quarters 1st W.T.C.[11]
> Bethel Tenn. Sept. 13th 1863
>
> His Excellency Andrew Johnson
> Military Governor of the State of Tennessee
>
> Reposing special confidence in the integrity and Patriotism of Wm. K.M. Breckenridge of Wayne County, Tennessee I do hereby nominate and appoint him Lieutenant Colonel First Regiment, West Tennessee Cavalry Volunteers raised under the act of Congress approved July 22nd, 1861, and I do hereby recommend him to the Honorable Andrew Johnson for commission to bear date from this day. Hoping this will meet your approval and that you will send his commission immediately.
>
> I remain yours
> Fielding Hurst
> Col. Comdg.
> 1st West Tenn Cav

Breckenridge made no journal entries or recorded any correspondence for the dates of September 7 through September 17. Information regarding his activities must be gleaned from the *Official Records*. It is known that he left camp for Toone's Station in Hardeman County, Tennessee. Breckenridge issued his report on the scout from Grand Junction, Tennessee, on September 25.

> HDQRS. SECOND BRIGADE, CAVALRY DIVISION
> *La Grange, Tenn., September 25, 1863*
>
> Lieut. J.K. Catlin,
> *Acting Assistant Adjutant-General, Cavalry Division*
> Lieutenant: I have the honor to transmit herewith the report of a scout to Toone's Station by this bridge, under Lieutenant-Colonel Breckenridge, Sixth Tennessee Cavalry.

11. Ibid.

Very respectfully, your obedient servant,

L.F. McCRILLIS,
Colonel, Commanding Brigade.

CAMP 6TH TENN CAV., Grand Junction, Tenn., Sept. 19, 1863

Sir: In pursuance to special orders, No. —, ordering all the available forces of the brigade to advance to Toone's Station, where 800 of the enemy were reported to be locating, at 3 P.M. on the 13th of September, 1863, Maj. W.J. Smith, with a detachment of 200 men from the Sixth Tennessee Cavalry, was ordered to proceed by the most direct route to Bolivar, Tenn., to take possession of the ferry across the Hatchie River, and hold it until he was joined by the remainder of the brigade.

At 6 p.m. I left camp at La Grange in command of the brigade *en route* for Toone's Station. I reached the Hatchie River at sunrise on the 14th, and had the entire command crossed over by 9 A.M. I was then in 4 miles of the reported position of the enemy. I so disposed of the troops under my command as to surround their position, which was done about 11.30 A.M., but the enemy was not to be found. The citizens reported to me that Newsom, with about 500 men under his command, had abandoned his position at that place on the evening previous, and went off in the direction of Jack's Creek, Tenn., by way of Clover Creek and Medon Station.

Finding the enemy too far in the advance for immediate pursuit, I decided to proceed on after them as far as Clover Creek, and camp for the night. I sent two companies, under the command of Captain Hodges, out on the trail of the enemy with instructions to go as far as Medon Station, and to ascertain, if possible, the direction taken or location of the enemy. The most reliable information I could obtain from that place was that Newsom's command had been divided about half proceeding in the direction of Jackson, Tenn., and the other half in the direction of Jack's Creek, Tenn.

And on the 15th, I moved with the command about 8 miles on the Jackson road, to where it was intersected with the

Denmark and Mifflin Road. I then decided that farther pursuit was vain, as we had left camp with but one day's rations.

Turning my course in the southeast direction, with the Sixth Tennessee Cavalry thrown out on the left, with instructions to reach Pocahontas at 6 P.M. on the 16th. The Seventh Tennessee Cavalry was thrown out to the right with the same instructions, covering a space of about 6 miles on each side of the road. The brigade was composed of the Third, Ninth, and Eleventh Illinois Cavalry, and the Sixth and Seventh Tennessee Cavalry, and I, with the Third, Ninth, and Eleventh Illinois Cavalry, proceeded to Medon Station, and from thereon to Montezuma, and when in about 5 miles of Montezuma the advance guard met up with a squad of the enemy and killed 8 of them and took 14 prisoners, and the remainder of them made their escape through the woods and brush. I then proceeded on to Montezuma with the prisoners and camped for the night, and the next morning [the 17th], about 6 o'clock, I proceeded to Pocahontas with the command. I got there about 4.30 P.M. and camped for the night. The Sixth and Seventh Tennessee Cavalry rejoined the command at about 6.30 P.M. The next morning [the 18th], about 8 o'clock, I left Pocahontas for camp at La Grange, Tenn. I did not come up with any more of the enemy, but there are several bands of them over the country, plundering and taking everything that is left in the country for the Union families to live upon.

I arrived at La Grange about 4 A.M., thus closing the expedition.

W.K.M. BRECKENRIDGE.

[Col. L.F. MCCRILLIS, *Commanding Cavalry Brigade*.]

Breckenridge is now identifying the regiment as the Sixth Tennessee Cavalry, whereas previously he had referred to his unit as the First West Tennessee Cavalry. In July 1863, the companies comprising the regiment had been redesignated as the U.S. Sixth Tennessee Cavalry.[12] Yet in his journal entries from July 1863 to September 19, 1863, he continued to call it the First West Tennessee Cavalry. However, from this

12. *Tennesseans in the Civil War, Part 1*, 334.

point forward, the unit will be referred to in this work as the U.S. Sixth Tennessee Cavalry.

The various regiments camped for the night in Montezuma, Tennessee. This village was the hometown of Dr. Hugh Hollis and Thomas W.S. Morgan as well as the site of the mercantile firm Hollis & Cason. Given the allegations and controversy a couple of months earlier, one can only imagine the stir caused by their presence in this village of stalwart secessionists. Yet this stopover appeared to be peaceful and uneventful. Breckenridge made no observations in his journal and his report contains no mention of any strife or irregularity which might have arisen. Again, this casts doubt on the earlier allegations.

Following the excitement of September 13–18, the regiment enjoyed a few peaceful days the following week. The men were primarily concerned with moving their camp from LaGrange to Grand Junction. The new camp was not ideal. As the men put up their tents and cleaned up the area, they discovered the water was not fit for use and had to carry their water from a source about one-half mile from the actual campsite.[13] With the exception of hospital tents and stores, the men got their tents erected on September 20.[14]

The next morning, Breckenridge was ordered to put his blacksmiths to work shoeing horses and preparing themselves to scout towards the Tennessee River.[15] The next three days were quiet and activities in camp were routine. On September 24, a small scout went out to Holly Springs but returned having seen no enemy troops.[16] After a few days' rest, word was received that some of the regiment would be sent on a scout down into Mississippi. Lieutenant William Chandler Webb, a native of Middle Tennessee, was selected to lead the men.[17] They had been expecting to head east to the Tennessee River but were disappointed with rumors of a possible order to march to Iuka, Mississippi, instead.[18]

On September 26, Lieutenant Webb and forty men under his command traveled some fifteen to twenty miles down into Mississippi to scout

13. Ibid.
14. Ibid.
15. Ibid, 220.
16. Ibid.
17. Ibid, 221.
18. Ibid.

for Rebel activity.[19] They captured a lone Confederate soldier, two guns, four cartridge boxes, and two horses. Finding no other enemy troops, they returned to camp.[20] The next day, fifty men were sent to Memphis to receive fresh horses. Captain Nathan M.D. Kemp was chosen to lead them. Kemp had joined the newly formed First West Tennessee Cavalry on September 11, 1862, and was made a captain upon his enlistment.[21] A tall man, standing six feet, he was a native of McNairy County.[22] There were a number of sick in camp and they were sent to the hospital in Memphis, some by train.[23] On the evening of September 28, Breckenridge received word that the regiment was under marching orders but he wasn't sure of the veracity of those reports.[24]

On September 28, Breckenridge penned a report in his journal that may also be found in the *Official Records*. It pertains to the events of July 14 at Jackson, Tennessee. There are slight differences between them. The report demonstrates the importance that Breckenridge appears to place on the individual property rights of citizens. The statements of Lieutenants Samuel Lewis and Edward L. Harden further illustrate that Breckenridge's viewpoint was exactly opposite of Fielding Hurst and William Jay Smith. However, Lewis indicates that Hurst also gave orders to refrain from interrupting "anything in town." Breckenridge's statement as written by him in his journal on September 28 is as follows:

Grand Junction, Tenn., September 28, 1863
Statement of Lt. Col. Breckinridge in reference to Col. Hatch's fight at Jackson.[25]

---

19. Ibid.
20. Ibid.
21. Compiled Service Record of Nathan M.D. Kemp. Compiled Service Records of Volunteer Union Soldiers Who Served in Organizations from the State of Tennessee. Records of the AGO, 1780s–1917. Record Group: 94, Series Number M395, Roll 0055. National Archives and Records Administration, Washington, D.C.
22. Ibid.
23. Breckenridge Daybook, 221.
24. Ibid.
25. Ibid, 224. All words contained in brackets are those found in Breckenridge's copy or draft. The same communication has been substituted in the official draft.

Our regiment was in the rear, and, after crossing the river. I was ordered to take charge of all the wagons and lead horses, as the men was mostly dismounted, and as the command advanced, I moved up the lead stock until I got on the edge of town. I there got an Order from an orderly to take charge of the prisoners and picket the town. I then rode up to the court-house, where the prisoners were, and while there a citizen come to me and said that the citizens was a carrying out whisky by the bucket-full and giving it to the men, and I rode over to where they was and had the whiskey all spilt that I could find. I then rode to where my reserve was and sent Lieutenant Lewis with ten men to destroy all the liquor they could find. In a short time, he come to me and said that the men were breaking into the houses and I told him to go and stop them and to arrest every man he found in a house. He then went off, and in a short time returned and told me of Mrs. A.A. Newman's millinery shop or store, and I told him to put a guard over the house. There was a good many stragglers around town, and after dark me and an officer of the Command, I don't know his name or regiment, heard a noise at a door, and started to see about it, and on the way I found about 30 men, I suppose, in and in front of a store. He said they belonged to his regiment, and I ordered them out, the owner then shut the door and we went on and in a few minutes returned; they was trying to get in again. I sent the officer to send them off, and I spent the most of my time that night in running from place to place trying to keep everything quiet and seeing to the wounded. And in the morning, when Col. Hatch returned to town, the men broke open houses and taken] all they wanted, and took buggies and wagons and loaded them with goods and boots, and so forth. I stood in the court-house yard and saw a portion of his staff pass, and nearly every man had something that had been taken out of this place.

W.K.M. BRECKENRIDGE
Lieutenant Colonel, Sixth Tennessee Cavalry

Addenda

Statement of Lieut. Samuel Lewis, Sixth Tennessee Cavalry

Grand Junction, Tenn., October 4, 1863.

I was in command of my company, and was held back in charge of some prisoners. When the regiment advanced I moved up into the edge of town. Colonel Breckenridge being informed by a citizen that the citizens were giving our men whisky, Colonel Breckenridge ordered me to take some men and proceed to all suspicious places in town and destroy all the whisky I could find; and while I was searching for whisky, I went into one millinery store belonging to a widow lady, and found her very much excited about the soldiers carrying out her goods. She demanded of me a guard. I went to Colonel Breckenridge and related her circumstances to him, and he told me to give her a guard. I then advanced to the court-house and took charge of the prisoners, with James J. Smith, lieutenant of the same company. I remained there all night, writing paroles for prisoners. Next morning I went out some distance north of the court-house, where the wounded were, and fell in company with Colonel Hurst. We had a conversation about the way the soldiers were treating the citizens. He ordered me to go and tell my men not to interrupt anything in town. As I was returning to my command, I saw Colonel Hatch's men, of the Third Michigan, or the Second Iowa Cavalry, breaking open store-house doors and carrying out goods of almost every description.

Samuel Lewis,
Lieutenant[,] Company A, Sixth Tennessee Cavalry Volunteers (First West Tennessee Cavalry, USA)

Statement of Lieut. Edward L. Harden, Sixth Tennessee Cavalry

Grand Junction, Tenn., October 4, 1863

In reference to Colonel Hatch's fight at Jackson, Tenn., on the 14th of July, 1863, I was in command of my company that day, and was held back to support one of our guns, and remained there until the fight was over. When I was ordered back to town it was getting dark. About the time I returned to town, one company of the Third Michigan Cavalry was there, and was breaking open houses and taking what they wanted. I saw them taking goods out of the houses myself. Colonel Breckenridge ordered me to go and stop them, and I went and ordered them away, and they went off. But just as soon as I went away they went back to breaking open others, and taking what they could carry. I went, then, and told the captain commanding them, and he turned round and yelled out to them to take those horses away from the doors, and not let them kick them down, and that was all he would say to them. The next morning, when Colonel Hatch and his command came through, his men would stop all along the line, and run to the houses and take what they wanted; and at Mrs. A.A. Newman's millinery shop I saw the Third Michigan Cavalry carrying the things out and burning them, and taking what they wanted with them.

Edward L. Harden,
Company F, Sixth Tennessee Cavalry

The statements of Lewis and Harden confirm the steps that Breckenridge took to protect the rights of the citizens of Jackson. Despite the actions of other Union Army regiments, it is clear that he expected the his men to refrain from looting and unnecessary destruction.

Interestingly, the *West Tennessee Whig*, a Jackson newspaper, published a story on Mrs. A.A. Newman's predicament in its December 2, 1865, edition.

Mrs. A.A. Newman.

This lady was engaged in the millinery business in this city for several years before the war, and after the Federals occupied the place she continued her business the night after the fight here between Col. Jeff. Forrest and Col. Hatch. That night, Col. Hurst's regiment was placed in guard of the town, when Mrs. Newman's establishment was entered by Federal soldiers and all her goods destroyed, worth some five thousand dollars. She then went to Memphis and laid her complaint before Gen. Hurlbut, who promised to have the pay of Hurst's regiment stopped until she was [paid]. Thereupon Hurst returned to Jackson, and with a threat to burn the town, unless the citizens paid him, by [...] day, something over five thousand dollars, and thus extorted that amount from a defenceless [sic] town, [...] citizens had previously taken the oath prescribed by Gen. Logan, the Federal commander, and according to all honorable rules of war, a right to be protected by the Federal Army. Anyhow Hurst got the money from the people of Jackson, and Mrs. Newman has never received a cent. Such was the conduct of soldiers fighting, as they said, for "the best government the world ever saw."

We are pleased to announce to the ladies of Jackson and the surrounding country that Mrs. Newman has returned and opened a new millinery House. She well merits a liberal patronage.[26]

The incident of extorting an equal sum of money from the people of Jackson as Hurst and the regiment were to be penalized for the damage to Mrs. Newman's business in interesting. This extortion took place in early 1864, some three to four months after the death of Breckenridge.[27]

Breckinridge wrote to Col. W.L. Lathrop on or about September 28. It is not know the exact background or purpose of this letter other than

---

26. Jackson TN *West Tennessee Whig*, December 2, 1865.

27. The final chapter of this work will further examine the potential connection between his death and the subsequent activities of the regiment he helped to establish.

to speculate that some question had arisen regarding some firearms that had come into the possession of the regiment.

>Head Qrt. 6th Tenn Cav.
>Lagrange, Tenn.
>
>Col. W.L. Lathrop
>   Sir, in obedience to an order of Sept. 20th, [18]63
>I wish to explain as well as I can the position I am in in reference to some old arms that I have before I went in to the service and the time the Rebels burnt the boats on Tennessee River in '62. I got those old guns and took some citizens and went down to see about the burning and when I come back to Hamburg the arms was put in the armory there and in a few days the rebels burnt the ferry and captured the ord. sergt. [sergeant] and his crew and 2 guns and he had all the papers showing what I had got before and I then taken some of the guns and went down to try and recapture them and the guns but couldn't and had to leave some of the arms on the gun boat Robb and some was left at Hamburg and when I returned the [...][28] and I have never been able to learn what had become of the Segt. as I had forgotten his name and the Rebels got my memorandum book.[29] I have a piece of the guns here and have tried at every post that I have been at to turn them over but have failed so far. Those arms never were invoiced to me. If you can give me any information about the above guns I will take it as a great favor. The guns were picked up on the Shiloh battlefield.
>
>>Yours very respectfully
>>Wm. K.M. Breckinridge
>>Lt. Col. 6th Tenn. Cav.[30]

This correspondence may not have been written until this time because Breckenridge was preoccupied with his various duties and now it

28. A portion of the sentence is illegible in the Breckenridge Daybook.

29. Breckenridge mentions that Rebels have taken his Memorandum Book. Perhaps he had more than one, but he does not elaborate.

30. Breckenridge Daybook, 225.

is apparent that his health is failing. He was using his downtime to catch up on reports and correspondence. In fact, he was not the only person sick in camp. There were a fair number of men who had to be sent to the Army hospital in Memphis, perhaps Washington Hospital. Although in failing health, Breckenridge continued to make strenuous efforts to do his duty. On September 29, he mentioned passing trains full of Union soldiers on their way to aid General William S. Rosecrans. The regiment's camp was in LaGrange, Tennessee. It was located on the Memphis and Charleston Railroad, an east-west line that was essential for shuttling both men and supplies to their needed destinations.[31]

On September 30, Breckenridge wrote that he was mending slowly.[32] It is not known exactly what was wrong with him. Neither his journal nor his military records divulge that information. It became obvious that his health was declining in October. The first three days of the month found the U.S. Sixth Tennessee Cavalry cooperating with the U.S. Seventh Tennessee Cavalry. On the 2nd, Breckenridge wrote that three hundred men were ordered to accompany Colonel Issac R. Hawkins and his regiment to Union City, Tennessee.[33] They were ordered back to camp, however, because of concerns that the enemy was nearby and close to the camp itself.[34]

On October 4, it appears for the first time that Breckenridge's illness was severe enough that he could not leave his room. This implies that he was staying at a home or boarding house in LaGrange. He writes that Hurst was leading a scout in the direction of Holly Springs, Mississippi.

Despite being infirmed and confined to his sickbed, Breckenridge recorded a rather detailed account of Hurst's scouting activities in his journal. After scouting for the enemy in north Mississippi, Hurst heads back toward the camps at LaGrange on October 7. It is approximately thirteen miles from Lamar, Mississippi, to Grand Junction, Tennessee. The road between the two settlements lay along the route of the Mississippi Central Railroad. Grand Junction was the junction between the Mississippi Central Railroad and the Memphis and Charleston Railroad. Breckenridge mentioned the order to return was given by a Colonel McCrillis. Colonel

31. Ibid, 221.
32. Ibid, 222.
33. Ibid.
34. Ibid.

Lafayette McCrillis was the commander of the Second Cavalry Brigade in the District of Corinth, which was composed of the Third, Fourth, and Fifth Illinois Cavalry. He was brevetted as a brigadier general for services rendered during the war though never appointed to full rank.

Breckenridge reports in his journal the events of October 5–8:

> Oct. 5th [1863]
> This morning the command stopped and fed their horses and rested about 1 hour & ½ and from there it proceeded on to Cold Water & there encamped for the night the men were all nearly worn out for they had not been out of the Saddle from 10 o'clock on the fourth till 5 o'clock [on the 5th] So they put out their pickets and rested for the night.[35]
>
> October 6th [1863]
> This morning about 6 o'clock the enemy attacked our pickets and drove them in after firing several rounds. Then Col. Hurst ordered one Company…A…of the Regiment to cross the creek and dismount and hold the Rebels in check until the battery come up. The Battery soon came and the dismounted Company "A" was thrown to the left and the forces drawn up in line before the enemy as they were forming the firing commenced and after the enemy got within about 100 yards of our Battery it turned loose at them but the Rebs kept their lines well closed up and undertook to charge but were repulsed. The fight commenced at 5 minutes after 8 o'clock A.M. and ended at 10 o'clock A.M. They found that the enemy (Rebs) outnumbered them about 4 to 1 and they commenced a retreat after finding out the Rebs was flanking them. The retreat commenced at 10 o'clock A.M. and retreated to […].[36]

It should be pointed out that Breckenridge's writing in his October 7 entry is somewhat confusing. From the first-person language he employs, it gives the impression that he was present though that doesn't seem plau-

---

35. Ibid, 223.
36. Ibid, 226. The last portion of the sentence is illegible.

sible given the previous two entries. Still, he will later make statements that again seem to imply he was present in Salem as well.

> October 7th [1863]
> This morning Col. Hurst in command of our regiment left Lamar by order of Col. McCrillis[37] for camps at Grand Junction. Had some little Skirmishing on the way. We were in the rear of the enemy and would dash on them and fire a few rounds and then fall back on the account of the Enemy outnumbering us 4 to 1. We got to camps about ten o'clock A.M. and got dinner and then some of the men lay down to Sleep but at 2 o'clock was ordered out again. They marched about 9 miles and lay over for the night.

As with his journal entry of October 7, Breckenridge employs language in his subsequent entry that is interesting. Given that he had spent so much time and effort building and organizing the First West Tennessee Cavalry (now the U.S. Sixth Tennessee Cavalry) and his frustrating relations with Hurst, he now refers to Hurst "with his regiment." He mentions an engagement at Salem, a small settlement in northern Mississippi now located in present-day Benton County.[38] Salem was settled in 1836 and incorporated by the Mississippi Legislature in 1837.[39] It was a small yet thriving village of influential and wealthy planters with an academy for young ladies, two hotels, and more than a dozen places of business.[40] Among those who were raised and lived nearby was Confederate General Nathan Bedford Forrest.[41] Breckenridge wrote:

> October 8th [1863]
> This morning about 4 o'clock Col. Hurst with his Regiment was ordered on the advance and moved on Salem and was attacked about ½ mile of Salem at about 10 o'clock A.M. Comp.

---

37. Warner, *Generals in Blue*, 589.

38. Franklin L. Riley, *Extinct Towns and Villages of North Mississippi* (Oxford: Mississippi Historical Society, 1902), 5:320–321.

39. Ibid.

40. Ibid.

41. Ibid.

"A" of our Reg. was dismounted and advanced up the hill to the enemy's advance then the balance of the Reg. followed. They fought about 1 hour with small arms and artillery when the Rebs left with our whole command after them through the town but they were too strong for us & our forces fell back ½ mile and Rebs attacked them again & the 9th Ill. Infantry pitched in to them and then (in about fifteen minutes) the whole Cav. force —— them 3 hours and our Reg. was ordered to charge on the enemies right [wing] & when they charged the enemy charged them but our boys broke their line and repulsed them and then our boys began to shell them out of the Hollows no sooner than done our boys followed on after them and dismounted and fought them until 4 o'clock. None killed out of our regiment but Maj. Boswell was wounded in the Shoulder very badly. Lt. Deford of Co. H wounded in the thigh very badly. Nine commissioned officers and men were wounded slightly, some very bad making in all ____ wounded of our Reg.[42]

Breckenridge mentions the injuries to Major Thomas H. Boswell during the fight at Salem. Boswell, in fact, was wounded grievously. According to the regimental surgeon, Dr. Thomas Williams, his wounds were:

...a gunshot wound to the right-shoulder joint, received at Battle of Salem, Miss., Oct. 8th, 1863, by Carbine ball passing through joint from front, and out of back of same shoulder. Ball entry inner edge of Deltoid muscle (in front) and passing through neck of Humerus, completely shattering head and neck of said bone, passing out with direction of backwards, downwards, and outwards, producing anchyloses (since recovery)...[43]

---

42. Though the last portion of the sentence is illegible, the names Col. H[urst] and Smith can be discerned.

43. Boswell Compiled Service Record.

Ultimately, Boswell's wounds would end in his military career in September 1864.[44]

Breckenridge continued to make entries in his journal, but also disclosed that he was still sick and confined to his bed. It was apparent that he made the ride himself to Grand Junction. It is not known if he was taken by ambulance or if he managed to ride on his own. His writing and his actual situation create a certain amount of confusion about the events. Still, Breckenridge was engaged and keeping up with events. On October 9, he left an unidentified camp and traveled to Grand Junction, arriving at 9:00 A.M.[45] The wounded had been taken there as well and he noted they were all sleeping or resting as they had little sleep for a week.[46] In the meantime, orders were received that the regiment was to be ready to march at daylight the next morning, October 10, with five days' rations.[47] Breckenridge wrote:

> ...The most of the men are wearied nearly down for they have been riding nearly all the time for 7 or 8 days. This evening we received orders to be ready to march at one minute's warning with five days rations. I am still sick and confined to my bed.[48]

The march did not occur at daylight. Instead, the men were instructed to be prepared to march at 1:00 P.M. Just as they were ready, new orders told them they would march at 7:30 A.M. on the 11th on the Ripley Road.[49]

Breckenridge was still confined to his bed the next day. It is likely that he was staying at either The Percey Hotel or The Railroad Hotel (later renamed The Commercial Hotel) in Grand Junction. The Percey Hotel, assuming it was still in business in 1863 and operating under the same name, was the site of a riot and insurrection on August 2, 1861.[50] The Railroad Hotel was a three-story brick structure with a cupola above the

---

44. Ibid.
45. Breckenridge Daybook, 228.
46. Ibid.
47. Ibid.
48. Breckenridge never divulges the nature of his illness, but it is apparent that it is both enduring and serious.
49. Breckenridge Daybook, 228.
50. "Grand Junction Insurrection," Memphis *Daily Appeal*, August 2, 1861.

third floor. It was constructed in or about 1858 and also served as a railroad depot. There were sitting rooms as well as a baggage room, dining room, and barber shop, all on the first floor. The rooms were located on the second and third floors.[51]

As his life faded, Breckenridge took a more tolerant view of Hurst. He gave a far more patriotic impression of his rival on October 11:

> This morning 8 o'clock I saw the regiment pass by my room at the Hotel in command of Major Smith.[52] They all seemed to be merry and willing to fight. Before they left their camps, Col. Hurst said he did not want any man to go that did not want to fight for his country but every man said they was willing to die for it and they all went that was able to get about and had a horse to ride and some got up out of their beds sick and said they would go with them if they had to be hauled back in the wagons.[53]

This would be the final entry of Breckenridge's journal. He mentions being sick in his bed and confined to his hotel. There are no further entries and no further correspondence or accounts by him. Breckenridge's story ends here. Or does it?

---

51. Cheri LaFlamme, *Landscape and Memory at Grand Junction, Tennessee: A Reconnaissance Resource Survey*. MTSU Center for Historic Preservation, May 2011, 34–35. http://www.sitemason.com/files/bPKvTO/Grand%20Junction%20Resource%20Study.pdf

52. William J. Smith

53. Breckenridge Daybook, 229.

THE RAILROAD HOTEL, ONE OF TWO POSSIBLE HOTELS IN GRAND JUNCTION WHERE LT. COL. WILLIAM K.M. BRECKENRIDGE MAY HAVE DIED.

DRIFTING *into* HISTORY'S SHADOWS

As William K.M. Breckenridge penned his last journal entry on October 11, 1863, one wonders how the next four days—the last ones of his life—were spent. He left no record in his journal. He never left Grand Junction, dying there from an unspecified disease on October 15.

According to available records, he was first buried at Saltillo, Tennessee, in what was termed the "citizens burying ground 2½ miles Southwest of the village."[1] The burial ledgers note that he was laid to rest in a "metallic case" with his name "engraved on the coffin top."[2] Breckenridge remained there for some time until his body was exhumed

---

1. Burial Ledgers, The National Cemetery Administration, Washington, D.C. Original records transferred to NARA: Burial Registers, compiled 1867–2006, documenting the period 1831–2006. ARC ID 5928352. Records of the Department of Veterans Affairs, 1773–2007. Record Group 15. National Archives and Records Administration, Washington, D.C.

2. Ibid.

Lt. Col. William K.M. Breckenridge Tombstone
Author's Collection

and reinterred at the National Cemetery at Pittsburg Landing in what is now Shiloh National Military Park.

Ultimately, the death of Breckenridge cast him into obscurity. Worse still, he fell back into the shadow of Fielding Hurst. His death on October 15, 1863, silenced him. No longer was there a dissenting voice within the leadership of the Sixth Tennessee Cavalry. His absence was felt in the coming months. An examination of the activities and history of the regiment from August 1862 until October 1863, compared with what transpired from the time of Breckenridge's death until the end of the war, offers a stark and drastic contrast.

While Breckenridge exercised leadership, the incidents of destruction and what was tantamount to war crimes were isolated to a few scattered incidents, all of which Hurst, Smith, or their most trusted subordinates were directly involved. Given the evidence that the alleged Mile Marker murders never occurred, looting and burning were the major crimes committed by Hurst and Smith. Further, each of these incidents was addressed by Breckenridge both personally and with his and Hurst's superiors. Breckenridge remained in contact with the Union Army command; with his guidance, the mission of the regiment appeared clear and in keeping with the larger goals of the 16th Army Corps.

But now Breckenridge was dead. One might be bold enough to say that as his spirit fled his body, the guiding conscience of the regiment departed as well. Now the men who had been forced to contend with Breckenridge's sense of duty and answer for their illegal actions when not in keeping with the true purpose of the Union Army found themselves in total control of the Sixth Tennessee Cavalry. Soon, the dangers in that situation would make themselves evident as well.

Breckenridge's death allowed Hurst to make changes to regimental command that suited him far more than the previous arrangement. He immediately elevated William Jay "Petticoat" Smith to the rank of Lieutenant Colonel to replace Breckenridge on October 16, 1863.[3] That would certainly have seemed extremely perverse to Breckenridge. Other promotions followed, including Captain Orlando Shearer to the rank of major, Adjutant Stanford L. Warren to captain of Company I, and Elijah J. Hodges to the rank of adjutant.[4]

3. Compiled Service Record of William J. Smith.
4. McCann, *Hurst's Wurst*, 48.

Within days of Breckenridge's death, the course was being set for the Sixth Tennessee's historical reputation as a rogue group. Well aware of Hurst's and Smith's past behaviors, Major General Hurlbut ordered Hurst to confine his operations to the area east of the Memphis and Ohio Railroad to suppress Confederate guerilla and conscription activities.[5] Hurlbut took the added precaution of warning Hurst that pillaging or looting by the men or officers of the Sixth Tennessee Cavalry would not be tolerated. Neither would the scattering of men from the regiment be tolerated, likely a direct order intended to prevent sending men like Walker, McIntyre, and others out on their nefarious missions.[6]

More particularly, Major General Hurlbut issued Special Orders, No. 264:

> The Sixth Tennessee Cavalry, Colonel Hurst, will move upon Bolivar and Jackson, covering the country east of the Memphis and Ohio Railroad, and suppressing with all necessary severity the guerilla and conscripting parties south of Trenton. They will draw supplies from the country giving receipts, to be settled at the close of the war. No plundering or pillaging by men or officers will be allowed. Colonel Hurst will report weekly, through the commanding officer at LaGrange, to the chief of cavalry. The men of this regiment will not be permitted to scatter, but will move actively in organized force...[7]

On November 1, 1863, Brigadier General Grenville Dodge—who it can be reasonably surmised did not trust Hurst loose anywhere—suggested to Hurlbut that the Sixth Tennessee remain at LaGrange to prevent the enemy from cutting the Union communication lines.[8] Dodge explained his thoughts:

---

5. Ibid.
6. Ibid, as to Hurlbut's order itself.
7. *O.R., Series I, Volume 31, Part 1*, 750–751.
8. *O.R., Series I, Volume 31, Part 3*, 12.

> Corinth, November 1, 1863.
>
> Major-General Hurlbut:
>
> I am informed that the Sixth and Seventh West Tennessee Cavalry move to-morrow. Would it not be well to hold them there until I get some of the rolling-stock back to Memphis, or until I cut loose at Iuka, so that I can have communication with you until the last moment? I don't think, if a show is kept up by our cavalry in active scouting, that the enemy will try us for several days. But if we leave such long gaps the guerillas will do the damage.
>
> G.M. Dodge,
> Brigadier-General.[9]

Keeping Hurst within sight was considered the safest option for all, but Hurst would have none of it. In fact, he abandoned his assigned position and he and his men could not be located.[10] They had struck out on their own. Here begins the true deterioration of the regimental order that Breckenridge had worked so hard to establish and maintain. Less than one week later after apparently having heard nothing from Hurst, Major General Hurlbut wrote to Brigadier General J.D. Stevenson, telling him to "try and find where Hurst is and get him under your command." He then informed Stevenson that both Hurst's Sixth Tennessee and Hawkins's Seventh Tennessee regiments were behaving badly.[11] Although both Hurst and Hawkins were in danger of removal from their regiments by Hurlbut, they were saved ultimately by Military Governor Andrew Johnson, who basically rewarded them for their early ability to raise troops among the Unionists in West Tennessee.[12]

So, what does all this mean? The implications are simple. First, within two weeks of Breckenridge's death, Hurst was already straying from the direct commands of his superiors. He was going rogue with no one in the regiment to check or influence his behaviors. Second, the old behaviors that Breckenridge had struggled so hard to inhibit and discipline were reemerging, again largely unchecked.

9. Ibid.
10. *O.R., Series I, Volume 31, Part 3*, 82.
11. Ibid.
12. McCann, *Hurst's Wurst*, 49.

Hurst began regularly to be out of touch with his superiors.[13] In early February 1864, he went back to Jackson, Tennessee, and extorted more than $5,000.00 from the town's citizens to cover the penalty imposed upon him by Major General Hurlbut for the losses Hurst and his men caused Mrs. A.A. Newman.[14] Afterward, he and his command looted and burned sections of Brownsville before returning to Jackson and burning some fourteen buildings in downtown Jackson despite having already been paid off by the citizens.[15] These war crimes—as they cannot be couched in any other term—came to the attention of Major General Nathan Bedford Forrest. Yet there were more serious allegations, resembling those previously alleged by Wisdom. Those allegations would be new charges of murder, this time of some seven individuals: six soldiers and one teenage civilian.

Aside from extortion and alleged murder, Hurst continued a pattern of following his own course. That course involved direct insubordination. The most serious instance was his failure to follow certain orders by Brigadier General Benjamin Grierson, which led to Hurst's court martial following the Sixth Tennessee Cavalry's humiliating defeat at Bolivar, Tennessee, by Confederate forces under the leadership of Colonel James J. Neely.[16] That defeat and Hurst's insubordination would cost him his command and his career as a soldier. In fact, it could be argued that the Sixth Tennessee's ultimate decline as an effective unit began with the death of its conscientious lieutenant colonel, William K.M. Breckenridge.

Missing since October 1863 was Breckenridge's sense of responsibility in the regiment's leadership, but that absent voice has been most noticeable and damaging to the course of history as we have known it. Without his journal, the regiment's legacy and that of Fielding Hurst was missing vitally important information and a meaningful viewpoint. That could not be helped. Now, with his voice freed from the prison of anonymity and the murky fog of history, a new light can be shed upon a subject many thought closed. In the end, perhaps the justice sought by Breckenridge in life has been attained in a most poetically just fashion.

13. *O.R., Series I, Volume 31, Part 3*, 331-332.
14. Williams, *Historic Madison*, 178–179.
15. Ibid.
16. McCann, *Hurst's Wurst*, 76.

This work would never have been written but for the release of Breckenridge's journal as contained in his Daybook. It provided a catalyst to bring about its study and ultimately a study of the man himself. Breckenridge's place in history had been tenuous and long hidden. Like an unknown presence in the shadows of a mystery, Breckenridge slowly emerges as the quietly heroic gentleman soldier simply doing his duty. In the course of transcribing his journal in full for a study of the man, the author noticed an interesting fact. There was never even a hint of obscenity or real ill will recorded in the journal. Certainly, he called out the transgressions of Hurst, Smith, and their faithful surrogates without hesitation. But he did so with professionalism befitting a career military officer. In that journal, he was recording his private and innermost thoughts and yet, he never truly spoke ill of anyone and he never employed the use of profanity for profanity's sake. He seemed to be simply reporting the truth as he saw it and in a gentlemanly way.

There is something quite telling about this man who was too long lost to history or, more appropriately, buried within it. Many times, the author walked through that peaceful and historically moving campground of the dead, Shiloh National Cemetery, through the impressive iron gates, down the brick paved paths, and stood beside the tall flagpole and looked out over the Tennessee River. One day, he stood in that spot and turned to his right. He looked over his shoulder to see a grave beside the path and within feet of the flagpole flying the great Stars and Stripes of the Union. The grave was that of William K.M. Breckenridge. Knowing he was a lieutenant colonel of the First West Tennessee Cavalry/Sixth Tennessee Cavalry, the author often wondered why so little was known of him.

The answer was simple but elusive. Death obscured this man whose name was once known to the Union high command in West Tennessee and beyond. There was nothing pretentious about Breckenridge—nothing boastful, nothing less than humble in his approach to leadership. As he drifted into the oblivion of death on October 15, 1863, he also drifted into history. The layers of history and the fables surrounding the ostentatious Hurst slowly obscured Breckenridge it seemed forever. The leadership of his regiment became personified largely by Hurst and, to a lesser degree, William Jay Smith.

Perhaps that would have bothered Breckenridge far less than knowing the reputation largely assigned to his regiment was that of a gang of outlaws. Indeed, the reputation of the First West Tennessee Cavalry/Sixth Tennessee Cavalry has become grossly overgeneralized and its accomplishments obscured largely by legends, lore, myths, and untrue renderings of stories told and retold over generations. Few truly know the real story of the regiment from the perspective of the soldiers themselves. Certainly none can ever know the entire story despite the diligent efforts that have been made.

There remains hope that with this work, all come closer to the truth of the circumstances, the passions, the hatred, the emotions, and the ultimate story of not only Breckenridge but also the regiment from perspectives other than those found in the *Official Records*. The author has sought to treat this entire work as a sort of historical mystery for which an archeological excavation of facts and circumstances was warranted. At the end of the proverbial day, it is hoped that the life and contributions of William K.M. Breckenridge will finally be recognized and assessed as they should. The recuperative processes may take longer for the regiment itself. Still, it is hoped that eventually the reputation of the regiment as a whole will be restored to a more positive position. Many good men served. A few selfish and bitter ones tainted an otherwise dedicated unit. One can only hope that these good fighting men are vindicated with the passage of time.

Finally, it should be clearly understood that the goals of this work did not include any effort to vindicate Fielding Hurst. As with Breckenridge and the regiment itself, the goal had been to clarify as many facts and circumstances as possible so that Hurst may, in time, be evaluated in the light of historical fact and not in the shadows of myth and popular folklore. Hurst was an entirely different individual from Breckenridge. In fact, they could not have been any more different than they were. Perhaps Hurst will have his own opportunity to find redemption or renewed criticism based upon a clearer picture of the facts. The goal of this work is to allow the reader to hear a new voice from an old conflict. If William K.M. Breckenridge eventually receives the credit for his hard work in forming, equipping, and leading the First West Tennessee Cavalry/Sixth Tennessee Cavalry, then the goal of this work has been achieved.

EPILOGUE

The death of William K.M. Breckenridge on October 15, 1863, may have been a watershed moment for the U.S. Sixth Tennessee Cavalry. His death removed the sense of restraint that leaders like Hurst and Smith felt regarding their unsanctioned activities. Even so, it must be understood that the men of the regiment were a diverse and fascinating group of individuals. Some had striven to uphold a cause and a duty. Others had sought to enrich themselves shamelessly by taking undue advantage of the greatest crisis to have befallen the nation. The war had brought out the best in some men and the worst in others. Some survived intact and moved on to greater things. Others simply survived and continued to survive. Some died, never to see the peace. Of course, even the concept of peace was a fragile and tenuous concept following the American Civil War. Reconstruction was not peace, but many of the men and officers of the regiment played a part in that tumultuous series of policies and events.

Here are the continued stories of some of the men whose lives were brought to view in the search for the story and life of Lt. Colonel William K.M. Breckenridge.

ISAAC T. McINTYRE ca. 1844–APRIL 23, 1864

Isaac T. McIntyre is one of the individuals whose history was long hidden until the discovery of Breckenridge's journal and subsequent research into it. Although he was never mentioned specifically by Breckenridge, McIntyre came to light from the shadows of the journal. Interestingly, he was the elder brother of the author's great-great-grandfather, John Absalom McIntyre. Family history always remained quiet on this collateral ancestor who died young. Isaac McIntyre was only 18 years old when he left home and joined the First West Tennessee Cavalry. His father, Robert Thompson McIntyre, was the grandson of a Revolutionary War veteran and Isaac's namesake and grandfather was a childhood witness to the Battle of McIntyre's Farm near Charlotte, North Carolina. His father was an ardent Unionist and justice of the peace in north McNairy County, Tennessee.

Isaac's involvement in the activities of the First West Tennessee Cavalry had remained buried for more than 155 years until 2020, when research on this work was coming to a close. The discovery was somewhat of an accident that opened new avenues in the search for factual and historical accuracy. The red-headed youth continued as a soldier in the regiment and it is unknown how many other acts of violence and deliberate destruction he committed. It is likely it extended beyond the crimes committed against Gardner Gill and A.A. Saunders. In January 1863, McIntyre was transferred from Company A to Company B, the same company as Lieutenant Benjamin Thomas "Tom" Walker "by order of Col. Fielding Hurst."[1] Further, there was a notation in McIntyre's service record that in June 1863, he was "absent on detached service by order of Col. Hurst with Lt. Walker."[2] Given Walker's usual activities, as alleged by the record, by Breckenridge himself, and Breckenridge's further

---

1. National Archives and Records Administration, Washington, D.C. Record Group Title Records of the AGO, 1780s–1917, Record Group 94, Series Number M395, Roll 0057.
2. Ibid.

journal entries of June 20 and 22, 1863, McIntyre was likely detached to assist Walker in his looting and arson activities.

Interestingly, McIntyre family tradition held that Isaac died in action at the Battle of Bolivar. There may be some truth to that tradition though it cannot all be accurate. The battle occurred at the end of March 1864. According to his service record, he died in the hospital in Memphis on April 23, 1864, of pneumonia and typhoid fever.[3] Perhaps he was wounded in the humiliating defeat of his regiment at Bolivar and then died subsequently in the hospital. A single daguerreotype was the only image of Isaac that ever existed. His service record states that his eyes were yellow, his hair red, and his complexion fair.[4] The daguerreotype itself is lost, but a photograph of the original was fortunately taken some twenty-five years ago and exists today. Ultimately, the wayward young McIntyre was buried in the National Cemetery in Memphis, Tennessee, in Section B, Plot 1175.

BENJAMIN THOMAS "TOM" WALKER ca. 1836-1864

Benjamin Thomas Walker had been completely obscured over the years. Breckenridge's journal has introduced us to this loyal subordinate of Fielding Hurst and William Jay Smith. Born about 1836, he joined the First West Tennessee Cavalry at the age of 26.[5] Little else is known about him. It is thought he was a McNairy County native, the son of Hardridge and Mary (McCann) Walker, who lived in the area around Purdy.[6] His father died prior to 1860.[7] The exploits of Walker—if one could call them that—were well documented by both Breckenridge and Walker's own service record. His wartime activities only make one more curious about his background.

Enlisting as a private in 1862, Walker rose to the rank of first lieutenant. During the course of the war, he made himself a useful tool to

3. Ibid.

4. Ibid.

5. Benjamin T. Walker Compiled Service Record.

6. Seventh Census of the United States, 1850. District 7, McNairy County, Tennessee. Roll 888, Page 10A, National Archives and Records Administration, Washington, D.C.

7. Eighth Census of the United States, 1860. District 7, McNairy County, Tennessee. Page 431. National Archives and Records Administration, Washington, D.C.

Hurst and Smith by basically terrorizing certain areas of West Tennessee. Hurst promoted him no fewer than three times during his military career. Walker was arrested at least twice: the 1862 arrest with Hurst and McIntyre and again in March 1864 at the order of Major Thomas H. Boswell. He died in the hospital at Memphis, Tennessee, of smallpox on June 20, 1864.[8] Walker was buried in the National Cemetery in Memphis, Tennessee, in Section B, Plot 1115, just a few yards away from Isaac McIntyre.[9]

STEPHEN J. THOMAS ca. 1840–?

Stephen J. Thomas was unknown until research conducted for this work. He was born in Tishomingo County, Mississippi. A short man of only 5' 6½" tall, he was a farmer by occupation. He was recruited into the regiment by Captain Horry Hodges and enrolled in the First West Tennessee Cavalry on October 13, 1862, at Bethel, Tennessee. He was mustered in formally that same day as a private in Company B. By January 1863, Thomas had been promoted to the rank of corporal. As a member of Company B, he served directly and closely with Isaac McIntyre and Benjamin Thomas "Tom" Walker. His service record reveals that he was detached by order of Hurst to accompany Walker on an unspecific mission. In March and April 1864, he was among a group of men detached to Helena, Arkansas, by special order of Major General Stephen A. Hurlbut. Apparently, he was sent to a convalescent camp in Memphis and left without leave. On August 25, Thomas was ordered confined at the military prison at Memphis. His pay for the months of July and August 1864 was forfeited by Special Order No. 231 dated September 23, 1864, and he was punished for being absent without leave. The charges and specifications were brought by his company commander, Captain Elijah J. Hodges. What became of Thomas after the war is not known.[10]

8. Ibid.

9. Nationwide Gravesite Locator, https://gravelocator.cem.va.gov, Memphis National Cemetery. The grave of Benjamin T. Walker is marked as Benjamin F. Walker, likely a transcription error from his service record.

10. Compiled Service Record of Capt. Stephen J. Thomas. Compiled Service Records of Volunteer Union Soldiers Who Served in Organizations from the State of Tennessee. Publication Number M395, National Archives Catalogue ID 300398, Record Group: 94, Roll 0061. National Archives and Records Administration, Washington, D.C.

HORRY HODGES 1833-1864

Captain Horry Hodges, often referred to as Harry Hodges, was born into an old and prominent family. His father, Elisha Hodges, was one of the early settlers of McNairy County, Tennessee. His grandfather, Jesse Hodges, had been a waggoneer during the American Revolution. The family had a record of military service. Horry Hodges was born in McNairy County on September 25, 1833. Prior to the war, he married Sarah Elizabeth Dodd in 1855. The couple had children, but the marriage was short-lived as Sarah died in 1858. He married a little more than a year later in 1859 to Mary Lain. The couple also had children. When the First West Tennessee Cavalry was organized, he enlisted on August 25, 1862. He officially mustered into the service at Bolivar, Tennessee, on November 13, 1862. Interestingly, Hodges' service record indicates that he was under arrest in January 1863, but does not specify the reason.[11] Hodges recruited many young men to serve in the regiment and was the officer who rescued Fielding Hurst after his capture in July 1863.

In March 1864, Hodges was detached to Helena, Arkansas, with a number of other members of the First West Tennessee Cavalry, by then known as the Sixth Tennessee Cavalry. He was sent by command of Major General Stephen A. Hurlbut. Like his brother, Hodges was tall and imposing. He stood six feet tall and carried on his person two Navy Colt pistols and a silver hunting case pocket watch.[12] While serving in Helena, Hodges grew ill and died of smallpox on May 5, 1864. He is buried in the National Cemetery in Memphis, Tennessee, in Section B, Plot 1240, within yards of McIntyre and Walker. He left behind three young children, a son and two daughters, as well as his second wife. His widow lived another sixty-five plus years, before she died in 1930.

ELIJAH J. HODGES 1831-1913

Elijah James Hodges was born to Elisha Hodges and Millie (Ward) Hodges on the family farm near present-day Finger, Tennessee, on May 18, 1831. He was the elder brother of Captain Horry Hodges. Whether he was educated at home or obtained some formal schooling is not known,

11. Horry Hodges Compiled Service Record.
12. Ibid.

but Hodges was a well-read man of literary pursuits. He has been described as such, "the Captain was an intellect and a great literary and Bible reader."[13]

Elijah and brother Horry enlisted in Company B of the First West Tennessee Cavalry on August 25, 1862, at Bethel Station.[14] On November 17, Elijah received a promotion to sergeant. Upon the death of Breckinridge on October 15, 1863, Hodges received a promotion to adjutant. He made the rank of first lieutenant on February 29, 1864. Upon his brother's death, he was elevated to captain on July 1, 1864, a rank he would hold until the war's end. Hodges was discharged at Pulaski, Tennessee, on July 26, 1865.[15] Captain Elijah Hodges made an impressive sight leading his troops, standing six feet, six inches tall, an unusual height for a man in the nineteenth century.

Following the war, Hodges pursued a career as a politician, farmer, and preacher. He was elected to the Tennessee State House of Representatives on the Unionist ticket in 1867 and represented McNairy County in the Thirty-fifth General Assembly until 1869. He was also a well-known Primitive Baptist preacher, leading among others the congregation at Mount Carmel Church near his home.

Elijah married Nancy Jane Dodd on December 29, 1852, and to this union were born eleven children: Tabitha F. Hodges (December 28, 1854–August 29, 1855), Sarah Ann Hodges (August 24, 1857–July 27, 1858), John Hodges (January 27, 1862–April 18, 1862), Elizabeth Ellen Hodges Peeples (1860–1939), Mary Hodges Robertson (1866–1941), Horry Hodges (March 19, 1868–September 23, 1940), William Henry Hodges (September 19, 1869–November 16, 1941), Harmon E. Hodges (December 3, 1871–November 17, 1957), Rozetta Jane "Jennye" Hodges Scott (June 12, 1873–September 14, 1956), Maggie Hodges (March 27, 1876–October 30, 1955), and Harvey G. Hodges (March 17, 1878–September 1, 1922).

---

13. Elijah J. Hodges obituary, published in the *McNairy County Independent*, April 25, 1913.

14. Compiled Service Record of Capt. Elijah J. Hodges. Compiled Service Records of Volunteer Union Soldiers Who Served in Organizations from the State of Tennessee. Publication Number M395, National Archives Catalogue ID 300398, Record Group 94, Roll 0055. National Archives and Records Administration, Washington, D.C.

15. Ibid.

Elijah often spoke at Union Army reunions and other events in his later years. More than a year prior to his death, he lost his eyesight, but according to his obituary, "everyday he was read to by some member of the family."[16] Elijah James Hodges died on April 21, 1913, at his home just east of the town of Finger. He was buried in Mount Carmel Cemetery. Following the Captain's death, the remaining single Hodges' children—Horry, Henry, Harmon, Maggie, and Harvey—allegedly signed a pact requiring each of them to remain single and to provide for their widowed mother and the family estate. Over the years, one of the guests who visited the Hodges home was William Jay Smith.[17]

WILLIAM JAY SMITH 1823-1913

Perhaps William Jay Smith, the man to whom Breckenridge derisively referred as "Petticoat" Smith, is the one character in this saga who deserves a closer inspection. He has long been afforded a far more positive reputation in history, but that reputation may have been more of a mirage than reality. Despite Smith's questionable and apparently deplorable behaviors during the war, he somehow managed to escape a negative judgment of history. Sometimes referred to as "Jerusalem" Smith, he did not himself escape controversy in the ensuing years.[18]

Eventually taking command of the Sixth Tennessee Cavalry, Smith was, in time, breveted a brigadier general. Despite many glowing postwar accounts, his rise through the ranks and his military service record were tainted by his behaviors, most thoroughly documented by Breckenridge. Before moving to a discussion of his postwar years, Smith's service record deserves a closer look. Indeed, Breckenridge's own feelings on Smith's motives—that they were primarily for his own enrichment or continued enrichment—are reinforced in a letter that Smith himself penned on July 4, 1863, wherein Smith sought permission to confiscate cotton from Secessionists around him. His alleged purposes for such takings were to recompense himself for his own losses.

---

16. *McNairy County Independent*, April 25, 1913.

17. John E. Talbott, J.D., *Let's Call It Finger: A History of North McNairy County & Finger, Tennessee & Its Surrounding Communities* (Dickson TN: BrayBree Publishing Company LLC, 2015), 314.

18. *Daily Memphis Avalanche*, March 31, 1885, 4.

Capt. Elijah James Hodges
(*Author's Collection*)

The Federals first came to Grand Junction on the 12th of June, 1862. On that occasion, I raised the Federal Flag on my plantation and acted as guide for Col. Dickey of the 4th Regt. Ill[inois] Cav. The next day the Divisions of Gen'l. Sherman came down and I was selected by the Gen'l. to repair the R.R. from Grand Junction to Bolivar. Col. (now Gen'l.) Leggett became Commander of the post. I rendered him all the assistance I could and he knowing that I had twenty-eight bales of cotton, told me one day to take it into town that he would have it shipped for me as he was going to evacuate the place.

I went to the freight Ag't. paid him the freight and he promised to see that it was shipped. A cotton buyer by the name of Hix monopolized all the cars for his cotton. My cotton was left. The Ag't. left my money with some of the citizens. Two hours after the Federals the guerillas came in, cut open my cotton, and burnt it. Lark McKenzie, Zeke Walls and his sons who burnt my cotton have plantations near mine. The former being nine miles southwest and the latter three miles south of me. They also burnt one hundred (100) bales in quantities as they found it. I would also state that with a great deal of trouble I made my way to Gen'l. Sherman's Hd-Qr's at Memphis, Tenn. When I told him about my losses, he promised me that when Federal troops again occupied Grand Junction, I should be doubly remunerated. I can prove by Secession-citizens that this is the amount of cotton I had burnt by guerillas. My Nursery, fences, etc. have been almost wholly destroyed by Federal troops.

I have the honor to remain Col.
Your Ob't. Serv't.
W.J. Smith
Major 1st Reg't. West Tenn. Cav."[19]

This letter is interesting in that Smith is not only complaining about alleged destruction by Federal troops—of which he is one himself—but is also stating that his contentions can be proved by Secessionists, an interesting contradiction.

19. Smith Compiled Service Record.

Smith had become regimental commander of the Sixth Tennessee Cavalry upon the resignation of Fielding Hurst on January 8, 1865. He had already been promoted earlier to the rank of lieutenant colonel upon the death of Breckenridge. Like his predecessor and friend, Hurst, he was prone to misconduct even as a senior officer. Aside from all of the allegations made by Breckenridge in his journal, Smith's service record demonstrates his level of intemperance as well. In March 1865, he was court-martialed for a number of alleged offenses. His charges included: 1) conduct unbecoming an officer and a gentleman and prejudicial to the benefit of the United States Army; and 2) conduct to the prejudice of good order and military discipline.[20]

The first charge against Smith involved an incident at Edgefield, Tennessee, in which Smith, on January 17, 1865, "did in violation of all articles of war, cut from the shoulders of 2nd Lieut. James A. Mangum, Co. M, 6th Regiment of Tennessee Cavalry Volunteers, his shoulder straps in a most vicious and unbecoming manner." The second charge against him involved Smith tying Mangum "fast and secure to a tree for the period of five or six hours" in "cold and disagreeable winter weather" at 4 o'clock P.M. and kept him "closely confined to a tree until 9 o'clock" causing Mangum to have a protracted and severe illness from which he came near losing his life and the effects of which he still labors under."[21] Mangum's witnesses were Dr. Job Bell (regimental assistant surgeon), John Huddleston (hospital steward), Risden D. Deford (Captain, Company H), John W. Barham, 2nd Lieutenant, Company K), John H. Thorrington (1st Lieutenant and Adjutant), and James H. Ross (1st Sergeant, Company M).[22]

The outcome of Smith's court-marital in not revealed in his service record. However, the day after Mangum's charges against Smith, he, Smith, had Mangum arrested and court-martialed.[23] Interestingly, there is no document in Mangum's file setting forth the charges and

20. Ibid.
21. Ibid.
22. Ibid.
23. Compiled Service Record of James A. Mangum. Compiled Service Records of Volunteer Union Soldiers Who Served in Organizations from the State of Tennessee. Publication Number M395, National Archives Catalogue ID 300398, Record Group 94, Roll 0056. National Archives and Records Administration, Washington, D.C.

specifications against him. There is only a letter dated July 11, 1865, setting forth the recommendations of the court-martial inquiry. It states that Mangum was guilty of conduct unbecoming an officer, that he should be dismissed from the service, and the findings should be published in Court Martial Orders No. 39.[24] There was no indication of the specifications of Mangum's charge.

By May 1865, Smith was absent from the regiment attending the session of the Tennessee Legislature.[25] He was about to embark upon his postwar political career. He served in the Tennessee House of Representatives until 1867, when he stood for election to the Tennessee State Senate and was elected on William G. "Parson" Brownlow's ticket.[26] Interestingly, it wasn't until the height of his senatorial campaign that Smith was breveted as a brigadier general on June 22, not during the war itself.[27] He ran for the U.S. House of Representatives in November 1868 on the coattails of Ulysses S. Grant and Schuyler Colfax.[28] He would serve from March 4, 1869 until March 3, 1871.[29]

After the election, on February 20, 1869, two separate stories appeared in the Memphis *Evening Post* pertaining to Smith. One told about a large crowd that had assembled in front of Smith's Linden Street home in Memphis to welcome him home from the state senate before he was to leave for Washington, D.C., to take his seat in Congress.[30] According to the story, the crowd was accompanied by a band and Smith gave an impromptu speech, the text of which the newspaper printed.[31] The other article was more controversial. Apparently, an investigation was being conducted regarding a school fund and the Tennessee National Bank in Memphis. Smith was implicated with a swindle and corruption during his tenure as senator. The issues revolved around the propriety of votes

24. Ibid.

25. Ibid.

26. Biographical Directory of the United States Congress, 1774–present, William Jay Smith, R-Tennessee, www.bioguideretro.congress.gov/Home/MemberDetails?memIndex=S000632. Memphis *Daily Post*, July 6, 1867, 4.

27. Smith Compiled Service Record.

28. Memphis *Evening Post*, October 3, 1868, 1.

29. Smith Biographical Directory.

30. Memphis *Evening Post*, February 20, 1869, 4.

31. Ibid.

that he cast pertaining to a Mr. Rutter and a Mr. R.S. Parham that were before the legislature. The *Evening Post* published Smith's deposition transcript.[32] Like his old colleague Hurst, controversy seemed to follow Smith.

Just three months earlier, the *Evening Post* hinted at corruption by others attempting to prevent blacks from voting for Smith. The lengthy article alleged that the "grossest frauds were perpetrated, and even wholesale perjury was committed in making spurious [election] returns." The newspaper went on to discuss election irregularities at Mason's Depot, Tennessee, that deprived Smith of black votes.[33] Ultimately, he only served one term in Congress before being defeated.[34]

After 1871, Smith returned to Tennessee and entered private business as well as serving as Surveyor of Customs.[35] He was identified as part of a Tennessee political machine in 1877 and one of many Federal officeholders in the state who were also members of the state Republican Executive Committee.[36] A year later, the Memphis *Daily Appeal* reprinted a story that first appeared in the Little Rock, Arkansas, *Democrat* that revisited allegations pertaining to his wartime activities. The columnist wrote:

> Sunday forenoon a little unpleasantness at the Capital hotel occurred between Captain Robinson and General William J. Smith, surveyor of customs and United States commissioner at Memphis, being the concluding chapter of a difficulty of the night before. Captain Robinson assaulted his opponent with a hickory cane, just inside the main hotel entrance, but, when striking, slipped and fell, at the same time receiving two or three blows on his head from a loaded stick in the hands of Smith. The men were separated; Robinson's wounds were dressed; he was wasn't satisfied, and returned shortly with a loaded revolver, which he presented at Smith's head. The chief-of-police happened to be present, rushed in, arrested Captain Robinson, and prevented further trouble. Both parties were interviewed by a *Democrat* reporter. Captain Robinson is well

32. Ibid.
33. Ibid, December 3, 1868, 1.
34. Smith Biographical Directory.
35. Ibid. Nashville *Daily American*, June 15, 1877, 2.
36. Ibid.

known in this city and greatly esteemed. He is agent for the house of Kirtland, Humphreys & Mitchell, St. Louis, and has a room in the *Gazette* building. He says the cause of the trouble dates back to the days of the war; the place, Salisbury, Tennessee, where Smith was first a Confederate and afterward a Federal officer. As a Federal, the captain charges him with stealing his mules and other property, under pretense of a demand from the Federal army, and converting them to his own use and benefit. General Smith we met in room No. 41, a few moments previous to the departure of the Memphis train. He disclaimed all knowledge of the alleged thefts, and said he only knew Captain Robinson by reputation; did not know him when he was attacked. He continued: "Robinson said my soldiers stole sixty dollars from him during the war, and I told him I knew nothing of it. My wife's home was burned by the 'rebels' at Grand Junction, and the Federal army corps commandant made a levy on the Confederate residents to reimburse her. He may have been assessed, although I knew nothing about it. I have held five commissions in the United States army, working myself up from a private to a general. I don't know Robinson, am innocent of his charges, and have never sought a difficulty with him."[37]

Smith was not truthful with the reporter in this instance. That should not really come as a surprise. It will be recalled that Breckenridge wrote in his June 20, 1863, journal entry:

> This morning Major Smith got up a detail of about 20 men to go with Thomas Walker out in the country and take sixty dollars' worth of property from each citizen until they collect one Thousand Eight hundred Dollars to pay the Major for what Sol Street taken from him. He said he had an order from General Hurlbut but if he did he could not show it…[38]

37. Memphis *Daily Appeal*, August 1, 1878, 1.
38. Breckenridge Daybook, 169.

In his interview, Smith claimed the protection of an unnamed superior officer. That begs the question: why not name the officer if his actions were sanctioned? It should be noted that no such order can be found to exist. Even so, Smith also claimed ignorance as to the taking of sixty dollars from Robinson. However, fifteen years before, Breckenridge wrote that Smith himself sent his men out to extract exactly the sum of sixty dollars per citizen. His claims of ignorance were not credible, despite his protestation. Further, Smith made claims as to the loss of real property at the end of the war and this home was not among them.[39]

Smith also mentioned his promotions from private to general. That boasting is more than a bit pretentious under the circumstances as established by Breckenridge in his journal so many years before. All of Smith's promotions in the early years have the appearance of opportunism for both himself and Hurst, that of quartermaster especially. His rise to lieutenant colonel only came about with the death of Breckenridge. Given the trails of corruption that constantly followed both Hurst and Smith from 1862 forward, claims of wrongdoing on their part deserve careful scrutiny.

Smith continued in his work as the surveyor of customs through the 1870s and into the early 1880s. By 1885, he found himself embroiled in personal controversy. He had been elected once again to serve in the Tennessee State Senate, but no sooner had his term started than his wife of many years, Mary Ann (Ross) Smith, filed for divorce.[40] Mrs. Smith filed her divorce action in Shelby County Chancery Court on March 30, 1885, and alleged grounds of cruel and inhumane treatment, neglect, and abusive and indecent language by Smith towards her in the presence of others.[41] According to Mrs. Smith, her husband referred to her in the presence of the children and servants as a "d—d b—", a "damned traitress," and a "d—d street walker," as well as failing to support his family.[42] She alleged that the couple owned several rental properties and derived significant income from them, but her husband had failed to contribute such income to the family to the point that she had to take in sewing to

---

39. Smith Compiled Service Record.
40. *The Daily Memphis Avalanche*, March 31, 1885, 4.
41. Ibid.
42. Ibid.

support herself and the couple's children. According to the newspaper reporting the divorce cause of action:

> The announcement of this suit will no doubt occasion surprise among the large circle of acquaintances of Gen. Smith and his wife, though persons most acquainted with the private life of the couple know they have been at outs for some time, and it is said the general has not been at home but once since the meeting of the legislature, and then he came to consult with his constituents concerning some local matter.[43]

The parties indeed divorced and the alimony portion of their case eventually made its way to the Tennessee Supreme Court in 1889, in the case of Mary A.R. Smith vs. W.J. Smith.

Relations and matters from his war years continued to rise with Smith's advancing years. One of these matters made for strange bedfellows. That was the case of Robert M. Thompson, who had been a prominent officer in the First West Tennessee/Sixth Tennessee Cavalry. After the war, he held various positions, including County Court Clerk of McNairy County, and was employed as an attorney who represented many claimants before the U.S. Claims Commission. All of the claimants referred to within this work were indeed represented by Thompson. In 1886, he was charged with wrongfully withholding the pension funds from the minor heirs of the late Thomas McCall.[44] Smith had posted bond for Thompson but he wasn't alone in acting as a bondsman. Another individual posted bond for Thompson as well: Dew Moore Wisdom. How strange that the very man who accused the regiment of such heinous murders would assist its former commander in posting bond for another senior officer of an outfit he referred to as a "renegade regiment."

In July 1888, Thompson's case came up before the District Court in Washington, D.C., where Thompson was then living.[45] He had previously been arrested in Tennessee where Smith and Wisdom posted his bond. He then left the state and fled to Washington, D.C., of all places.[46]

43. Ibid.
44. McCann, *Hurst's Wurst*, 125.
45. Nashville *Daily American*, June 9, 1888, 1.
46. Ibid.

BREVET BRIG. GEN. WILLIAM J. SMITH TOMBSTONE

Thompson was arrested again by E.D. Fitch and Smith himself. Smith wanted to take Thompson back to Tennessee and surrender him to the authorities. At the time Smith and Fitch arrested Thompson, it was Thompson's fourth arrest.[47] In 1902, the matter was mentioned again by the press when the Nashville *Daily American* reported that Congress had recently passed a bill relieving Smith and Wisdom from the three thousand dollar bond of Thompson back in Tennessee.[48] Why it took almost fifteen years for the matter to be resolved for the two men is not known.

For the last decade of his life, Smith was engaged in banking and private business. As the years progressed, he continued to dabble in politics and became active in Union veterans matters. He eventually lived with his niece, Kate M. Hainer, and not his children.[49] In September 1913, he was identified by the *Chattanooga Daily Times* as a member of

47. Ibid.

48. Ibid, May 7, 1902, 5.

49. Thirteenth Census of the United States, 1910. Memphis Ward 6, Shelby County, Tennessee. Roll T624-1520, page 3B, Enumeration District 0130. National Archives and Records Administration, Washington, D.C.

the National Council Grand Army of the Republic, the official Union veterans' association.[50] On November 29, 1913, Smith was walking down a street in Memphis when he collapsed and fell dead from heart failure. He was ninety years old.[51] He was buried in Elmwood Cemetery in Memphis. Interestingly, his former wife, Mary Ann (Ross) Smith, was buried there as well upon her death in 1921 at the age of ninety-one.[52]

Like Hurst, Smith was controversial throughout his life. His deeds followed him. Perhaps because he lived in an urban area and could offer a more presentable image, he escaped much of the criticism leveled at Hurst. Perhaps he simply lived long enough to rehabilitate his image. Whatever the case may be, Breckenridge gave history an early glimpse at the character of William Jay Smith. It may be that Smith has just been lucky enough that history and historians haven't bothered to reexamine him in the century since his death. That may yet change.

FIELDING HURST 1810-1882

Fielding Hurst never stopped being controversial. His personality was one that seemed to enjoy stirring up others and raking up some form of strife. Following Breckenridge's death, the contentions surrounding Hurst continued to grow. In 1864, new charges of murder and mayhem were lodged against him. He was accused of no less than seven murders—those of Lieutenants Willis Dodds and Joseph Stewart, Privates Alexander Vale, John Wilson, Samuel Osborn, and Martin, as well as Lee Doroughty, a teenage civilian. In fact and in fairness, there are significant discrepancies with these allegations. Ones made by Nathan Bedford Forrest were never repeated during the postwar years, even by the most virulent of anti-Radical Republican newspapers. Still, Hurst was never far from controversy.

Following Breckenridge's death, Hurst's leadership of the Sixth Tennessee Cavalry was questionable at best. Following his humiliating defeat at Bolivar, Tennessee, his direct insubordination, and the many allegations lodged against the regiment, the unit was looked upon by

50. *Chattanooga Daily Times*, September 16, 1913, 7.

51. Bristol TN *Herald Courier*, November 30, 1913, 6.

52. William Jay Smith & Mary Ann Ross Smith Burials, www.findagrave.com/memorial/7787024/william-jay-smith and www.findagrave.com/memorial/8494205/mary-ann-smith.

the Union command as both largely ineffective and troublesome.[53] On December 10, 1864, Hurst resigned his command due to bad health which included scurvy and physical unfitness. Charges of personal corruption and theft made by civilians and Breckenridge as well as suspicion by his superior officers plagued him throughout his service. Referring to the matter of the "ransom" paid by the citizens of Jackson, Tennessee, they believed he retained the five thousand dollars in gold for his own benefit rather than turning it over to Federal authorities.[54] Such charges would occur again after the war under different circumstances.

Of course, Hurst always charged that he was reacting to similar acts committed against him by Confederates and Rebel guerilpas. In a letter to Major W.H. Morgan, Acting Adjutant General, dated September 15, 1864, he accused local Rebels of stealing seventeen horses and mules, more than a thousand bushels of corn, hay, fodder, and oats as well as eight to ten thousand pounds of bacon from his farm in 1862.[55] He further accused them of stealing and using hundreds of bushels of corn, more mules and horses, hogs, fowl, and sheep as well as "kidnapped and carried to Miss[issippi] twenty Africans who had been my property."[56] The veracity of those claims may never be proven conclusively.

Hurst's postwar career was colorful. Following his resignation, he served as a state senator representing the Twenty-First Senatorial District. He took an active role during his time in the state senate, serving on the Military Affairs, Elections, and Judiciary committees. He voted to ratify the Thirteenth Amendment to the U.S. Constitution and for measures that were representative of the so-called "Brownlow Assembly."[57] To some degree, Hurst may have established his foundation for election to the senate at his regimental camp at Edgefield, Tennessee, on January 5, 1865, when he and the men he had formerly led met to appoint delegates to the State Convention, which was to be held on January 9. The group elected delegates from different of the counties represented within the regiment. Some of those delegates were men mentioned by Breckenridge in his journal, including Sergeant Houston Roberts, Lieutenant W.C.

53. McCann, *Hurst's Wurst*, 78.
54. Hurst Compiled Service Record.
55. Ibid.
56. Ibid.
57. McCann, *Hurst's Wurst*, 86–87.

Webb, Lieutenant Robert F.O. Boswell, Captain Nathan M.D. Kemp, Lieutenant Colonel William J. Smith, and other key regimental figures including Dr. Job Bell, Captains Stanford L. Warren, Elijah J. Hodges, and Samuel Lewis.[58]

Hurst chaired the meeting and a number of resolutions were passed. Among them was a recommendation that Tennessee's state government be reorganized under Federal control, calling for the laying down of arms by Rebels in the state, the abolition of slavery within its borders, that William G. Brownlow replace eventual Vice-President Andrew Johnson as Military Governor of Tennessee, and that the delegates appointed by this meeting be seated at the upcoming State Convention.[59]

Hurst served in the state senate for only a short time. He resigned when he was appointed Circuit Judge of Tennessee's Twelfth Judicial District (Decatur, Hardin, Henderson, Hickman, McNairy, and Wayne counties) in July 1865.[60] Even that tenure was controversial. He was added as a party defendant in the case of Union Bank v. Smith, one of a few lawsuits against him during the postwar years. Still, it didn't slow down his political activities. In September 1866, he attended the Loyalists' Convention in Philadelphia as a delegate. His old war colleague, Robert M. Thompson of Purdy, also served.[61] Hurst was active in the Loyalist and Radical Republican cause.

While Congressman Henry Emerson Etheridge was speaking to a group in Purdy, Tennessee, in June 1867, it was alleged that Hurst interrupted him in a "vile, savage and demonical manner."[62] The Nashville *Republican Banner* described Hurst and mentioned an alleged incident that Breckenridge never recorded in his journal. The newspaper stated that "It is known to all that a doughty warrior by the name of Fielding Hurst, the valiant commander of the notorious robbing, burning and pillaging 6th Tennessee Cavalry—the same that chased little General W.J. Smith into his quarters at Grand Junction for selling salt to the Confederates, now wears, as a mark of Brownlow's favor, the judicial

58. Nashville *Daily Union*, January 8, 1865, 3.
59. Ibid.
60. McCann, *Hurst's Wurst*, 90.
61. New York *Tribune*, September 3, 1866, 8.
62. Nashville *Republican Banner*, June 23, 1867, 1.

ermine of the Eighth District, once presided over by such good and true men as Haskill, Turley, Reed, Totten, and others."⁶³

According the *Republican Banner*—undoubtedly a newspaper biased against Hurst—Ethridge began discussing the Radicals in Tennessee when Judge Hurst became enraged.⁶⁴ Aside from the comments quoted earlier, Hurst also allegedly screamed the following pertaining to his war years: "'…G—d d—m the rebels! See h-h-h-here' – sticking his fingers under his right upper lip '—see—see—see—here—the God d—n rebel s—n b—s shot out two of my teeth. God d—n the Rebels.'"⁶⁵ Allegedly, Ethridge dressed Hurst down. "You are a judge, I believe. You are sworn to preserve the peace, sustain the dignity and sanctity of the law. Are you not now perjuring yourself here before high Heaven—here in this sacred building—here before this alter, where all meet to worship the one living God, regardless of all political differences and animosities?"⁶⁶ Hurst allegedly grew more violent but was supposedly berated by Ethridge for his uncouth behavior.⁶⁷

In December, 1867, the same Nashville newspaper attacked Hurst's conduct as a jurist. In a distasteful article entitled "Sambo Supreme," the *Republican Banner* excoriated Hurst:

> During the session of his court at Purdy, last Saturday, a negro named James Hardin, a pestilent disturber of the peace in those parts, and a mighty man among the Leaguers, was arraigned for having deliberately murdered Samuel Lewis, Sheriff of McNairy County, who served during the war, with much credit, as a captain in the Federal army. When he met his death, the late Gubernatorial campaign being in progress, Sheriff Lewis was attempting to restrain the fury of a negro mob, led by Hardin and one or two others. But the Loyal Leaguer was not to be spared from the work which had been

---

63. Ibid, June 25, 1867, 1.

64. The Clarksville *Chronicle* reported on the intemperate and profane language of one Captain Winters at Pulaski, Tennessee, in March 1869 and stated the "valiant captain has doubtless taken lessons in profanity from Judge Fielding Hurst." Clarksville *Chronicle*, March 13, 1869, 2.

65. Nashville *Republican Banner*, June 25, 1867, 1.

66. Ibid.

67. Ibid.

> planned by Judge Hurst and a few Radical whites of that section. It was necessary to reserve his murderous skill for other deeds of blood, and as a white jury, irrespective of party, would certainly have hung the accused, a safe means of escape was provided in the "unconstitutionality" of the 16th section. By rejecting all "rebels" and securing a negro jury Hardin's acquittal would be of course assured. In accordance with this plan a pannel [sic] of over 100 had, at last accounts, been exhausted, and but two jurors had been obtained—one a full blooded negro and the other a Radical white man. Thus has a Radical law been nullified by a Radical Judge for the sole purpose of defeating the ends of justice; thus has a precedent been established of which the result must be, at best, disastrous to the peace and welfare of this State.[68]

If true, this action certainly would have aroused the anger of many in the state. According to the Bolivar *Bulletin*, Hurst had passed his own judgment on the franchise laws stating:

> Judge Fielding Hurst has decided the sixteenth section of the franchise law which prohibits negroes from holding office or sitting on juries, as unconstitutional and void. In the court now being held at Purdy, McNairy county, Tennessee, he has admitted negroes to the jury box, and peremptorily refused to allow any disfranchised whites to be sworn as jurors.[69]

There was a rumor in the summer of 1868 that Hurst had been murdered. Perhaps the story was only wishful thinking for many former Rebels and secessionists. According to the *Republican Banner*, a newspaper decidedly against him, Hurst was reportedly called upon by a man one night and asked to accompany him on a stroll.[70] Hurst refused to comply and the man told him that if he didn't go voluntarily, Hurst would have to go with a hundred men. A large party seized him and carried him about a mile from his house, where they allegedly cut out his tongue and

68. Ibid, December 21, 1867, 4.
69. Bolivar TN *Bulletin*, January 4, 1868, 1.
70. Nashville *Republican Banner*, July 3, 1868, 4.

"outraged his person in various ways."[71] The *Republican Banner* reported a few days later that the story turned out to be a hoax. "[A] correspondent at Purdy, a friend of Judge Hurst, writes us that the Judge is in good health, and attending to the business of his circuit."[72] In other circles, it was apparently reported that Hurst was more than injured but had in fact been assassinated.[73] The St. Louis *Times* went so far as to compose Hurst's obituary, not a flattering piece of work.[74]

In the latter part of July 1868, the Nashville *Union and American* reported on Hurst's politics. From Grand Junction, the old headquarters of the former Sixth Tennessee Cavalry, the reporter wrote about changes in the Democratic Party in Hardeman County and elsewhere in that section.

> Moreover, it is currently reported, at Corinth and Iuka, that Judge Fielding Hurst, of Purdy, Tennessee, has changed his politics again (according to his habit, in times past, of changing sides at least once in every six or seven years), and had signified his intention of rallying to the Conservative banner, with all his henchmen and retainers.[75]

A change in his radicalism could have coincided with the decline of Radical Republican fortunes in Tennessee. By 1868 and 1869, the political shift was definitely in favor of a more conservative government. In late 1869, Hurst resigned from the bench.[76] He was appointed collector of internal revenue for the Sixth District of Tennessee by the Grant administration.[77]

That tenure was especially controversial. During the approximately two years that Hurst filled this post, he did not escape the newspapers or the attention of his detractors. His actions as tax collector made news occasionally as in July 1870 when the Memphis *Daily Appeal* reported that the large distillery of Randolph and Alexander in Maury County, Tennessee,

71. Ibid.
72. Ibid, July 8, 1868, 4.
73. Grenada MS *Sentinel*, July 11, 1868, 3.
74. St. Louis *Times*, reprinted in the Memphis *Public Ledger*, July 20, 1868, 3.
75. Nashville *Union and American*, July 28, 1868, 1.
76. McCann, *Hurst's Wurst*, 92. Nashville *Republican Banner*, December 11, 1869, 3.
77. McCann, *Hurst's Wurst*, 92.

whose contents and fixtures were valued at $30,000, were confiscated by Hurst for "alleged violation of the revenue and illicit distilling."[78]

Just a little more than a year into his appointment, Hurst was suspended on the charge of fraud and neglect in January 1871.[79] The Columbia, Tennessee, *Herald and Mail* reported on the rumors of his dismissal on both sides in what appears to be an effort at unbiased reporting.[80] More than a year later, the Fayetteville, Arkansas, *Weekly Democrat* reprinted a *New York Tribune* story that listed the "federal robberies and defalcations under the present administration," which included Hurst.[81] Indeed, the Grant Administration is remembered today for the level and depth of the graft and corruption present within it.

Despite problems during his tenure as tax collector, Hurst could not escape from his past either. The Bolivar *Bulletin* reported on a wartime incident that resulted in a lawsuit in 1870.

> Ex-Judge Fielding Hurst, now Revenue Collector for the Columbia District, is destined to be 'brought up a standing' for one of his many tyrannical acts during the war. The facts in the case, as we learn them from the best of authority, are as follows: In the winter of 1863, while cohorting around with his notorious regiment, the 7th [sic] Tennessee, Federal, he came to Bolivar and demanded of Dr. George Wood, fifteen or sixteen hundred dollars in gold, and said if the money was not furnished, that he would burn the houses of Geo. Wood, Robt. H. Wood, J.H. Bills, R.P. Neely and J.J. Neely. Now, it must be borne in mind that Dr. Wood did not owe Hurst one cent, but that his son, who was then over twenty-one years of age, and doing a mercantile business in this place, or had been, was endorser on a note for $1000, which note was held by a member of Hurst's regiment, named T.E. Reynolds, who died, or was killed during the war. Knowing the desperate character of Hurst, the unwarrantable demand was complied with and he departed with the money. Mrs. Reynolds

---

78. Memphis *Daily Appeal*, July 21, 1870, 2.
79. Baltimore *Sun*, January 18, 1871, 1.
80. Columbia TN *Herald and Mail*, February 3, 1871, 2.
81. Fayetteville TN *Weekly Democrat*, September 7, 1872, 2.

says that her husband never received the one thousand dollars thus forcibly collected by Hurst, and the inference is that the doughty Colonel pocketed the coin. Dr. Wood has brought suit for the recovery of his gold, and will no doubt be able to recover it. H.M. Hill, of Bolivar, is counsel for Dr. Wood. We suppose the case will be tried at Columbia.

Mr. Hill is now in Columbia looking after the interest of his client, and we wish him every success.

"O Colonel, O Judge, O United States Revenue Collector! How are you, now?"[82]

Even in such biased reporting are echoes of the behaviors that Breckenridge recorded in his private journal. Interestingly, at the end of 1870, an article appeared in the same newspaper discussing a federal lawsuit against former Confederate General Gideon J. Pillow and J.W. Murphy for conversion of property during the war, resulting in proposed legislation for the relief of Pillow and Murphy. The *Bulletin* then took the position that if Pillow and Murphy were entitled to relief, then Hurst could do the same "with as much propriety as Murphy and Pillow."[83]

Hurst was often accused of being the influence for others who committed disgraceful or allegedly disgraceful acts. In the summer of 1871, a group of five alleged former Sixth Tennessee Cavalrymen were accused of regularly descending upon Toone's Station in Hardeman County, Tennessee, and harassing the town.[84] According to the Nashville *Republican Banner*, one of many anti-Hurst newspapers, these men were arrested by townspeople after they allegedly "shot an inoffensive negro, and cut an old man named Willoughby, without provocation."[85]

Another lawsuit against Hurst was reported upon, this one with a judgment. On December 17, 1872, the Honorable C.F. Trigg, presiding Judge of the Federal Court, awarded $840.10 in the case of United States vs. Fielding Hurst, et al.[86] No study of lawsuits against Hurst has been conducted for purposes of this work but in 1878, a U.S. Marshal's

82. Bolivar TN *Bulletin*, January 8, 1870, 2.

83. Ibid, December 24, 1870, 2.

84. Nashville *Republican Banner*, June 23, 1871, 2.

85. Ibid,

86. *The Daily Memphis Avalanche*, December 18, 1872, 4.

Sale was held to sell a parcel of real property for purposes of satisfying a judgment in the case of United States v. Fielding Hurst, et al.[87]

The last decade of Hurst's life was filled with turmoil. He continued to practice law and his surveying skills and expertise were still sought after. In late 1871, there arose discussion of a railroad to be built between Bolivar and Savannah and running through Purdy and Adamsville.[88] According to the Bolivar *Bulletin*, Hurst's knowledge of the geography of the country between Bolivar and Savannah was called upon to determine the feasibility of laying out a railroad from Spring Creek bottom to Savannah without the necessity of making extensive cuts into the landscape.

> From Bolivar across Spring Creek to Big Hatchie bottom; up the valley of Big Hatchie to Wade's Creek; up the valley of Wade's Creek to Rose's Creek; up the valley of Rose's Creek to within two miles of Bethel, thence down a branch bottom to the valley to Sandy Creek, and up the valley of Sandy to Purdy, then strike the head waters of Snake Creek and follow the valley to Adamsville, where a level country extends all the way to Savannah. The one cut of ten feet referred to will be near the north corporate line of Purdy where a small elevation turns the water that falls in the public square of Purdy, right and left—one portion going into the Tennessee while the other flows westward to Big Hatchie.[89]

The railroad he and its supporters proposed was never built.

Hurst's legal skills made the local newspapers as well. In March of 1878, he was in Bolivar defending two men, Phillips and Burrow, on charges of murder. He continued to practice law late into his life. Yet he saw setbacks and reversals of his earlier good fortune during this time. He was forced to sell his two-story home in Purdy and move permanently to his home in the Mt. Gilead community in northwestern McNairy County.[90] It was there in the heart of the Hurst Nation that he died on

---

87. Ibid, November 6, 1878, 4.
88. Bolivar TN *Bulletin*, September 22, 1871, 2.
89. Ibid.
90. McCann, *Hurst's Wurst*, 92.

April 3, 1882, at the age of seventy-two. The cause of death was reported to be "an affection of the brain."[91] This diagnosis is interesting in that an "affection" of the brain refers to an abnormal state of mind. Some medical authorities of that time refer to the same as being anything from an inflammation to Parkinson's disease or similar affliction. Some even refer to mental and emotional disturbances.[92] Such gives one pause to consider Hurst's actions over his lifetime.

Fielding Hurst was buried in the Mt. Gilead Cemetery, though he has never fully faded into the shadows. To this day, his reputation remains in question and he still looms large. Perhaps he always will.

---

91. Ibid. Milan TN *Exchange*, April 15, 1882, 5.

92. *Webster's Encyclopedic Unabridged Dictionary of the English Language* (New York: Portland House, 1989), 24.

BIBLIOGRAPHY

GOVERNMENT/OFFICIAL RECORDS

Barred and Disallowed Case Files of the Southern Claims Commission, 1871–1880. Records of the U.S. House of Representatives, 1789–2015. Record Group Number 233, Series Number M1407. National Archives and Records Administration, Washington, D.C.

Burial Ledgers, The National Cemetery Administration, Washington, D.C. Original records transferred to NARA: Burial Registers, compiled 1867–2006, documenting the period 1831–2006. ARC ID 5928352. Records of the Department of Veterans Affairs, 1773–2007, Record Group 15. National Archives and Records Administration, Washington, D.C.

College Student Lists. Worcester, Massachusetts: American Antiquarian Society.

Deposition of Fielding Hurst. Southern Claims Commission, Claim No. 17782. Claim of Pitser M. Cheshier. Claim Date: December 5, 1872. NARA Publication Number M1407, Roll No. 014. National Archives and Records Administration, Washington, D.C.

Deposition of Jessie J. Clemmons. Southern Claims Commission Approved Claims, 1871–1880. Claim No. 17793. Claimant: Nancy Webster. Claim Date: December 5, 1872. National Archives and Records Administration, Washington, D.C.

Deposition of John Webster. Southern Claims Commission Approved Claims, 1871–1880. Claim No. 17793. Claimant: Nancy Webster. Claim Date: December 5, 1872. National Archives and Records Administration, Washington, D.C.

Deposition of Mary Swain. Barred and Disallowed Case Files of the Southern Claims Commission, 1871–1880. Records of the U.S. House of Representatives, 1789–2015. Record Group Number: 233, Series Number M1407. National Archives and Records Administration; Washington, D.C.

Deposition of Nancy Webster. Southern Claims Commission Approved Claims, 1871–1880. Claim No. 17793. Claimant: Nancy Webster. Claim Date: December 5, 1872. National Archives and Records Administration, Washington, D.C.

Dew M. Wisdom to Col. Philip D. Roddey, July 23, 1863. NARA M474, RG 109, Reel 88, Frames 167–169. National Archives and Records Administration, Washington, D.C.

Eighth Census of the United States, 1860. Series Number M653. Records of the Bureau of the Census. District 8, Lawrence County, Tennessee. National Archives and Records Administration, Washington, D.C.

Letter from Colonel E.W. Rice to Major General Richard Oglesby, April 16, 1863. Compiled Service Records of Volunteer Union Soldiers Who Served in Organizations from the State of Tennessee. Series Number M395, Roll 0055. National Archives and Records Administration (NARA); Washington, D.C.

Military Record of William K.M. Breckenridge. Compiled Service Records of Volunteer Soldiers Who Served During the Mexican War in Organizations from the State of Tennessee. Records of the Adjutant General's Office, 1762–1984. Record Group Number RG 94,

Series Number M638, NARA Roll 7. National Archives and Records Administration; Washington, D.C.

Ninth Census of the United States, 1870. McNairy County, Tennessee. U.S. Census Population Schedules. NARA Microfilm Publication M593, National Archives and Records Administration, Washington, D.C.

Record of Appointment of Postmasters, 1832–1971. NARA Microfilm Publication M841, 145 rolls. Records of the Post Office Department, Record Group Number 28. National Archives and Records Administration, Washington, D.C.

Records of the Internal Revenue Service. Record Group 58. National Archives and Records Administration, Washington, D.C.

Register of Enlistments in the U.S. Army, 1798–1914. National Archives Microfilm Publication M233, Roll 81. Records of the Adjutant General's Office, 1780s–1917. Record Group 94. National Archives, Washington, D.C.

Register of Enlistments in the U.S. Army, 1798–1914. National Archives Microfilm Publication M233, Roll 81. Records of the Adjutant General's Office, 1780s–1917. Record Group 94. National Archives and Records Administration, Washington, D.C.

Service Record of A.J. Wharton. Compiled Service Records of Confederate Soldiers Who Served in Organizations from the State of Tennessee. Record Group 109, Series Number M268, Roll 74. National Archives and Records Administration, Washington, D.C.

Service Record of Benjamin T. Walker. Compiled Service Records of Volunteer Union Soldiers Who Served in Organizations from the State of Tennessee. Records of the AGO, 1780s–1917. Record Group 94, Series Number M395, Roll 0061. National Archives and Records Administration; Washington, D.C.

Service Record of C.M. Cason. Records Showing Military Service of Soldiers Who Fought in Confederate Organizations, compiled 1903–1927, documenting the period 1861–1865. National Archives Catalogue ID: 586957, Record Group 109, NARA M268, Tennessee. Roll 0245, National Archives and Records Administration, Washington, D.C.

Service Record of Calvin Roberts. Compiled Service Records of Volunteer Union Soldiers Who Served in Organizations from the State of Tennessee. Records of the AGO, 1780s–1917. National Archives Catalogue Id 300398, Record Group 94, Series Number M395, Roll 0059. National Archives and Records Administration; Washington, D.C.

Service Record of David J. Dickerson. Compiled Service Records of Volunteer Union Soldiers Who Served in Organizations from the State of Tennessee. Records of the AGO, 1780s–1917. Record Group 94, Series Number M395, Roll: 0052. National Archives and Records Administration; Washington, D.C.

Service Record of Private Edmond M.V. Ferguson. Compiled Service Records of Volunteer Union Soldiers Who Served in Organizations from the State of Tennessee. The National Archives and Records Administration, Publication Number M395. National Archives Catalogue ID 300398, Record Group 94, Roll 0053.

Service Record of Capt. Elijah J. Hodges. Compiled Service Records of Volunteer Union Soldiers Who Served in Organizations from the State of Tennessee. Publication Number M395, National Archives Catalogue ID 300398, Record Group 94, Roll 0055. National Archives and Records Administration, Washington, D.C.

Service Record of Capt. Horry Hodges. Compiled Service Records of Volunteer Union Soldiers Who Served in Organizations from the State of Tennessee. Publication Number M395, National Archives Catalogue ID 300398, Record Group 94, Roll 0055. National Archives and Records Administration, Washington, D.C.

Service Record of Elijah Roberts. Compiled Service Records of Volunteer Union Soldiers Who Served in Organizations from the State of Tennessee. Publication Number M395, Catalogue Identification Number 300398, Tennessee, Roll 0059. National Archives and Records Administration, Washington, D.C.

Service Record of George Brown. Compiled Service Records of Confederate Soldiers Who Served in Organizations from the State of Tennessee. National Archives Publication No. M268, NARA, Catalogue No. 586957, Record Group 109, Tennessee, Roll 0065. National Archives and Records Administration, Washington, D.C.

Service Record of Hugh Hollis. Compiled Service Records of Confederate Soldiers Who Served in Organizations from the State of Tennessee. Series Number M268, Roll 170; National Archives and Records Administration, Washington, D.C.

Service Record of Isaac T. McIntyre. Compiled Service Records of Volunteer Union Soldiers Who Served in Organizations from the State of Tennessee. Records of the AGO, 1780s–1917. Record Group: 94; Series Number M395, Roll 0057. National Archives and Records Administration; Washington, D.C.

Service Record of John Ambrose Wharton. Compiled Service Records of Confederate Soldiers Who Served in Organizations from the State of Tennessee. Record Group 109, Series Number M268, Roll 172. National Archives and Records Administration, Washington, D.C.

Service Record of Nathan M.D. Kemp. Compiled Service Records of Volunteer Union Soldiers Who Served in Organizations from the State of Tennessee. Records of the AGO, 1780s–1917. Record Group 94, Series Number M395, Roll 0055. National Archives and Records Administration, Washington, D.C.

Service Record of Capt. Sol G. Street. Compiled Service Records of Confederate Soldiers Who Served in Organizations from the State of Mississippi. Series Number M269, Roll 15. National Archives and Records Administration, Washington, D.C.

Service Record of Stanford L. Warren. Compiled Service Records of Volunteer Union Soldiers Who Served in Organizations from the State of Tennessee. The National Archives and Records Administration, Publication Number M395, National Archives Catalogue ID 300398, Record Group 94, Roll 0061.

Service Record of Stephen J. Thomas. Compiled Service Records of Volunteer Union Soldiers Who Served in Organizations from the State of Tennessee. Publication Number M395, National Archives Catalogue ID 300398, Record Group 94, Roll 0061. National Archives and Records Administration, Washington, D.C.

Service Record of T.K. Cason. Records Showing Military Service of Soldiers Who Fought in Confederate Organizations, compiled 1903–1927. documenting the period 1861–1865. National Archives Catalogue ID 586957, Record Group: 109, NARA: M268, Tennessee, Roll 0245. National Archives and Records Administration, Washington, D.C.

Service Record of Thomas H. Boswell. Compiled Service Records of Volunteer Union Soldiers Who Served in Organizations from the State of Tennessee. Records of the AGO, 1780s–1917. Record Group

94, Series Number M395, Roll 0051. National Archives and Records Administration, Washington, D.C.

Service Record of Thomas Stark. Compiled Service Records of Confederate Soldiers Who Served in Organizations from the State of Tennessee. Series Number M268, Roll 96. National Archives and Records Administration (NARA); Washington, D.C.

Service Record of W.G. Brown. Compiled Service Records of Confederate Soldiers Who Served in Organizations from the State of Tennessee. National Archives Publication No. M268, NARA, Catalogue No. 586957, Record Group 109, Tennessee, Roll 0073. National Archives and Records Administration, Washington, D.C.

Service Record of W.T. Hollis. Records Showing Military Service of Soldiers Who Fought in Confederate Organizations, compiled 1903–1927, documenting the period 1861–1865. National Archives Catalogue ID 586957, Record Group 109, NARA M268, Tennessee, Roll 0246. National Archives and Records Administration, Washington, D.C.

Service Record of William A. Newsom. Compiled Service Records of Volunteer Union Soldiers Who Served in Organizations from the State of Tennessee. Records of the AGO, 1780s–1917. Record Group 94, Series Number M395, Roll 0057. National Archives and Records Administration, Washington, D.C.

Service Record of William C. Webb. Compiled Service Records of Volunteer Union Soldiers Who Served in Organizations from the State of Tennessee. Records of the AGO, 1780s–1917. Record Group 94, Series Number M395, Roll 0062. National Archives and Records Administration, Washington, D.C.

Service of William F. Hance. Compiled Service Records of Volunteer Union Soldiers Who Served in Organizations from the State of Tennessee. Series Number M395, Roll 0055. National Archives and Records Administration, Washington, D.C.

Service Record of William J. Smith, Record Group Title: Records of the AGO, 1780s–1917. Record Group 94, Series Number M395, Roll 0060. National Archives and Records Administration, Washington, D.C.

Service Record of William K.M. Breckenridge. Compiled Service Records of Volunteer Union Soldiers Who Served in Organizations from the State of Tennessee. Publication Number M395, NARA Catalogue

No. 300398, Record Group 94, Roll 0051. National Archives and Records Administration, Washington, D.C.
Seventh Census of the United States, 1850. McNairy County, Tennessee. NARA Microfilm Publication M432, Records of the Bureau of the Census. Record Group Number 29. National Archives and Records Administration, Washington, D.C.
Tennessee Confederate Applications, Soldiers and Widows, 1891–1965. filed by soldier, No. 2193–2241. Tennessee State Library and Archives, Nashville, Tennessee.
Tennessee Death Records, 1908–1958. Roll Number 9. Tennessee State Library and Archives, Nashville, Tennessee.
Tennessee Probate Court Books, 1795–1927, McNairy County, Tennessee. Inventories, 1865–1890, Volume E. www.familysearch.org and from the files of the McNairy County, Tennessee, Archives, Selmer, Tennessee.
Tennessee State Marriages, 1780–2002. Tennessee State Library and Archives, Nashville, Tennessee, microfilm.
Tenth Census of the United States, 1880. District 4, McNairy, County, Tennessee. Page 394. Family History Library Film 805262. National Archives and Records Administration, Washington, D.C.
U.S. City Directories, 1822–1995 (database on-line). Ancestry.com Operations, Inc., Provo, Utah, 2011.

BOOKS

Abernathy, Thomas Perkins. *From Frontier to Plantation in Tennessee: A Study in Frontier Democracy*. Memphis TN: Memphis State College Press, 1955.
Brazelton, B.G. *A History of Hardin County, Tennessee*. Nashville TN: Cumberland Presbyterian Publishing House, 1885.
Burton, E. Milby. *The Siege of Charleston, 1861–1865*. Columbia: University of South Carolina Press, 1970.
Carter, Claude A., *Lawrence County, Tennessee Marriage Records, 1818–1923*. Self-Published, 1979. Reprinted by permission by The Family Tree Press, Lawrenceburg, Tennessee, 1992.

Corlew, Robert E. *Tennessee: A Short History*. 2nd Edition. Knoxville: The University of Tennessee Press, 1990.

Crutchfield, James A. *The Natchez Trace: A Pictorial History*. Nashville TN: Rutledge Hill Press, 1985.

Davison, Eddy W. and Daniel Foxx. *Nathan Bedford Forrest: In Search of the Enigma*. Gretna LA: Pelican Publishing Company, 2007.

Dodd, Jordan, Liahona Research, comp. *Arkansas Marriages, 1851–1900*.

Dodd, Jordan R., et al. *Early American Marriages: Virginia to 1850*. Bountiful UT: Precision Indexing Publishers, 1990.

Dyer, Gustavus W. and John Trotwood Moore. *The Tennessee Civil War Veterans Questionnaires, Volume One, Federal Soldiers (Accuff–Wood) Confederate Soldiers (Abbott–Byrne)*. Easley SC: Southern Historical Press, Inc., 1985.

Eisenhower, John S.D. *So Far from God: The U.S. War with Mexico, 1846–1848*. Norman: University of Oklahoma Press, 1989.

Elliot, Sam Davis. *Confederate Governor and United States Senator Isham G. Harris of Tennessee*. Baton Rogue: Louisiana State University Press, 2010.

Foote, Shelby. *The Civil War, A Narrative: Fort Sumter to Perryville*. New York: Random House, 1958.

Forester, Cathy Tudor, ed. *Tennessee Historical Markers*. Nashville: Tennessee Historical Commission, 1996.

Harbert, P.M., *Early History of Hardin County*. Memphis TN: Tri-State Printing and Binding Co., 1968.

Henry, Robert Selph. *First with the Most Forrest*. Indianapolis IN: The Bobbs-Merrill Company, 1944.

Hill, Sarah Jane Full and Mark M. Krug, eds. *Mrs. Hill's Journal—Civil War Reminiscences*. Chicago: The Lakeside Press, R.R. Donnelley & Sons Company, 1980.

History of Tennessee: From The Earliest Time to the Present; Together with an Historical and a Biographical Sketch of the Counties of Henderson, Chester, Decatur, McNairy and Hardin, Besides a Valuable Fund of Notes, Original Observations, Reminiscences, Etc., Etc., Illustrated. Nashville TN: The Goodspeed Publishing Co., 1887.

Hughes, Nathaniel Cheairs Jr. *The Battle of Belmont: Grant Strikes South*. Chapel Hill: The University of North Carolina Press, 1991.

Kennedy, Nancy Wardlow. *Antiquities of McNairy County, Tennessee: McNairy County History 1823–1876, Notes of Ancil Walker Stovall.* Selmer TN: Self-published, 2001.

Kennedy, Nancy Wardlow, ed. *Hollis & Cason Merchant's Accounts, ca. 1857–1861.* Selmer TN: Self-published, 2005.

Killebrew, J.B., A.M. and J.M. Safford, PhD, M.D. *Introduction to the Resources of Tennessee.* Nashville TN: Tavel, Eastman & Howell, 1874.

LaFlamme, Cheri. *Landscape and Memory at Grand Junction, Tennessee: A Reconnaissance Resource Survey.* Murfreesboro TN: MTSU Center for Historic Preservation, May 2011.

Mathes, Capt. J. Harvey. *General Forrest.* New York: D. Appleton and Company, 1902

McCann, Kevin D. *Hurst's Wurst: Colonel Fielding Hurst and the Sixth Tennessee Cavalry, U.S.A.* Dickson TN: McCann Publishing Company, 2007.

Morris, Eastin. *The Tennessee Gazetteer or Topographical Dictionary, 1834.* Nashville TN: W. Hassel Hunt & Co., 1834.

Oliva, Leo E. *Fort Larned: Guardian of the Santa Fe Trail.* Topeka: Kansas State Historical Society, 1982.

Pitts, John A. *Personal and Professional Reminiscences of an Old Lawyer.* Kingsport TN: Southern Publishers, Inc., 1930.

Riley, Franklin L. *Extinct Towns and Villages of North Mississippi.* Publication of the Mississippi Historical Society, Vol. 5. Oxford: Mississippi Historical Society, 1902.

Simmons, Marc, ed. *On the Santa Fe Trail.* Lawrence: University of Kansas Press, 1986.

Simon, John, ed. *The Papers of Ulysses S. Grant.* Vol. 5. Carbondale: Southern Illinois Press, 1973.

Sistler, Byron and Barbara Sistler. *Early Middle Tennessee Marriages, Volume 1, Grooms.* Self-published, 1988.

Sistler, Byron, and Barbara Sistler. *1890 Civil War Veterans Census: Tennessee.* Santa Maria CA: Janaway Publishing, Inc., 2014.

Sulzer, Elmer G. *Ghost Railroads of Tennessee.* Bloomington: Indiana University Press, 1975.

Talbott, John E., J.D. *A Sacred High Place: A History of Mount Carmel Cemetery & Meetinghouse, McNairy County, Tennessee.* Dickson TN: BrayBree Publishing Company, LLC, 2012.

Tennesseans in the Civil War: A Military History of Confederate and Union Units with Available Rosters of Personnel, Part I. Nashville TN: Civil War Centennial Commission, 1964.

Tennesseans in the Civil War: A Military History of Confederate and Union Units with Available Rosters of Personnel, Part II. Nashville TN: Civil War Centennial Commission, 1965.

The War of the Rebellion: A Compilation of the Official Records of the Union and Confederate Armies, Series I, Volume 17, Part II. Washington, D.C.: Government Printing Office, 1894.

The War of the Rebellion: A Compilation of the Official Records of the Union and Confederate Armies, Series I, Volume 23, Part II. Washington, D.C.: Government Printing Office, 1894

The War of the Rebellion: A Compilation of the Official Records of the Union and Confederate Armies, Series I, Volume 24, Part I. Washington, D.C.: Government Printing Office, 1894.

The War of the Rebellion: A Compilation of the Official Records of the Union and Confederate Armies, Series I, Volume 24, Part III. Washington, D.C.: Government Printing Office, 1894.

The War of the Rebellion: A Compilation of the Official Records of the Union and Confederate Armies, Series I, Volume 31, Part 1. Washington, D.C.: Government Printing Office, 1890.

The War of the Rebellion: A Compilation of the Official Records of the Union and Confederate Armies, Series I, Volume 31, Part 3. Washington, D.C.: Government Printing Office, 1890.

The War of the Rebellion: A Compilation of the Official Records of the Union and Confederate Armies, Series II, Volume 2. Washington, D.C.: Government Printing Office, 1891.

The War of the Rebellion: A Compilation of the Official Records of the Union and Confederate Armies, Series II, Volume 5. Washington, D.C.: Government Printing Office, 1899.

The War of the Rebellion: A Compilation of the Official Records of the Union and Confederate Armies, Series II, Volume 6. Washington, D.C.: Government Printing Office, 1899.

Walker, Dale L. *Pacific Destiny: The Three-Century Journey to the Oregon Country*. New York: Forge Press, 2000.

Warner, Ezra J. *Generals in Blue: Lives of the Union Commanders*. Baton Rogue: Louisiana State University Press, 1964.

Webster's Encyclopedic Unabridged Dictionary of the English Language. New York: Portland House, 1989.
Williams, Emma Inman. *Historical Madison: The Story of Jackson and Madison County, Tennessee, From the Prehistoric Moundbuilders to 1917.* Jackson TN: McCowat-Mercer Press, Inc., 1972.
Woodward, C. Vann, ed. *White House Under Fire: Responses of the Presidents to Charges of Misconduct.* New York: Dell, 1974.
Wright, General Marcus J. and John E. Talbott, J.D. and Kevin D. McCann, eds. *Reminiscences of the Early Settlement and Early Settlers of McNairy County, Tennessee.* Dickson TN: BrayBree Publishing Company, LLC, 2012.

ESSAYS/PAPERS

Sickles, John. "A Chronological Sketch of the Life of William Kibben Matthews Breckenridge." Merrillville IN: Self-published, 2011.

ARTICLES

Fahey, Captain John H., MC USN (Ret.). "Bernard John Dowling Irwin and the Development of the Field Hospital at Shiloh." *Military Medicine*, 171, no. 5, May 2006.

NEWSPAPERS

Daily American, Nashville TN,
Memphis Bulletin, July 31, 1863.
Memphis Daily Appeal, August 2, 1861.
Memphis Daily Appeal, March 17, 1863; March 31, 1863; April 30, 1863.
Jonesboro Evening Sun, March 27, 1934.
New York Times, July 24, 1864.
Republican Banner, Nashville, TN, June 23, 1867; June 25, 1867; June 27, 1867; December 21, 1867; July 3, 1868, July 8, 1868.
West Tennessee Whig, Jackson, Tennessee, December 2, 1865.

JOURNALS/DIARIES

Breckenridge, Lt. Col. William K.M. Civil War Daybook, 1862–1863. Tennessee State Library and Archives, Nashville, Tennessee.

PRIVATE PAPERS/COLLECTIONS

1880 Confederate Veterans' Reunion Attendance Rolls, Henderson TN. Private Papers of Joanne Talley Van Cleave, unpublished and private.
1893 Confederate Veterans' Reunion Attendance Rolls, Henderson, TN. Private Papers of Joanne Talley Van Cleave, unpublished and private
1894 Confederate Veterans' Reunion Attendance Rolls, Horner TN. Private Papers of Joanne Talley Van Cleave, unpublished and private.

WEBSITES

Biographical Directory of the United States Congress, 1774-present, William Jay Smith, R-Tennessee, www.bioguideretro.congress.gov/Home/MemberDetails?memIndex=S000632.
Family Search, https://www.familysearch.org/tree/pedigree/landscape/K81N-7L8.
Political Graveyard, William Jay Smith, www.politicalgraveyard.com/bio/smith9.html.

INDEX

A

Abolitionist, 54
Adams Express Company, 30, 30n
Adamsville, Tennessee, 50, 51, 106, 107, 108, 109, 110, 230
Alabama, state of, 96, 151
Alabama and Tennessee Railroad, 98
Alexander, J.A.L., 161
Alton, Illinois, 113
Alton, Illinois Military Prison, 105n
American Civil War, xiv, 3, 10, 137, 140, 206
Andersonville Prison (Georgia), 21
Arkadelphia, Arkansas, 153
Arkansas, state of, 136
Arkansas Gazette, 218
Army of the Mississippi, 169
Army of the Tennessee, 28n
Atlanta, Georgia, 98

B

Barnum, Acting Asst. Adj. Gen. W.L., 47
Bath Springs, Tennessee, 33
Bay Springs, Mississippi, 98
Bear Creek camp, 96
Bell, Dr. Job, 215, 224
Belmont, Battle of, 28n, 71
Benton County, Mississippi, 193
Berry, Capt. Joseph G., 107, 108
Bethel Station, Tennessee (*also* Bethel, Tennessee), 29, 32, 32n, 35, 36, 37, 40, 56, 61, 65, 84, 96, 97, 103, 106, 106n, 107, 108, 109, 181, 209, 210, 230
Biffle, Col. Jacob B. (Confederate), 48, 52, 107, 108, 116, 117, 138, 149
Biffle's Battalion, 107
Big Hatchie Bottom, 230
Big Hatchie River, 60, 138, 230

245

246   IN THE SHADOW OF THE DEVIL

Bill, J.H., 228
Binmore, Lt. Col. Henry, 96, 118
Blankenship, Gary R., x
Bolivar, Tennessee, 25, 30, 46, 47, 52, 54, 55, 56, 59, 61, 62, 66, 71, 72, 81, 84, 86, 87, 88, 89, 90, 91, 92, 93, 94, 95, 97, 103, 118, 119, 136, 138, 149, 182, 201, 208, 210, 214, 222, 228, 229, 230
Bolivar, Battle of, 208
Bolivar and Purdy Road, 136
Bolivar *Bulletin*, 226, 228, 229
Bolivar Road, 118
Bonaparte, Napoleon, 171
Boswell, Lt. Robert F.O., 224
Boswell, Maj. Thomas H., 180, 194, 195, 209
Bowling Green, Kentucky, 147
Bragg, Gen. Braxton (Confederate), 51, 52, 140, 143, 144
Brayman, Brig. Gen. Mason, 47, 55, 56, 59, 60, 61, 62, 63, 71, 72, 73, 84, 104
Breckenridge, David, 4, 7
Breckenridge, Dicey (Wilson), 6, 7
Breckenridge, Hannah, 4
Breckenridge, James N., 7
Breckenridge, John C. (U.S. Vice Pres.), 10
Breckenridge, William Daniel, 6, 7
Breckenridge, Lt. Col. William K.M.
　Generally, x, xi, xii, xiii, xiv, xv, xvi, 3, 4, 22, 23, 24, 28, 29, 34, 35, 36, 38, 40, 42, 46, 47, 48, 50, 52, 53, 55, 56, 60, 61, 62, 63, 71, 72, 72n, 77, 78, 79, 80, 81, 82, 83, 86, 88, 89, 90, 91, 92, 93, 107, 108n, 112, 113, 116, 129, 130, 136, 138, 150, 166, 169, 177, 178, 185, 190, 190n, 197, 199, 204, 205, 207, 208, 219, 222, 223
　Army commission and difficulties with, 25, 63, 125, 126, 180, 181
　Arsonist activities by Fielding Hurst as reported by Breckenridge, 99, 103
　Arrest and imprisonment for being a secessionist, 10, 10n, 11, 12
　Arrest by Hurst, 66, 67, 70, 71, 71n
　Arrest of Benjamin Thomas Walker, 87
　Breckenridge's humanity with prisoners, 112
　Being punished for holding transgressors responsible, 76n
　Concerns over looting and arson, 28
　Concerns over loyal citizens and their families, 44
　Concerns over camp prostitution, 120, 121
　Dealings with Confederate guerillas, 46, 139
　Defeat at Clifton, Tennessee, 49
　Depiction of the battle of Jackson, Tennessee, 185, 186, 187
　Depictions of William Jay Smith and Fielding Hurst, 70, 72, 126
　Dissatisfaction among troops over activities Hurst and subordinates, 42, 78, 124, 125
　Drunkenness among the First West Tennessee Cavalry, 109, 110, 175
　Enlistment in the Dragoons, 7, 8
　Expedition up Horse Creek, 102
　Experience and knowledge of military rules & bureaucracy, 23, 25
　Experience in the Indian Territories, 64, 138
　Frustrations over conditions of First West Tennessee Cavalry, 50, 78, 87, 91, 125
　Frustrations over lack of pay for men of First West Tennessee Cavalry, 122
　Health and physical condition of, 119
　Hurst's lack of cooperation with Breckenridge, 35
　Hurst's and Smith's wartime activities as viewed by Breckenridge, 35, 65, 88, 122, 212
　Illness and/or death, 195, 198, 202, 203, 211, 222
　In pursuit of Nathan Bedford Forrest, 44
　Journal/Daybook, 24, 25, 30n, 40, 42, 59, 62, 64, 66, 69, 70, 72, 76n, 78, 79, 80, 83n, 88, 90, 94, 125, 127,

128, 138, 150, 169, 184, 196, 198, 204, 215, 219
Leave of absence at Memphis, Tennessee, 150
Meeting with Gen. Richard James Oglesby, 104
Mexican War experience, 5, 64, 138
Mustering Issues, 29
Objections of men of the First West Tennessee Cavalry to activities of Hurst and Smith and subordinates, 128
Observations about citizens showing up in Union camps, 177
Operations along the Tennessee River, 47, 52, 53, 71, 100, 102, 104, 109, 115, 177
Operations in North Mississippi, 192
Photograph of Breckenridge, 27
Private life, 5, 6, 7
Prostitution in camp addressed by Breckenridge, 90
Raid on Linden, Tennessee, 105, 106
Report on skirmish at Clifton, TN, 49, 50
Reports on Rebel sightings, 131, 175
Reporting on activities in Hardin County, Tennessee, 51
Respected by the men of the First West Tennessee Cavalry, 126
Sense of duty as an officer, 31, 63
Stationed at Fort Larned, 8, 9, 10
Struggles to lead First West Tennessee Cavalry, 31, 55, 66, 87, 125, 132, 203
Travels and efforts to supply regiment, 26, 29, 30, 32n, 35, 95, 176, 178, 179
Treatment of prisoners of war by Breckenridge, 167, 176
Britain, 67
Brooks, Joe C., 159, 159n, 160
Brown, George, 140, 142, 146, 147, 149, 156, 158, 162
Brown, Ichabod (Achabod), 39, 39n, 156
Brown, W.G., 148, 156, 157
Brownlow Assembly, 223

Brownlow, William G. "Parson," 171, 216, 224
Brownsville, Tennessee, 154n, 203
Bryant, James, 156
Buchanan, James (U.S. Pres.), 28n
Buffalo *Bulletin*, 71
Buffalo, New York, 71
Bull Run, Battle of, 19, 28n
Bulliner, George, 17
Bunker Hill, Battle of, 67
Burnsville, Mississippi, 98
Burrow, Mr. (alleged murderer), 230

C

Cairo, Illinois, 105
Californias, the, 9
Camden (*now* Rose Creek, McNairy County, Tennessee), 136, 138, 149, 166
Camp Davis, 96
Camp Trousdale, 105n
Canaan, 69
Capt. Leftwich's Co., 6
Capitol Hotel (Little Rock, Arkansas), 217
Carmichael, Capt. Eagleton, 115, 117
Carroll, W.H., 146, 153
Catlin, Lt. J.K., 181
Cartmell, Robert, 135, 136
Cason, C.M., 154, 155
Cason, Second Lt. T.K. (Confederate), 155
Centerpoint, Tennessee, 148
Chalk Bluff (Hardin County, TN), 106, 109
Chalk Creek (Hardin County, TN), 106
Chalmers, Gen. James Ronald (Confederate), 117
Chambers Creek, 53
Charleston, Mississippi, 98
Charleston Harbor, South Carolina, 16
Charlotte, North Carolina, 207
Chattanooga *Daily Times*, 221
Chattanooga, Tennessee, 51
Cherry, Mr., 108
Chester County, Tennessee, 152

248 IN THE SHADOW OF THE DEVIL

Chewalla outpost (McNairy County, Tennessee), 96
Churchwell, Lt. G.W. (Confederate), 146
Cincinnati, Ohio, 14, 32
City Point, Virginia, 105n
Civil War, 30n, 63, 77, 154, 159
Clarksville, Tennessee, *Chronicle*, 225n
Clay County, Mississippi, 84
Clayton, Thomas M., 155
Clear Creek Cemetery (McNairy County, Tennessee), 99
Clemmons, Elijah, 21
Clemmons, Jessie J., 21, 22
Clifton Road, 116
Clifton, Tennessee, 47, 48, 49, 50, 51, 52, 106, 107, 109
Clover Creek (Tennessee), 182
Coffee Bottom (Hardin County, Tennessee), 106
Coldwater, Mississippi, 58, 192
Coleman, Isabel Jane, 17, 18
Coleman, John, 18, 155
Colfax, Schuyler, 216
Collierville, Tennessee, 168
Columbia (female personification of the United States), 67, 69
Columbia *Herald and Mail*, 228
Columbia, Tennessee, 229
Columbia District (Tennessee Revenue Collection District), 228
Columbus, Kentucky, 15, 31, 32, 32n, 35, 64
Columbus, Mississippi, 97, 98
Confederates (generally), 17, 19, 39, 46, 47, 78, 89, 153, 166, 223
Confederate Army (*also* Confederate forces), 12, 14, 17, 19, 22, 44, 46, 99, 107, 139, 146, 151, 160, 180, 204
Confederate government (authorities), 14, 15, 26, 147, 150, 163
Confederate partisans, 119
Confederate regime, 20
Confederate States of America (Confederacy), 12, 129, 146
Confederate States of America War Department, 143

Confederate (Rebel) sympathizers, 76
Congress (U.S.), 28n
Contrabands, 90
Corinth, Battle of, 108n, 115, 169
Corinth, District of (Union Army district), 52, 115, 192
Corinth, Mississippi, 33, 44, 84, 94, 95, 96, 97, 100, 102, 103, 118, 138, 178, 202
Cotam's Ferry, 111
Cotton-gin Port, Mississippi, 97
Cotton Grove, Tennessee (Madison County), 110
Covey, C.B., 155
Cox, Col. Nicholas N. (Confederate), 107, 108
Cox's Battalion, 107, 116
Cox's Raid, 107
Craighead County, Arkansas, 161
Cross, Alphonso, 147
Cumberland River, 15

D

Damron, Capt. (Confederate), 147
Davis, Jefferson (C.S. Pres.), 68, 144
Davison, Eddy W., 49
Deberry, Mr., 112
Decatur County, Tennessee, 224
Decaturville Road, 50
Decaturville, Tennessee, 109, 110, 111, 112, 113
DeFord, Lt. Risden D., 111, 171, 172, 194, 215
Denmark and Mifflin Road, 183
Desoto, Mississippi, 175
Dickerson, Capt. David J., 61, 61n, 62, 99
Dickerson, Mrs., 100, 102
Dickey, Col., 63, 214
Dibbrell, Col. (later Gen.) George G. (Confederate), 48, 107, 108, 108n
Dodds, Lt. Willis (Confederate), 222
Dodge, Gen. Grenville, 33, 49, 50, 51, 52, 65, 66, 84, 96, 97, 104, 115, 201, 202
Doroughty, Lee, 222

INDEX 249

Douglas, Stephen A., 28n
Duck River (Tennessee), 109
Duke, Fountain P., 136

E

East Perryville (Tennessee), 109
Eastport, Mississippi, 14, 96
Edgefield, Tennessee, 215, 223
Eighth Illinois Infantry, 108n
Eighth Tennessee Cavalry (CSA), 108n, 147
Eighty-first Ohio, 53
Eldridge, Capt. John Wesley (Confederate), 146
Eldridge's Artillery Company, 146
Eleventh Illinois Cavalry, 183
Elliot Farm, 52
Elmwood Cemetery (Memphis, Tennessee), 222
Etheridge family, 22
Ethridge, Henry Emerson (U.S. Congressman), 136n, 224, 225

F

Fayette County, Tennessee, 120
Fayetteville, Arkansas, *Weekly Democrat*, 228
Federal Government (authorities), 89, 131, 223
Ferguson (Furgasen), Edmond M.V., 88, 88n
Ferguson, Lucinda, 158
Ferguson, William R., 157
Fifth Illinois Cavalry (USA), 192
Fifth Ohio Cavalry, 76
Fifteenth Illinois Cavalry
  Company A, 117
  Company B, 117
  Company C, 117
  Company D, 117
  Company G, 117
  Field and Staff, 117
Fifteenth Illinois Cavalry, 115
Fifth Tennessee Cavalry (CSA), 147
Fifty-second Illinois, 53
Finger, Tennessee, 210, 212

First West Tennessee Cavalry, x, xi, xii, xiii, xiv, xv, 3, 8, 20, 23, 24, 29, 30, 31, 32, 36, 37, 42, 44, 46, 47, 50, 51, 53, 54, 56, 59, 60, 61, 62, 64, 66, 69, 72, 72n, 73, 77, 78, 80, 81, 82, 87, 88, 90, 91, 92, 93, 94, 98, 104, 109, 112, 115, 116, 117, 118, 119, 120, 122, 127, 128, 129, 130, 131, 132, 139, 141, 146, 148, 150, 151, 152, 154, 155, 156, 161, 163, 167, 169, 170, 173, 175, 179, 181, 185, 187, 193, 204, 205, 207, 208, 209, 210, 214, 220
  Company A, 36, 37, 129, 187, 192, 194, 207
  Company B, 37, 56, 100, 123, 126, 129, 172, 173, 180, 207, 209, 211
  Company C, 42, 129
  Company D, 42, 70, 129, 180
  Company E, 42, 70, 81, 88, 103, 106n
  Company F, 42, 61
  Company G, 106
  Field and Headquarters Staff, 29, 40
  First Battalion, 73
  Regimental Commissary, 40
  Regimental Quartermaster, 72
  Regimental Wagon master, 88
Fitch, E.D., 221
Ford, G.W., 30, 30n
Forest Hill, Tennessee, 168
Forked Deer River, 138
Forrest, Col. Jeff (Confederate), 189
Forrest, Gen. Nathan Bedford (Confederate), 33, 44, 48, 49, 51, 52, 108n, 138, 149, 163, 193, 203, 222
Fort Dodge, 9
Fort Donelson, 14, 15, 28n, 71, 128
Fort Henry, 14, 15, 128
Fort Larned, Kansas, 3, 8, 9, 9n
Fort Sumter, 9, 16
Forty-Eighth Illinois Infantry, 35, 37
Forty-Ninth (49th) Illinois Infantry, 107
Forty-Third Ohio, 96
Foster, Enos, 154
Fourteenth Tennessee Cavalry (CSA), 174
  Company H, 174

Fourth Illinois Cavalry, 34, 192, 214
Foxx, Daniel, 49
Frederick County, Virginia, 151
Free Soil Democrat, 28
Frierson, Lt. Col. William (Confederate), 105, 105n
Fugate, James M., 9
Fuller, Mr., 96
Fulton, Mississippi, 98

G
Gattis, W.L., 155
Germantown, Tennessee, 168
Gertrude, Queen, 142
Gettysburg, Pennsylvania, 129, 130
Gill, Gardner, 37, 38, 39, 40, 47, 207
Glendale outpost (Hardin County, Tennessee), 96
Grand Junction, Tennessee, 55, 60, 73, 78, 84, 122, 123, 176, 181, 182, 184, 185, 187, 188, 191, 193, 195, 197, 198, 214, 227
Grant Administration, 227, 228
Grant, Maj. Gen. Ulysses S., 4, 28, 32, 33, 40, 51, 52, 63, 70, 99, 100, 120, 129, 130, 150, 216
Graves, Mr., 103
Green, Col. John Uriah (Confederate), 119
Grenada, Mississippi, 84
Grierson, Brig. Gen. Benjamin H., 31n, 83, 203
Guerillas (Confederate/Rebel), 23, 44, 46, 47, 50, 51, 58, 59, 61, 65, 66, 71, 123, 139, 149, 163, 168, 170, 173, 178, 179, 201, 223
Guinn, Rev. Enos, 67

H
Hainer, Kate M., 221
Halleck, Gen. Henry W., 30
Hamburg Road, 116
Hamburg, Tennessee, 52, 96, 100, 102, 106, 111, 190
Hamlet, 142
Hance, William F., 70
Hannes, William M., 70

Hardeman County Democratic Party (Tennessee), 227
Hardeman County, Tennessee, 54, 58, 60, 96, 181, 229
Hardeman, Dr. John B., 157
Harden, Lt. Edward L., 185, 188
Hardin County, Tennessee, 16, 47, 102, 106, 115, 224
Hardin, James, 225, 226
Harris, Isham G. (Tennessee Gov.), 16, 17, 68, 78
Harris, Mr., 46
Harrison, Mr. H (Union scout), 106
Haskill (Haskell), Judge Joshua, 225
Hassle, Mr., 111
Hassle, Mrs., 111
Hassle's Tannery, 110
Hatch, Col. Edward, 136, 139, 149, 150, 185, 186, 187, 188, 189
Hatchie Bridge, 136
Hatchie River, 67, 83, 84, 136, 149, 182
Hawkins, Col. Isaac R., 18, 20, 191
Hawkins' Tories, 18
Hayes, Capt., 32, 32n, 42
Haynie, Col. Isham Nicholas, 35, 37
Helena, Arkansas, 209, 210
Henderson, Capt. John, 99
Henderson, Tennessee, 154, 156
Henderson County, Tennessee, 22, 48, 153, 224
Henderson Station, Tennessee, 19, 20, 107
Henry, Dr. C.A., 10
Henry, Robert Selph, 48
Hickman County, Tennessee, 224
Hightower, Harrietta, 159
Hill, Abraham, 157
Hill, H.M., 229
Hill, James, 157, 158
Hill, Lucinda, 157
Hill, Martha, 157
Hodges, E.M.R., 155
Hodges, Capt. Elijah James, 56, 126, 155, 200, 209, 210, 211, 212, 213, 224
Hodges, Elisha, 210
Hodges, Harmon E., 211, 212
Hodges, Harvey G., 211, 212

Hodges, Capt. Horry (*also known as* Harry Hodges), 36, 37, 55, 56, 57, 123, 155, 172, 173, 180, 182, 209, 210, 211
Hodges, Professor Horry (*son of* Elijah J. Hodges), 211, 212
Hodges, Jesse, 210
Hodges, John, 211
Hodges, Maggie, 211, 212
Hodges, Mary (Lain), 210
Hodges, Millie (Ward), 210
Hodges, Nancy Jane (Dodd), 211
Hodges, Sarah Ann, 211
Hodges, Sarah Elizabeth (Dodd), 201
Hodges, Tabitha F., 211
Hodges, Dr. William Henry, 211, 212
Hollis and Cason, 154, 156, 184
Hollis family, 162
Hollis, Elizabeth, 152
Hollis, Dr. Hugh Lawson White, 140, 142, 146, 147, 148, 149, 152, 153, 154, 156, 158, 162, 184
Hollis, James C., 152, 153, 154, 155
Hollis, James Wilson, 152, 154
Hollis, Sallie W. "Mamie" (Wilson), 153, 154
Hollis, Third Lt. W.T. (Confederate), 155
Holloway, James, 156
Holloway, W.D., 156
Holly Springs, Mississippi, 184, 191
Hooker's Bend, Tennessee, 51
Horner, Tennessee, 154
Horse Creek (Hardin County, Tennessee), 102, 115n
Houghton, Major (Confederate), 14
Houston, Capt. William E., 29, 30
Huddleston, David N., 161
Huddleston, John, 215
Hurlbut, Maj. Gen. Stephen A., 40, 60, 103, 118, 122, 123, 126, 128, 189, 201, 202, 203, 209, 210, 218
Hurst, Elza, 155, 156
Hurst, Col. Fielding, x, xi, xii, xiii, xiv, xv, 8, 11, 12, 13, 15, 16, 17, 20, 21, 22, 23, 24, 25, 26, 28, 29, 31, 32, 32n, 33, 34, 35, 36, 38, 39, 40, 42, 44, 45, 47, 53, 54, 56, 58, 59, 60, 61, 62, 63, 64, 65, 66, 67, 69, 70, 71, 73, 76, 76n, 77, 78, 79, 81, 82, 83, 84, 86, 87, 88, 89, 93, 94, 95, 96, 98, 99, 100, 102, 103, 104, 110, 119, 121, 123, 124, 125, 126, 128, 131, 135, 136, 136n, 138, 139, 140, 141, 142, 143, 144, 146, 148, 149, 150, 151, 152, 154, 156, 158, 161,162, 163, 164, 168, 169, 170, 171, 172, 173, 174, 175, 176, 180, 181, 185, 187, 189, 191, 192, 193, 194n, 196, 200, 201, 202, 203, 204, 205, 206, 208, 209, 210, 215, 217, 219, 222, 223, 224, 225, 226, 227, 228, 229, 230, 231
Hurst Nation, 230
Hurst's Wurst: Colonel Fielding Hurst and the Sixth Tennessee Cavalry, U.S.A., 15

I

Illinois, 14, 40
Illinois Central Railroad, 71
Illinois Senate, 108n
Indian Creek, 115, 116
Introduction to *Resources of Tennessee*, 103
Iuka, Battle of, 169
Iuka, Mississippi, 184, 202
Ivy, Long B., 156

J

Jack's Creek, Tennessee, 153, 154, 182
Jackson, John, 156
Jackson, Mississippi, 117
Jackson, Tennessee, 30, 31, 35, 40, 84, 96, 97, 108, 110, 112, 117, 128, 135, 136, 137, 138, 146, 149, 159, 182, 185, 188, 189, 201, 203, 223
Jackson, Tennessee, Battle of, 149
Jackson, Tennessee, *West Tennessee Whig*, 188
Jackson's Cavalry, 118
Johnson, A.M., 155
Johnson, Andrew (TN Military Gov., later U.S. Vice President), 22, 68, 78, 82, 181, 202, 224

Johnson's Island, Ohio, 105n
Johnson's Mill (north McNairy County, Tennessee), 21
Johnston, Gen. Joseph E., 108n
Jones, Lt., 146
Jonesboro, Arkansas, 161

K
Kansas, 9
Kemp, Capt. Nathan M.D., 51, 52, 112, 185, 224
Kerr, Thomas Baker (*also* Thomas Carr, Thomas Carrs, Thomas Car), 99
Kevold, Capt., 107
Killebrew, J.B., 103, 120
Kimball, Gen. Nathan, 83, 84
Kirtland, Humphreys & Mitchell (St. Louis, Missouri), 218

L
LaBelle Village, Tennessee, 120
La Grange and Memphis Railroad Company, 168, 184
La Grange, Tennessee, 60, 83, 84, 112, 120, 121, 122, 149, 150, 166, 167, 168, 169, 170, 171, 175, 178, 181, 182, 183, 190, 191, 201
La Grange, Tennessee Depot, 168
Lamar, Mississippi, 191
Landes, Capt., 102
Lathrop, Col. W.L., 189, 190
Lawler, Col. (later Brig. Gen.) Michael Kelly, 33, 104
Lawrence County, Tennessee, 6
Ledbetter, Mr., 114
Lee, Gen. Robert E. (Confederate), 129
Leggett, Gen. Mortimer Dormer, 214
Lexington, Tennessee, 112
Lewis, Lt. (later Capt.) Samuel, 185, 186, 187, 224, 225
Lewis, Mrs., 174
Lewis County, Tennessee, 6
Lick Creek (Tennessee), 111
Lincoln, Abraham (U.S. Pres.), 16, 17, 105, 130
Lincoln County, Tennessee, 99

Linden Street (Memphis, Tennessee), 216
Linden, Tennessee, 105
Little Rock, Arkansas, 217
Locke family, 140, 151, 162
Logan, Brig. Gen. John "Black Jack" Alexander, 28, 28n, 35, 189
Louisiana, state of, 68, 127
Love, Major, 55, 56
Lowland Scot, 4
Lowery, Dr., 102
Lowryville, Tennessee (*also* Loweryville), 102, 115, 115n
Loyalists, 224
Loyalists' Convention (Philadelphia), 224

M
Madison, Indiana, 168
Madison County, Tennessee, 128
Mangum, Second Lt. James A., 215, 216
Mars Hill Cemetery (McNairy County, Tennessee), 161
Martin (alleged victim of Fielding Hurst), 222
Martin's Mill, 115
Mason's Depot, Tennessee, 217
Mathes, Capt. J. Harvey (Confederate), 48
Matthews, William Kibben, 4
Matthewses (Tennessee), 109
Maury County, Tennessee, 4, 227
Meade, Gen. George, 129
Medon Station, Tennessee 182, 183
Meeks, Gen. John H., 99, 100, 101
Memphis and Charleston Railroad, 60, 168, 191
Memphis and Ohio Railroad, 201
Memphis *Bulletin*, 170, 171, 173, 174
Memphis *Daily Appeal*, 54, 58, 84, 217, 227
Memphis *Evening Press*, 216, 217
Memphis National Cemetery, 208, 209, 210
Memphis, Tennessee, 6, 18, 58, 73, 74, 76, 88n, 96, 118, 131, 150, 167,

168, 169, 176, 178, 180, 185, 202,
  209, 210, 214, 222
Meridian, Mississippi, 98
Mexican War, 4, 7, 28n, 64, 108n, 138
Mexico, 4, 5
Michie, Tennessee, 159
Michigan Cavalry, 109
Middle Tennessee, 8, 17, 25, 48, 49, 127,
  178, 184
Mile Marker Murders, 139, 141, 162,
  163, 200
Miller, Col. (Confederate), 61
Miller, John, 135
Mississippi, state of, 22, 52, 58, 68, 76,
  83, 96, 184, 223
Mississippi Central Railroad, 191
Mississippi Legislature, 193
Mississippi River, 21n, 32n, 119, 129,
  168
  "Gibraltar of the Mississippi," 32n
Mizner (*also* Misner *or* Misener),
  Col. J.K., 112, 175, 178
Mobile, Alabama, 97, 98
Mobile and Ohio Railroad, 32n, 35, 84,
  107
Molino Del Ray, Mexico, 6
Molino Del Ray, Mexico, Battle of, 6
Montevallo, Alabama, 98
Montezuma, Tennessee, 138, 151, 152,
  153, 154, 183, 184
Moors, G., 102
Morgan, Gen. John Hunt Morgan
  (Confederate), 47
Morgan, Ann, 152
Morgan, Franklin, 152
Morgan, Henry Abel, 152
Morgan, John (*son of* John R. *and*
  Lucinda), 152
Morgan, John R., 151
Morgan, Lucinda (Debell), 151
Morgan, Mary, 152
Morgan, Thomas W.S., 140, 142, 146,
  147, 148, 149, 151, 152, 158, 162,
  184
Morgan, Maj. W.H., 223
Morgan, William, 152
Mormons, 71
Morris, Eastin, 120

Morris, T.K., 76
Moscow, Tennessee, 168
Moss Creek (Tennessee), 111
Mount Carmel Cemetery, 18, 212
Mount Carmel Church (Primitive
  Baptist), 211
Mount Gilead (McNairy County,
  Tennessee community), 230
Mount Gilead Cemetery, 231
Muddy Creek, 59, 60
Murphy, J.W., 229
Murrell, John A., 76, 79
Murrell's, 135

Mc

McCall, Thomas, 220
McCann, Kevin D., x, 15, 173
McCann, R.M., 161
McClellan, Maj. Gen. George, 10, 10n
McCrillis, Col. Lafayette F., 182, 183,
  191, 192, 193
McFerran, Maj. John C., 9
McIntyre, Isaac T., xv, 36, 37, 38, 39, 40,
  41, 56, 135, 156, 201, 207, 208,
  209, 210
McIntyre, John Absalom, 17, 18, 39, 207
McIntyre, Robert Thompson, 18, 39,
  39n, 155, 156, 207
McIntyre, W.C., 155
McIntyre's Farm, Battle of, 207
McKenzie, Lark, 214
McNairy County Court Clerk, 220
McNairy County Quarterly Court, 39
McNairy County, Tennessee, 11, 12, 14,
  15, 16, 17, 17n, 18, 19, 20, 21,
  22, 26, 36, 37, 38, 39, 56, 60, 99,
  100, 128, 129, 136, 140, 147, 151,
  152, 155, 156, 157, 159, 160, 161,
  162, 163, 185, 207, 208, 210, 224,
  225, 230

N

Nashville *Daily American*, 221
Nashville *Republican Banner*, 136n, 224,
  225, 226, 227, 229
Nashville, Tennessee, 62, 104
Nashville *Union and American*, 227

254   IN THE SHADOW OF THE DEVIL

Natchez Trace, 79
Nathan Bedford Forrest: In Search of the Enigma, 49
National Cemetery (Memphis, Tennessee), xv
National Council Grand Army of the Republic, 222
Nauvoo, Illinois, 71
Nebraska Territory, 10
Neely, J.J., 228
Neely, Col. James J. (Confederate), 203
Neely, R.P., 228
Nelson, Hugh, 174
New Mexico, 9
New Orleans, Louisiana, 168
New York Stock Exchange, 30
New York *Tribune*, 228
Newman, Mrs. A.A., 135, 186, 188, 189, 203
Newsom, Col. John F. (Confederate), 138, 149
Newsom, Pvt. William A. (Confederate), 81
Newsom's Cavalry (CSA), 147, 156, 182
   Company F, 147
Newsome, Col. John (Confederate), 164
Nichols, Matthias, 111
Ninth Illinois Cavalry, 183
Ninth Illinois Infantry, 194
North Carolina, 39, 67
North Mississippi, 23, 59, 191
Northwest Mississippi, 127
Notes on McNairy County, 38

O

Official Records of the War of the Rebellion (Official Records), 10, 24, 31, 35, 46, 51, 55, 59, 60, 62, 66, 80, 83, 100, 104, 141, 181, 185, 205
Oglesby, Maj. Gen. Richard James, 84, 86, 96, 97, 107, 108, 108n, 117, 118
Okalona, Mississippi, 54
Old Capitol Prison, 11
Oldtown, Tennessee, 116
One Hundred Eighth (108th) Regiment, Tennessee Militia, 99
One Hundred Fifty-Fourth (154th) Senior Infantry (CSA), 147, 159
   Company H, 147
   Company I, 159
Osborn, Samuel, 222
Oxford's Creek (McNairy County, Tennessee), 99

P

Paducah, Kentucky, 110
Palo Alto, Mississippi, 84
Panola, Mississippi, 58, 117
Parham, Mr. R.S., 217
Parker's Crossroads, Battle of, 48
Pawnee fork, 9
Pawnee River, 8, 9
Peeples, Elizabeth Ellen (Hodges), 211
Pemberton, Lt. Gen. John C. (Confederate), 119
Percy Hotel, 195
Perry County, Tennessee, 105, 106
Perry County, Tennessee Courthouse (Rebel depot), 105
Perryville, Battle of (Kentucky), 105n
Perryville, Tennessee, 52, 53, 107, 109, 111, 113
Phelps, Lt. Cmdr. Seth Ledyard, 105
Philippi, Virginia, 169
Phillips, Mr. (alleged murderer), 230
Pillow, Gen. Gideon J. (Confederate), 229
Pinhook and Savannah Road, 115
Pinhook, Tennessee, 116
Pitts, Asst. Adj. Gen. John, 62
Pitts, Judge John A., 12, 99
Pittsburg Landing, Tennessee, 15, 18, 33, 44, 50, 51, 200
Pocahontas-Purdy Road, 139, 140, 148, 149, 150, 151, 156, 158, 161, 162, 166, 169
Pocahontas, Tennessee, 55, 59, 60, 61, 67, 138, 142, 144, 148, 149, 166, 183
Point Lookout, Maryland, 105n
Polk, James Knox (U.S. Pres.), 4
Port Hudson, Mississippi, 118
Porter, Brig. Gen. Fitz John, 10, 10n
Prince, Col. Edward, 83, 84

INDEX

Pulaski, Tennessee, 211, 225n
Purdy, Tennessee, 12, 15, 21, 34, 44, 45, 48, 55, 65, 84, 95, 99, 100, 102, 103, 112, 125, 136, 136n, 138, 139, 142, 144, 149, 160, 161, 162, 163, 224, 225, 226, 227, 230

R
Radical Republicans, 153, 224, 225, 227
Railroad Hotel (*also* The Commercial Hotel), 195, 197
Randolph and Alexander Distillery, 227
Rankin, Francis M., 156
Raymond (U.S. steamer), 52
Rebel Army (Rebel soldiers), 18, 19, 20, 33, 74, 76, 105, 108, 109, 139, 167, 168, 170, 179, 190, 225
Reconstruction, 153, 206
Red Sulphur Springs, 51
Reed, Judge, 225
Refugees (wartime), 128
Reminiscences of the Early Settlement and Early Settlers of McNairy County, Tennessee, 38, 39n, 82, 99
Report and Journal, 1865, 9
Republican Executive Committee (Tennessee), 217
Reynolds, T.E., 228
Reynolds, Mrs. T.E., 228
Revolutionary War, 39, 207, 210
Rice, Col. Elliot Warren, 52, 53, 84, 86, 106, 106n, 108, 108n, 109
Rich Mountain, 169
Richardson, Col. Robert V. (Confederate), 34, 83, 118, 119, 172
Richardson's Cavalry (12th [Richardson's/Green's] Tennessee Cavalry Regiment) (*also known as* 1st or 12th Tennessee Partisan Ranger Regiment), 118
Richmond, Virginia, 108n, 143, 144, 150
Ripley Road, 195
Ripley, Mississippi, 58, 59, 156, 175, 176
Robb (U.S. gunboat), 53, 190
Roberts, Capt. Elijah, 32, 32n, 42, 99, 118, 176, 177
Roberts, Sgt. Calvin, 103, 104, 104n

Roberts, Sgt. Houston, 223
Robertson, Mary Hodges, 211
Robertson, Dr. Christopher Wood, 173
Robinson, Capt., 217, 218, 219
Roche, Pvt. Robert F., 8
Rocky Knob community (McNairy County, Tennessee), 19, 21
Roddey, Col. Philip Dale (Confederate), 139, 140, 142, 143, 151, 156, 163
Rogers, Richard, 46
Rose Creek (McNairy County, Tennessee), 136
Rose Hill Cemetery (McNairy County, Tennessee), 157, 157n
Rosecrans, Maj. Gen. William S., 31n, 52, 169, 191
Rose's Creek, 230
Ross, First Sgt. James H., 215
Rossville, Tennessee, 168
Ruggles, Gen. Daniel (Confederate), 97, 98
Rutter, Mr., 217

S
Salem, Mississippi, 180, 193, 194
Salisbury, Tennessee, 218
Saltillo, Tennessee, 49, 51, 106, 107, 109, 110, 111, 198
Sanders, A.A. (*also* Aaron A. Saunders *or* A.A. Saunders), 37, 38, 39, 40, 47, 207
Sanders, Aaron, 38
Sanders, Andrew, 38
Sanders, Edward L., 38
Sanders, Elizabeth, 38
Sanders, Isabella M., 38
Sanders, Mary S., 38
Sanders, Rebecca E., 38
Sanders, Sargent D., 38
Sandy Creek, 230
Santa Fe Trail, 8
Savannah and Waynesborough Road, 116
Savannah, Tennessee, 51, 53, 116, 230
Scott, M.E., 115
Scott, Gen. Winfield "Old Fuss and Feathers," 6

Scott, Rozetta Jane "Jennye" (Hodges), 211
Scouting Adventures in 1853, 9
Second Cavalry Brigade, 136, 139, 181, 192
Second Iowa Cavalry, 127, 187
Second Infantry, 8
Second Mississippi State Cavalry 58
  Company A, 58
Second Seminole War, 7
Second Tennessee Cavalry, 32, 107
Second West Tennessee Cavalry (USA), 42
Seddon, James (Confederate Secretary of War), 140, 143, 144
Selma, Alabama, 97, 98
Seventh Illinois, 127
Seventh Illinois Cavalry, 127n
Seventh Illinois Infantry, 127n
Seventh Iowa, 53
Seventh Tennessee Cavalry, 18
Sevier (Seveere) County, Tennessee, 20
Shannonsville (Tennessee), 109
Sharp, Joseph Cannon, 135, 135n
Shaw, C.A.S., 174
Shearer, Capt. Orlando, 200
Shelby County Chancery Court (Tennessee), 219
Sherman, Maj. Gen. William Tecumseh, 214
Shenandoah Valley campaign, 169
Sherwin, Christopher, 147
Shiloh, Battle of, 16, 18, 22, 23, 47, 71, 115, 128, 159, 190
Shiloh National Cemetery, 200, 204
Shiloh National Military Park, 200
Shiloh, Tennessee, 138, 142
Sickles, John, 4, 6, 7
Sipes, Alfred, 156
Sixth District of Tennessee (revenue), 227
Sixth Indiana Volunteers, 169
Sixteenth (16th) Army Corps, 118, 175, 200
Skinner, (Confederate officer), 14
Smith, Capt. Francis A., 32, 32n, 42
Smith's farm/plantation (William Jay Smith), 73, 78
Smith, James J., 187
Smith, Mary A.R. *v.* W.J. Smith (1889 Tennessee Supreme Court case), 220
Smith, Mary Ann (Ross), 73, 73n, 74, 219, 222
Smith, William Jay "Petticoat" (or "Jerusalem"), xv, 40, 58, 61, 63, 65, 69, 70, 73, 74, 75, 76, 76n, 77, 78, 79, 80, 83, 86, 87, 88, 89, 96, 110, 112, 122, 123, 124, 125, 135, 168, 182, 185, 194n, 195, 200, 201, 204, 206, 208, 209, 212, 214, 215, 216, 217, 219, 220, 221, 222, 224
Smith, Gen. William Sooy, 61, 84
Smithville, Mississippi, 98
Snake Creek, 230
Somerville, Tennessee, 172, 174
South Carolina, 68
Southern Claims Commission, xiii
Southern Confederacy, 16, 168
Southern Illinois, 28n
Southern Railway, 60
Southern Unionists, 18
Southwest Tennessee, 47
Sparkman, J.C., 6
Spring Creek (Tennessee), 111
Spring Creek Bottom, 230
Spring Hill, Mississippi, 175, 176
St. Louis, Missouri, 7, 25, 26, 30, 31n, 32, 35, 64, 66
St. Louis *Times*, 227
St. Louis *Union*, 71
Stantonville, Tennessee, 99
Starks, Elijah W., 157, 158
Starks, Lucinda, 157
Starks, Nancy W., 157, 157n
Starks, Thomas (*also* Thomas Stark), 140, 142, 146, 147, 148, 149, 157, 158, 162
Starnes, Col. James W. (Confederate), 48
Stephens, Capt., 46
Stevenson, Brig. Gen. J.D., 202
Steward's Battalion, 103
Stewart, Joseph, 222
Still, Dr., 135
Stovall, A.W., 38

INDEX

Street, Maj. Solomon G. "Sol" (Confederate), 55, 58, 59, 61, 73, 73n, 74, 78, 122, 123, 218
Streight, Col. Abel, 97
Sullivan, Brig. Gen. Jeremiah Cutler, 47, 49, 60, 168, 169
Sutton's Tanyard, 111
Swain, Mary Martha Caroline (Alexander,) 14, 14n, 15
Swain, William W., 14, 14n
Swallow Bluff (Tennessee), 109

T

Talladega, Alabama, 98
Tallahatchie River, 58
Tarkington, James, 22
Taylor, Capt., 7
Tennessee (U.S. gunboat), 98
Tennessee, state of, 12, 16, 17, 22, 23, 54, 58, 68, 98, 157, 159, 168, 181, 220, 221, 227
Tennessee House of Representatives, 82, 211, 216
Tennessee Legislature, 32n, 216
Tennessee National Bank, 216
Tennessee River, 15, 17, 19, 21n, 33, 34, 44, 50, 52, 65, 66, 70, 71, 81, 100, 102, 104, 105, 106, 107, 110, 111, 113, 115, 131, 177, 184, 190, 230
Tennessee State Convention, 224
Tennessee State Senate, 216, 219
Tennessee Supreme Court, 220
Tennessee Valley Divide (Dividing Ridge), 21, 21n
Tennessee State Library and Archives, xi
Tenth Tennessee Infantry (CSA), 147
Texas, 4, 5, 6
"The Soldier's Dream," 64
Third Division Headquarters, 110
Third Illinois Cavalry, 183, 192
Third Michigan Cavalry, 96, 187, 188
Third Tennessee Infantry, 6
Thirteenth Amendment (U.S. Constitution), 223
Thirteenth Indiana, 169
Thirteenth Street Prison (Washington, D.C.), 10
Thirteenth (13th) Tennessee Regiment (CSA), 142, 146, 152
  Company F, 152, 159
Thirty-Fifth General Assembly (Tennessee), 211
Thirty-First (A.H. Bradford's) Tennessee Infantry Regiment, 154, 154n
  Company C, 155
Thomas, Pvt. Stephen J., 123, 135, 209
Thomas, Sgt. (Asst. Commissary General), 87
Thompson, Capt. Robert M., 36, 155, 158, 172, 220, 221, 224
Thorrington, First Lt./Adj. John H., 215
Tippah County, Mississippi, 58
Tishomingo County, Mississippi, 209
Tollivers, 135
Tombigbee River, 97
Toone's Station, Tennessee, 181, 182, 229
Tories, 54
Totten, Judge A.W.O., 225
Treaty of Guadalupe Hidalgo, 8
Trenton, Tennessee, 32, 42, 47, 154, 201
Trigg, Judge C.F., 229
Trunnels Cross Road (Trundle Crossroad), 20
Tupelo, Mississippi, 159
Turley, Judge W.B., 225
Turkey Creek (Tennessee), 116
Tuscumbia, Alabama, 97
Twelfth Cavalry Battalion (CSA), 147
Twelfth Judicial District of Tennessee, 224
Twenty-First Senatorial District (Tennessee), 223
Twenty-Fourth Tennessee Infantry (CSA), 147
Twenty-Seventh Tennessee Infantry, CSA, 105n

U

U.S. Claims Commission, 220
U.S. House of Representatives, 216
U.S. Sixteenth Army Corps, 96
U.S. Sixth Tennessee Cavalry, x, xi, xii, 4, 8, 48, 49, 82, 127, 181, 182, 183, 184, 186, 187, 188, 190, 191, 193,

258   **IN THE SHADOW OF THE DEVIL**

200, 201, 202, 203, 204, 206, 210, 212, 220, 222, 224, 227, 229
Company A, 187
Company F, 188
Company I, 200
Company M, 215
U.S. Seventh Tennessee Cavalry, 183, 191, 201
Union (generally), 11, 19, 23, 28n, 39, 55, 68, 69, 89
Union Army (armed forces and generally), xi, 11, 14, 15, 18, 19, 20, 21, 22, 23, 34, 44, 55, 77, 86, 107, 119, 121, 158, 188, 200
Union Bank *v.* Smith, 224
Union City, Tennessee, 191
Union gunboats, 19
Union Navy (naval forces), 15, 129
Union transport ships, 44
Union War Hymn of Measures, 67
Unionists (Union sympathizers), 17, 18, 71, 76, 82, 189, 211
United States *v.* Hurst, et al., 229, 230
United States Army, 6, 9, 11, 25, 144, 215, 218
United States Congress, 216, 217, 221
United States Constitution, 68
United States Government, 122
United States Navy, 168
University of Louisiana, 152

V

Vale, Alexander, 222
Verona, Mississippi, 97, 98
Vicksburg, Mississippi, 98, 129, 130
Virginia, state of, 151

W

Walker, Benjamin Thomas "Tom," xv, 36, 37, 38, 40, 43, 58, 76, 77, 86, 87, 122, 123, 124, 126, 126n, 135, 201, 207, 208, 209, 210, 218
Walker, Hardridge, 208
Walker, Mary (McCann), 208
Walker, William C., 156
Walls, Zeke, 214
War Department (U.S.), 24, 82

War of 1812, 38
Warren, Capt. Stanford L., 67, 82, 85, 200, 224
Washington, D.C., 10, 25, 26, 32, 35, 64, 66, 150, 216, 220
Washington, D.C. District Court, 220
Washington Hospital (Memphis, Tennessee), 18, 191
Wayne County, Tennessee, 7, 181, 224
Waynesborough Road, 115
Waynesborough and Florence Road, 115
Waynesborough and Savannah Road, 116
Webb, Lt. William C., 106, 106n, 107, 109, 110, 118, 177, 184, 223–224
Webster, Daniel, 18, 20, 21
Webster, John, 21
Webster, Marion, 21
Webster, Nancy, 18, 19, 19n, 20, 21, 22
Webster, William (*son of* Nancy Webster), 18, 19, 19n, 20
Webster, William (*husband of* Nancy Webster), 20
Weir, Capt., 103
Weir, Thomas B., 175
Welles, Secretary of the Navy Gideon, 105
West Point, Mississippi, 84
West Tennessee, x, xiii, xiv, xv, 12, 16, 17, 20, 21n, 22, 23, 25, 26, 39, 46, 48, 82, 90, 95, 127n, 128, 147, 171, 177, 202, 204, 209
West Tennessee District Headquarters (Union Army), 40
Wharton, A.J., 160
Wharton, C.R., 147
Wharton, Caleb F., 159, 160
Wharton, Charles R. "Charley," 159, 160
Wharton, Capt. John Ambrose "Dock," (Confederate) 140, 141, 142, 143, 144, 146, 148, 149, 151, 158, 159, 159n, 160, 161, 162
Wharton, John (*father of* Dock Wharton), 159
Wharton, John J. (*son of* Dock Wharton), 159, 160
Wharton, Kenneth McIntire "Kit," 160, 161

Wharton, Martha (Wilkerson), 159, 160
Wharton, Mary E. (*also* Mary A.), 159, 160
Wharton, Polly, 159
Wharton, W.H., 159n
Wharton, William "Bill," 159, 160, 161
White Oak Creek (Hardin County, Tennessee), 51, 52
White Oak Creek (McNairy County, Tennessee), 19, 21
White Oak Ridge (Hardin County, Tennessee), 47
White River (Arkansas), 136
Whiteville, Tennessee, 150, 168
Wiggins, Quartermaster, 83
Williams, Emma Inman, 164
Williams, Dr. Thomas, 194
Willoughby, Mr., 229
Wilson's Cavalry Regiment (21st Tennessee Cavalry, CSA), 142, 143, 146, 148, 158, 160, 162
Wilson, Elizabeth Y., 7
Wilson, John, 222
Winters, Capt., 225n
Wisdom, Celia (Shull), 163, 165
Wisdom, Col. Dew Moore (Confederate), 12, 139, 140, 141, 142, 143, 144, 145, 146, 147, 148, 149, 151, 152, 156, 157, 159, 160, 162, 163, 164, 203, 220, 221
Wisdom, William S., 162, 163, 165
Wolf River, 120
Wolholms, 135
Wolverton, James T., 173
Wood, Dr. George, 228
Wood, Robert H., 228
Woodard, Col., 109
Wright Boys, 152
Wright, Col. John Vines (Confederate), 12, 163
Wright, Gen. Marcus Joseph (Confederate), 12, 38, 39n, 82, 99, 163
Wright, Mr. (refugee), 97

Y
Yankee yawls, 58
Yazoo City, Mississippi, 117

Young, Lt. J.F., 117

ABOUT THE AUTHOR

John E. Talbott is an attorney, lecturer, author and former educator. A graduate of both Freed-Hardeman University (B.A. History/Secondary Education) and the University of Memphis, Cecil C. Humphreys School of Law (Juris Doctor), he has long held a special interest in the Civil War history of West and Middle Tennessee. He has spent eight years transcribing the journal of William K.M. Breckenridge as well as researching hundreds of records from the National Archives. He has also traveled as far as Fort Larned, Kansas, St. Louis, Missouri, Columbus, Kentucky, Washington, D.C. and numerous points across the South in search of the story of Breckenridge and the United States First West Tennessee Cavalry.

In this work on Breckenridge and the United States First West Tennessee Cavalry, Talbott used investigative techniques and conducted research into issues and controversies pertaining to both Fielding Hurst and his regiment. As a result, the emerging portrait of the regiment is a far different one than previously depicted by other writers and researchers. The author has sought to set the record straight as to many of the long-held and often repeated legends and folklore surrounding the regiment.

Talbott has practiced law in Henderson, Tennessee, for more than seventeen years and has taught and lectured on the subject of history on both the high school and university levels. A resident of Chester County, Tennessee, with longstanding ties to McNairy County, Tennessee, he is well-qualified to write about the history of the area. The author and/or editor of six previous works of history and two works of Southern fiction, he is also the editor of the works of the late Tennessee novelist and short story writer, Jack Happel Boone.

Other books written or edited by John E. Talbott

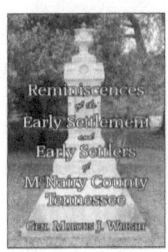 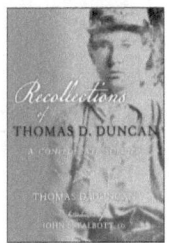

www.ingramcontent.com/pod-product-compliance
Lightning Source LLC
Chambersburg PA
CBHW030136170426
43199CB00008B/89